Charley Boorman's first film role was as Ed's Boy, Jon Voight's son in *Deliverance*, directed by his father John Boorman. Since then, he has appeared in *Excalibur*, *The Emerald Forest*, *Hope and Glory* and, more recently, *Karaoke*, *The Serpent's Kiss* and *The Bunker*. Born in London in 1966, he grew up in Ireland, spending much of his childhood riding motocross bikes. From 1998 to 2002, he ran a British motorcycle team with Ewan McGregor, winning the Superstock Series with David Jeffries.

In 2004 he travelled round the world with Ewan McGregor, and co-wrote a bestselling book with Ewan about their adventures, *Long Way Round*. In the summer of 2007, Charley and Ewan will start another journey: the Long Way Down, from John O'Groats to South Africa. The accompanying book will be available from Sphere in the autumn.

Married with two daughters, Charley rides a Ducati 748 and lives in London.

Race to Dakar

CHARLEY BOORMAN

with ROBERT UHLIG

Foreword by Ewan McGregor

sphere

SPHERE

First published in Great Britain in 2006 by Time Warner Books
This paperback edition published in 2007 by Sphere

A CIP catalogue record for this book
is available from the British Library.

ISBN 978-0-7515-3817-5

Papers used by Sphere are natural, recyclable products made from
wood grown in sustainable forests and certified in accordance with
the rules of the Forest Stewardship Council.

Typeset in Times by M Rules
Printed and bound in Great Britain by Clays Ltd, St Ives plc
Paper supplied by Hellefoss AS, Norway

Sphere
An imprint of
Little, Brown Book Group
Brettenham House
Lancaster Place
London WC2E 7EN

A Member of the Hachette Livre Group of Companies

www.littlebrown.co.uk

To Doone, Kinvara and Olivia for being there for me.

Also for Boubacar Diallo and Mohammed Ndaw, two spectators who were tragically killed on the rally. Our hearts go out to their families and friends.

And Andy Caldecott, who lost his life in this year's rally, and for all those brave riders that fell before him.

Contents

PART THREE: THE ROAD HOME

Foreword

by Ewan McGregor

We were in an office somewhere, and our book had just been brought into the room. There was real excitement. As we both shut our eyes and covered them with our hands, the copy was placed on a table. Then: *ta daa!* There it was, and there *we* were, on the cover, standing proud like two explorers from the past. Our first book. It was a first for both of us, and we smiled huge smiles at each other.

'Wow,' we said.

'Look at this . . . the picture goes all the way round the cover.'

'Cool.'

For a while we flicked through in silence, looking at the grouped photos and reading wee bits and pieces. A feeling of pride was swelling in my chest when Charley suddenly said, 'Oh, fuck.'

'What?' I asked.

'It says here I'm doing the Dakar in 2006.'

My best friend Charley has ridden motorbikes since he was seven, which makes him something of a hero in my eyes. His riding has always been really good – whether he was on the track or just going round town – but it was to get better. Much better.

On the Long Way Round trip I followed his lead through some of the rougher stuff, and it's true to say that we both improved. The terrain that tested us in Kazakhstan would have been a doddle had we faced it later on in Siberia. There were times when we both felt pretty good about ourselves. After such stretches the helmets would come off to reveal huge dusty grins and we would relive moments of motorcycling excellence. There was a name that was always mentioned to describe these times. Not to describe the actual techniques of riding on the dirt (certainly not in my case), but the *feeling* of it. When everything came together, the bike disappeared beneath you and you felt as if you were just flying along, no thoughts or decisions about which line to take, which gear to be in, everything automatic, leaving you free to experience true flow and exhilaration. The Dakar moments.

Now, I don't know if Charley had actually decided to race in the world's most gruelling rally or not when, in a moment of bravado shortly after arriving in New York, he said to our editor, 'Yeah, I'm doing the Dakar next.' But when he saw it in print on the flyleaf of our book, he more than rose to the challenge.

Over the following year I saw him change, seeing less and less of him as he threw himself into an extraordinary training schedule. I'd never seen him more driven, so all-consumed by anything before. He truly surprised people with his riding and his passion for this new, terrifying challenge.

A lot of friends and family – myself included – were nervous and worried for him. The training was really tough, and we all knew about the life-threatening dangers he could face on the rally itself. By the final week before the race, I know that Charley himself was scared too, but he never flinched from the job at hand.

I was many miles away when the race began in Lisbon in January 2006, but I know that, along with many others, my thoughts and prayers found him, sweating on the start line, engine gunning, his heart beating in his throat . . .

'GO ON, CHARLEY . . . GO ON!'

Ewan McGregor, July 2006

PART ONE

The Road to Lisbon

Chapter 1

EARLY DAYS

It's early in the morning of New Year's Eve and I am climbing into a taxi outside a luxury hotel in Lisbon, feeling strangely calm. The day I've dreamt about for years has finally come and the sheer terror that was paralysing me last night has given way to a calm feeling I've not felt for a long, long time. And I don't know why.

As usual, Simon is late, but even that doesn't wind me up. I've had a good night's sleep – a miracle considering I was in a blind panic only a few hours ago – and I feel relaxed as we head off to the start.

The Dakar Rally. Last night I could hardly utter those words without feeling sick. At dinner with my wife, children and friends, the cutlery in my hands was shaking as I struggled to force down some food. I felt like a man facing the firing squad in the morning. But this morning, everything seems to have fallen into place at last.

Kate Bush plays on the radio as Simon, Matt and I sit in silence, lost in our thoughts as the taxi moves quickly through deserted city streets. It feels like any other early morning start. Just like leaving for the airport before a holiday. Except we are dressed in several layers of protective motorcycle kit and about to embark on the most hazardous, tortuous, demanding race of all.

And then it dawns on me. After a year of breaking bones, preparing bikes, chasing sponsors, battling bureaucracy, getting visas and vaccinations sorted, learning to race off-road, finding funding, entering races I feared I would never finish, securing broadcast deals and convincing my teammates that I was up to scratch, at last life has become blissfully simple. No more hassles, just a simple future. Put on my helmet, get on my bike and ride to Dakar.

Two days earlier, shortly after we arrived in Lisbon, I'd felt that unbeatable feeling as I rode my BMW rally bike to the race compound. Just concentrating on the bike and the road, that sense of completeness I'd found on Long Way Round, travelling around the world with Ewan, came flooding back. There was nowhere else I would rather have been than on that bike – well, maybe in bed with my wife – right then, right there, riding past the ranks of racing trucks, rally cars and the coolest, meanest off-road bikes anyone has ever seen. Fuck! It didn't get any better than that!

I followed my team mates Simon Pavey and Matt Hall into a petrol station near the Lisbon docks. Shortly after we arrived a squadron of bikes decked in the colours of Repsol, one of the leading teams, arrived. Thrilled to be parking my bike alongside *real* professional Dakar riders, I watched as Simon chatted to a rider in Repsol kit.

'Who was that?' I asked when Simon returned.

'Andy Caldecott. Know him from previous Dakars. Nice guy.'

Like Simon, Caldecott was an Aussie. 'I thought he wasn't racing this year,' I said.

'Yeah, said it was a freak thing he's even here. Hadn't been expecting to ride but one of the factory riders got injured. Repsol rang him two weeks ago, just before Christmas. Said would you come and ride on a factory KTM. He hadn't been practising or training at all this year, but said yes straight away. Guess that's what Dakar does to you.'

I knew a little bit about Caldecott – in 2005 he'd won two Dakar stages and come sixth overall – and as I stood there looking at Andy and the other Repsol riders filling up their bikes beside me, I suddenly realised: this is it. For the first time I felt part of the rally.

We were all about to go into scrutineering, where our bikes would be examined to ensure they were up to race standard, and it would be the same for everyone. That was one of the things that made the Dakar so special. Once it got underway, everyone from the stars to the novices was equal. The stars had massive support and assistance teams, but they still had to fill up their own bikes, get them through scrutineering, ride them on the same tracks – and on the marathon stages, repair their bikes themselves – just like everyone else. Eighty trucks, 188 cars and 240 motorcycles were about to start in the world's greatest motor adventure and we were all in the same boat. And watching Caldecott across that petrol station forecourt also made me wonder how I'd wound up in the same race as someone who'd devoted most of their life to racing bikes. After all, less than a year ago I'd never ridden a dirt bike fast and with aggression.

That night, at a party held in a Lisbon blues club to celebrate the Race to Dakar team's participation in the rally, my oldest mate reminded me why I was there. Kaz had rung me a few days earlier to say that he, my neighbour Isaac and a couple of other friends were coming down to see me off.

Twenty-five years ago, Kaz Balinski was a fellow junior bike fanatic who lived across the river from my parents' farm in

County Wicklow. Kaz always had the top gear, whereas I always had the pants stuff. If I'd saved up enough money to buy myself a second-hand bike, Kaz would have the same bike but brand new. And Kaz had the one that I as a twelve-year-old craved more than anything: a motocross track. Kaz and I would race our bikes – his Yamaha YZ-80 and my 125 – around that track every day until long after dark. We'd hang out together in the school holidays, playing cops and robbers on our bikes, tearing across private land that wasn't ours.

Milling around the house one day, Kaz and I were asked by my mother to dig some potatoes out of the vegetable garden, her pride and joy. Kaz and I rode our bikes a couple of hundred yards down the hill from the house to a walled garden beside the stables, then stared at the long mounds of potato plants with a mixture of apathy and disdain. It was an amazing garden with strawberries, raspberries, rhubarb, tomatoes and berry trees, but as kids we regarded collecting produce from it as a punishment.

Then I had a brainwave. We could use Kaz's dirt bike, with its big knobbly tyres, to dig out the spuds. Kaz parked his front wheel on the soil, squeezed the front brake slightly and revved the engine so the back wheel would spin furiously while pushing the bike slowly along the trench between the potato plants. After Kaz had tested it I had a turn, riding the length of a row while Kaz stood behind the bike with a basket, trying to catch the spuds as they came flying out of the ground.

Kaz was covered in mud and the potatoes were gouged with cuts, but we were thrilled with what we thought was an inspired invention. It was only when we presented ourselves and our harvest to my mother that we realised we were in trouble.

When we weren't riding bikes or wrecking my mother's kitchen garden, Kaz and I would lie in the hay shed, smoking cigarettes and risking a major fire, or we'd hang around the house watching television. One afternoon we sat transfixed by something we'd never seen before. Dozens of motorcycles racing across an empty desert, trailing long plumes of Saharan dust in their wake. It was the first year of the Paris–Dakar rally.

In 1977 a French motorcyclist called Thierry Sabine got lost in the Libyan desert competing in the Abidjan–Nice rally, the first African rally. After a few days Sabine was rescued and airlifted to civilisation, but the desert had made a deep impression on him and he vowed to set up his own desert rally. The next year, 170 competitors set off from the Place du Trocadéro for Dakar. Riding via Algeria, Niger, Mali and Upper Volta then through Senegal, the best of them reached Dakar a fortnight later. It was a huge success.

The event grew every year until Thierry Sabine died in a helicopter crash during the 1986 rally. Thierry's father Gilbert took over the running of the Dakar, but it somehow lost its lustre. By 1993 the number of entrants had dwindled from a peak of 603 bikes, cars and trucks to just 154 vehicles. The Amaury Sport Organisation, organiser of the Tour de France, the Paris Marathon and more than a dozen other sports events, took over. ASO then built up the rally into one of the world's largest sports events.

Over the years, I watched the Dakar on television whenever I could. At first it was the four-wheel-drive trucks pounding through the sand that fascinated me, these ten-ton behemoths racing so fast and with so much power they went airborne over the sand dunes. But my fascination for the trucks was soon overtaken by the cars and, more than anything, the bikes.

I was hooked and whenever anyone mentioned the Dakar I'd recognise a kindred spirit. By the time I was in my mid-teens, I'd vowed to compete in the Dakar one day, although I suspected that, like many adolescent yearnings, it would remain no more than a distant dream.

Whenever I got the chance I'd speak to bikers who had taken

part. They all said the same thing: it's the toughest race in the world. That put the fear of God into me, but it also made me want to do it even more. It wasn't just the race, hard as it was. It was all the preparation that went into it. Most bikers spent years getting ready for it, earning their stripes in enduro races and desert rallies until the day came when they felt there was only one challenge left to face, until they had no choice but to enter the Dakar. Even then, they'd spend another six months to a year raising funds, sorting the paperwork, polishing their technique in sand dunes and getting their bike ready. Just getting to the start was a major achievement.

Riders who had 'done the Dakar' would tell me that no one could understand the rally until they'd competed in it. It wasn't just the distance and the physical demands. It was the mental strength needed to keep pushing when stuck in the middle of nowhere, exhausted and dejected. It was the drive to ignore that desperation to give up when there were 250 miles to ride across soft sand in darkness.

Dakar riders said the rally took you to the worst and best places you'd ever been – and most of them were in your head. It was a rollercoaster ride from the biggest highs to the deepest lows.

Like me, Kaz knew all that as we knocked back the beers at the party in Lisbon. With Simon nearby, matching some Scottish bikers drink for drink just thirty hours before the start because 'you can't let a couple of Scots drink an Aussie under the table,' I asked Kaz why he'd come all the way to Lisbon.

'To see you, Charley,' Kaz said. 'To wish you on your way.'

'But you could have said goodbye in London.'

Kaz looked me in the eye. 'I came because I thought I might not see you again. A lot of people die doing the Dakar. And, whatever happens, you'll come back a different person.'

*

My life felt like it had come full circle in the years since Kaz and I scrambled around the Wicklow mountains on our bikes and became obsessed by the Dakar rally. And now the biggest challenge I'd ever faced was less than forty hours away.

As the son of a film director, I had an unconventional and, occasionally, glamorous early life. By the age of five I'd appeared in a Hollywood movie, sitting on a sofa behind Jon Voight in one of the final scenes of *Deliverance*. Over the next decade I appeared in several other films directed or produced by my father, including *Excalibur,* my first proper acting role, *Nemo* and *The Emerald Forest*, in which I was chosen for the lead by a group of producers and studio executives who did not know I was the director's son.

The Emerald Forest was a huge success. Suddenly people were recognising me in the street and I was flying all over the world for premieres, promotion and press junkets. I moved to Los Angeles but the offers I thought would come rolling in failed to materialise. After six months I moved back to London, where I bumped into Olly, a girl who had recently split up with a mate of mine called Ian. As soon as she walked into the room my mouth dropped open. She is *gorgeous*, I thought. Although I didn't have a clue about proper romance, I could tell Olly needed a good old-fashioned courtship if I was to convince her that I was the right kind of guy. For months, we circled each other. We hadn't even kissed, but I felt completely in love and didn't want to blow it. After a few months of what seemed like the most protracted courtship on record, we went on holiday to Spain with some friends. Aided by the sun and Sangria, Olly and I got it together. I was twenty years old and felt like I'd hit the jackpot. Nineteen years later, married with two daughters, I still feel the same.

I moved in with Olly shortly after we got back from Spain and continued to make films and television shows, but each one was less distinguished than its predecessor. Even now I can't remember some of their names. By the mid-1990s I was making at most one film a year, keeping afloat by starting up a building and decorating business with a friend. In 1996, Doone, my first daughter, was born. Kinvara, her sister, was born the next year. From that point on, leaving my family at home to make films became even less appealing, but I still missed the adventure, the travelling and the money I'd tasted as a younger man.

In 1997 I got a part in a film that would eventually change my life. The part was relatively small – I was credited simply as Secretary – and the film was not a great success, but the actor playing the lead part in *Serpent's Kiss* was a fellow bike nut called Ewan McGregor. Ewan and I built a great friendship around our love of bikes and our families – we both had two daughters of similar ages – and when, a few years later, Ewan suggested riding two bikes around the world from London to New York, I leapt at the chance. Olly recognised it was a once in a lifetime opportunity and immediately said I should join Ewan. The only problem was that I couldn't afford it. But as we talked late into the night about the trip and thought about our wives' suggestions that we should keep a journal to remember it, the idea occurred to us that maybe we could finance the trip by filming it. And, with a production team on board, we'd have someone to help us with the bureaucracy – something at which we, as actors, were not particularly adept.

Gradually we pulled the trip together and in April 2004 set off from Shepherd's Bush. When the trip was underway I took some convincing that it would be a success. I was worried that we'd be seen as a couple of wanky actors poncing around on bikes. Even when we'd crossed Siberia I still felt there was some truth to that view. Before we set off from London I felt convinced that the trip wouldn't change me in the slightest. I didn't believe travel broadened the mind and I certainly didn't believe riding a bike from London to New York would change my life one little bit. Once it was over, I told myself, it would be back to building and decorating, with a film thrown in every few years if I was lucky.

I couldn't have been more wrong. After finishing Long Way Round, Ewan went straight back to his day job as a film star. No big change there. But Long Way Round taught me that a lot of things are possible if you believe in yourself and as we were approaching New York I was already hatching plans to avoid going back to my old life.

Many years earlier I'd filed away my childhood dreams of competing in the Dakar. In the days when I was fitting kitchens and painting living rooms it seemed a distant and unrealistic pipe dream. But, riding across America on open roads, I realised pipe dreams can come true provided you want them more than anything and if you focus totally on achieving them.

When we arrived in New York I told Russ Malkin, one of the Long Way Round producers, about my plan to do the Dakar. Russ is one of those eternally optimistic people. In Russ's world, anything is possible. In fact, the more impossible it seems, the more Russ wants to do it and his response was typical.

'Sounds interesting,' Russ said. 'Maybe we should do it.'

When Ewan and I were hatching our dream of riding around the world, I bumped into Russ, who I thought looked the spitting image of Rob Lowe, at a party in London. Russ told me about his background in organising and filming events, such as the Venice–Simplon Orient Express Challenge, which involved celebrities and professional drivers in Lamborghinis, Aston Martins and Ferraris dashing from London to Venice in a race to beat the Orient Express train. He'd recently produced the World's Fittest Woman, a competition in Hong Kong that was broadcast by Sky, and as a fellow biker who shared the same outlook as Ewan and me, Russ was the obvious choice to help us produce the Long Way Round documentary. Over the course of the fourteen-week trip, Russ did a fantastic job and we became very good friends, so when I thought of the Dakar, Russ was my only choice.

But Russ didn't mention the rally again that summer and I thought little more of it while I was on holiday with my wife and daughters. It was only in September, when Ewan and I received the first copies of the Long Way Round book, that I realised I'd been hoisted by my own big mouth. There, on the dust jacket, in the final sentence of my biography, were the fateful words: 'He rides a Ducati 748 and is preparing for the 2006 Paris–Dakar rally, if his wife lets him.'

Oh shit. I'd forgotten I'd ever written that.

A few weeks later, at a book signing, a member of the public pointed at the fateful sentence. 'You're doing the Dakar then?' he said. 'Good on yer.'

Oh no, I thought. I really was committed now.

I spoke to Russ again. Fortunately he was still interested.

'Sounds good, Charley, but you need to think about how you're going to do it,' he said. 'You could try on your own, but you'd have a better chance with someone who's done it before. If you want to do it that way, I'll help you.'

Even with Russ's encouragement, there was a part of me that was convinced my dreams might be quashed by the reality of having to earn a living to support my family. But, to my surprise, it soon became apparent that Long Way Round was going to be a huge success. The book reached number one in the bestseller charts and the television series sold around the world.

Ewan had been right all along. It was going to change my life.

And when I mentioned my Dakar dream to the people at BMW who had lent us three GS1150 Adventures for Long Way Round, or to the television executives at Sky who had bought the seven-part series from us, or to the people who had commissioned the book, none of them looked at me as if I was mad.

The BMW people tried to instil some reality. The questions came thick and fast. Did I realise the risks? Where would we get the money? They wanted answers. But they didn't say no. And the television and book people said yes straight away.

After feeling that I'd been part of a double act with Ewan for the last year, it was very reassuring to hear everyone's confidence in me. Maybe Long Way Round had been my OBE – Only Because of Ewan – but here was my chance to escape years of mind-numbing hard graft and do something I really wanted to do. I had to seize it.

At the end of October 2004, Russ and I travelled to Valencia for the final MotoGP race of the season. On the night before the race, shit-faced in a bar, I got talking to an Englishman with a massive smile called Chris Evans. Emboldened by maybe one beer too many, I grandly declared my ambitions to take part in the Dakar in 2006 and told Chris about wanting to make a documentary about Dakar privateers' experiences as all the coverage to date had focused on the professional factory teams.

'Well you better come and have a look at it in January, then,' Chris said. He went on to explain that he worked with ASO, as their English representative. Shouting above the music and the din of the club, Chris regaled me with dozens of stories about the Dakar and encouraged me to pursue my dream.

Christ, I thought, is no one going to tell me to abandon my Dakar ambition?

Starting to realise the scale of what I was taking on, I began to hope someone would say no. Then I'd be able to say that I had at least tried, without actually having to go through with it. But here was Chris Evans, a man with a direct connection to the heart of ASO, telling me that making a documentary would be no problem.

In January 2005 Russ and I boarded the first in a succession of planes that would take us to Tichit in eastern Mauritania. By now I thought I knew everything there was to know about the Dakar. But, as Russ liked to point out, I tend to think I know everything there is to know about everything anyway.

'What page is that on?' Russ would say whenever I piped up with some fact or anecdote about the Dakar.

'Whaddya mean *what* page is it on? What page of *what*?' I'd say.

'What page of the Charley Book of Everything?'

I knew the Dakar was tough. I knew it lasted fifteen days. I knew that it involved cars, trucks, bikes and support vehicles and helicopters and a travelling staff of more than 1000. But I had no concept of quite how tough and how big and how organised it was until we arrived at the bivouac in the Sahara desert.

Our pilot had flown us from Dakar through a dust cloud thick as custard in a single-engine ten-seat propeller plane. Flying blind, she dropped the plane as we approached the airfield outside Tichit, a God-forsaken dot on the map of west Africa, then looked for the bivouac in the swirling dust. Everyone in the plane was silent as she strained to see some sign of life. The instant she spotted the encampment below, the pilot pulled the plane into a tight downward spiral, not taking an eye off the runway until we slammed on to the ground. You could feel everyone in the plane holding their breath and tensing for the landing. As soon as the plane came to a stop, I flung the door open and threw myself on the ground. It had been a nightmare of a flight, but we were safe.

I wandered around the bivouac open-mouthed. The scale of the operation was so much larger than I had imagined. On the side of the airfield a huge Hercules transport aeroplane had been converted into an editing suite for twenty-seven editors. With its own air-conditioning, it had been made completely air-tight to keep out the desert dust.

The bivouac was like a carnival. There was activity everywhere, much of it chaotic. And everyone's attention was focused on the arrival zone. For hours we waited. Then, before we could see anything, the faint whine of a motorcycle engine cut through the desert dust. A minute or so later, we spotted a headlight and the first of the bikes arrived, a Yamaha ridden by David Frétigné, the stage winner.

It was early evening and only a handful of bikes had turned up. To everyone it was becoming clear that a scene of carnage was unfolding in the dunes before Tichit. The few bikers who had made it home were screaming at the ASO officials, shouting that people were going to die in the mayhem of the desert if they didn't take action immediately.

While I was standing there, asking myself if I seriously wanted to be part of this crazy event, a blue KTM from the Gauloises team rode in. The rider pulled off his helmet and standing right in front of us was Alfie Cox, a Dakar legend who was celebrating his birthday that day. As a South African, Alfie was one of the few English-speaking stars of the event.

'It's been a true day of the Dakar for sure,' Alfie said coolly, unfazed by the chaos surrounding him. 'Strenuous. Low vision. And lots of camel grass. A lot of the guys are going to spend some of the night coming out. The camel grass didn't stop all day – I mean five hundred kilometres non-stop.'

Clumps of prickly camel grass were a familiar sight on desert rallies. Usually about three feet wide and a couple of feet high, they were so tough and so deep-rooted they'd throw riders off their bikes and stop cars. I asked Alfie why riding between the clumps was so difficult. 'No rhythm,' he said. 'Up, down, up, down. You can't get going. Second gear, first gear, second gear, third gear. And if you hit them, you fly through the air.'

Whereas Alfie had taken about nine hours and twenty-three

minutes to ride the 669 kilometres from Zouérat to Tichit – just seven minutes slower than Frétigné – most of the riders would take nearly twenty-four hours. At 9 p.m. more than 80 per cent of the field was still out in the desert, many of them having run out of petrol because they hadn't received the news of an extra checkpoint.

By midnight the organisers realised they were facing a disaster. About a dozen trucks, the same number of cars and a few more motorbikes had reached the end of the stage. The remainder – several hundred vehicles in all – were stuck in the dunes, stranded because of mechanical failure, exhaustion or injury. I walked up to the medical tent to see what was going on and heard about a rider who had crashed and broken his arm. The medics had operated on him but he had now lapsed into a coma. Another guy had smashed most of the bones along the left side of his body.

A squadron of ASO trucks was loaded with fuel and sent off into the desert. Gradually the racers appeared. The next day's special stage was cancelled. Stage eight, from Tichit to Tidjika, still need to be ridden or driven, but it wouldn't be timed, and competitors were told that they would still be in the race, without time penalties, as long as they started stage nine by mid-morning on the following day.

In the early hours of the morning, just as I was about to search for somewhere to sleep, I spotted a familiar figure crouching over a bike in the pits. It was Simon Pavey, who had trained Ewan and me to ride off-road before Long Way Round. On his fourth Dakar attempt, Simon was struggling to repair a broken exhaust and sub-frame.

Simon told me what had happened to him. He'd had a problem with his bike early in the day and fallen to the back of the field. By late afternoon he'd made it to the checkpoint where they were giving bikes twenty litres of fuel, but Simon had damaged both his rear fuel tanks and insisted on filling up his bike. The official refused, but Simon ignored him. Although he had agreed to ride with two Irish lads, he knew there were still more than thirty miles of dunes to be crossed. The Irish riders were fannying around, so Simon thought, sod it, I'll just go on my own.

The ground around the checkpoint was so soft he had to get a push out of the refuel. Cars that had stopped to have their time cards stamped had to get their sand ladders out to move off again. It was crazy.

The dunes were a nightmare. Really hard. And to make matters worse, they were engulfed in a sandstorm. Closing his mind to everything around him, Simon rode in his little mental bubble, taking each dune one by one, never thinking too far ahead, just concentrating on what he could see in the beam of his headlight as the sun disappeared. Every so often, a car would pass by and Simon would stop, if he could, on the crest of a dune to watch the line the car had taken through the darkness. He'd try to memorise the dunes he'd glimpsed in the car's beams and work out a route.

It didn't take long for Simon to get stuck in a sand bowl – a deep hollow surrounded by dunes. While he was trying to dig out his bike a car got bogged down as well. It was a British team and Simon thought they'd help him get out, but the car left him behind. After maybe an hour of struggling, Simon managed to force his bike over the lip of the bowl, climb on to the saddle and move off, but he soon came to a stop on the upward slope of another dune. He made more than forty attempts to haul his bike over the dune, spending hours digging his bike out of deep sand then trying to get it moving before falling and sinking again.

The dune was too churned up and too soft to cross so he turned around and rode up the opposite slope, where he saw the headlights of some cars following another line. Trying to memorise what he'd seen in the beams of their lights, he attempted a different route, riding down into a valley between the dunes, bumping blind over tufts of camel grass and getting thrown off his bike several times. Needing to build up sufficient speed to power his bike over a distant dune, he was riding as fast as his bike would move in the soft sand but dunes create a short horizon and the range of his headlights couldn't keep up with the speed at which he was travelling. For most of the time he was riding almost totally blind. Three or four times that night he went straight over the bars of his bike.

It was nearly midnight and Simon had been riding hard since six that morning. He was so tired he was cresting dunes with his eyes shut. Just when he thought he couldn't ride any more, an American rider pulled alongside and found another line over the dune. Simon tried to follow him but he was so tired it took him three attempts. And, to make matters worse, the bike's air filter was clogged so the bike had no power.

Riding over the brow of the next dune, he came across more than twenty bikes caught in a sand bowl. They'd made a little camp. Physically incapable of continuing, Simon stopped with them and slept through the night. At dawn he started riding with the other bikers, but they were all on lighter KTMs and left him behind.

Simon stopped, changed his air filter and got moving again. A few miles further on, he met one of the Irish riders he'd left behind at the refuel, standing in the middle of the desert with no bike.

'Gary?' Simon said.

'My bike's about two ks over there. Can you help me?'

Gary jumped on the back of Simon's bike and they rode together to the Irish rider's abandoned bike, which had a flat battery. They jump-started it, then rode in tandem to the finish.

'Fucking hell!' I said when Simon finished telling me about his long, hard day. 'How d'you do it?'

'It's what Dakar's all about. Never giving up.'

To make things worse, it was a marathon stage. All competitors had to repair their own equipment. Simon looked exhausted so I grabbed some tools and dived in to help him. When we'd finished Simon handed me his road-book, a long roll of paper with directions for the rally, and signed it. 'See you here in '06,' it said.

'Yeah, hope I see you too.'

Chapter 2

I returned to England from Dakar wondering if I really was taking on more than I could handle. I'd seen hardened riders arrive exhausted at the Tichit bivouac and I'd trembled. They were among the best in the world and a lot of them were struggling. My only off-road experience was Long Way Round and there were many times on that trip when we'd averaged only sixty miles a day for a week. On one day we managed only fifteen miles, yet the terrain was no more difficult than anything on the Dakar. And if we were exhausted or fed up, we could simply stop and camp. There were no such luxuries on the Dakar. We'd have to average more than 370 miles a day for fifteen days with just one rest day at the halfway point. The longest day would involve riding nearly 550 miles, most of it across sand dunes, and if we didn't finish by the start time of the next day's stage, we'd be disqualified.

To make matters worse, I'd be trying to make a documentary at the same time. That multiplied the stress by a thousand. Aside from the complications involved with filming an event that never stands still, there would be more pressure on me to do well and much greater financial pressures. Most of all it meant my participation would take place under the full glare of television cameras. I knew there were already plenty of bikers who would like to see me fail, who regarded me as little more than a playboy on a bike. I wondered if I also needed a national television audience expecting the drama of injury or physical collapse.

But when I considered all my options, I realised that, as well as fulfilling a life-long ambition, the Dakar was an opportunity I couldn't ignore. I didn't want to return to installing kitchens and the Dakar was my only escape route. Even if it turned my Dakar dream into a nightmare, I had to make it work. I just couldn't see how. Fortunately, Russ, reliable as ever, had a sensible plan.

'I know you're passionate about doing it, but it's an incredibly dangerous race. You could enter on your own – it might be less hassle and it would certainly be less exposed – but I think you'd be a fool.

'Out there, on your own, you could get into serious trouble. You haven't the experience and you could get lost. You need a second rider to back you up, someone who's done it before. And, ideally, that second rider should train you too, and know all about the mechanics of BMW bikes.'

There was one obvious candidate: Simon Pavey.

I first met Simon in the spring of 2004, when he was nursing a broken collarbone after crashing out of the Dakar that year. With Nick Plumb, who had just finished the same rally, he took us on a two-day training course at BMW's off-road training ground in south Wales.

Simon liked to joke he was a native of south Wales – New South Wales. He'd grown up in the Southern Beaches district of

Sydney, near Bondi Beach, and got into bikes when a kid across the street let him have a ride on a mini bike he'd built himself. It had a lawnmower engine with a pull-cord start and no brakes, but Simon was hooked and from that moment on saved up all his pocket money until he had enough to buy a Honda XR75, a classic dirt bike. Aged thirteen, he rode his XR75 along footpaths, through sewers and drains to the Kurnell Peninsula, a vast area of sand dunes that formed the best playground any bike-obsessed kid could have wanted.

After hacking around on his own for a while, Simon joined a kids' mini-bike club, a kind of dune-khana, or Pony Club on two wheels, where he learned the skills of riding off-road. At sixteen he started racing in adult motocross races, winning the first race he entered. But ten-minute races around dirt tracks 'didn't float my boat much,' as Simon put it. As soon as he was seventeen – the minimum age requirement – Simon entered his first enduro, a day-long off-road event.

Young, enthusiastic, brave – and a bit reckless – Simon competed in all the state championship enduros, the East Coast Championship and dozens of desert races. He was never a top racer, but usually finished in the front of the field and won the state championship for hare scrambles one year. For Simon, it was more about the crack and discovering parts of the outback he never normally would have experienced than racing to win.

By the time he was nineteen, Simon was racing in six-day rallies in French Polynesia, the dirt-racing tropical paradise where he met Linley, who later became his wife. Having won a few stages and finished sixth overall, he was approached to race professionally in Japan.

Sponsored by the owner of a Sydney bike shop, Simon headed out to Yokohama, where he spent four months racing. Although the job was everything he could have wanted, he hated living in a Tokyo suburb and had a hard time dealing with the pressure put on him to win. There's a big difference between racing for yourself because you love it and racing to win for someone else. If Simon won, the Japanese owners of the team gave him a quiet pat on the back – after all, winning was his job – but if he came second or third no one on the team would speak to him and he was threatened with being sent back to Australia if he didn't win the next race. It took all the fun out of what had, until then, always been a passion. To any outsider, it looked like Simon was living the dream, but he was seeing the dream from its other side. It meant taking risks and being prepared to get hurt because your employer expected it of you. By the time his visa came up for renewal, he'd had enough.

In 1991 Simon packed his Honda XR600 in a crate, stuffed everything that he and Linley owned around it and came to England. His mother was English, so he had plenty of relatives to look up and no visa problems. He got a job in Catford, south London, training disadvantaged kids to be mechanics. He soon started entering British enduro races, representing the Victoria State team from Australia in the International Six-Day Enduro in 1993. In 1997, he scraped together enough money to enter the Atlas Rally in Morocco with some mates, including John Deacon, Britain's best enduro rider at the time. When he returned home, Linley took him aside.

'You better do the Dakar now,' she said.

'Where'll we get the money?' Simon replied.

'Just do it. We'll work it out,' Linley insisted. 'Don't talk about it any more. Just do it.'

With some help from the editor of *Bike* magazine and an XR600 loaned from Honda, Simon entered the Dakar as a true privateer – no support, no mechanic, just him – and finished. He was thirty years old and came fortieth, still his best result to date, but in the Dakar results don't really matter. Only getting to the beach in Dakar counts.

By the time I bumped into Simon on the 2005 Dakar, his record stood at two finishes (1998 and 1999) out of four, a very impressive record, given that only a third of all bikes got through each year. In 2003 he had a mechanical fault in southern Libya and ended the rally with a five-hundred-mile taxi ride to Tripoli. In 2004, Simon broke his collarbone less than twenty miles from the end of the ninth special stage. When I met Simon at Tichit in 2005, he was nursing his left wrist, having fractured the radius a few weeks before the race. Fighting against the pain, he made it to Dakar in seventy-eighth position, giving him a tally of three finishes in five Dakars.

A few weeks later, Simon was at the Alexandra Palace Bike Show, his wrist still strapped up. I knew that in Simon rested my best chance at the Dakar, but approaching him, particularly when I was asking someone who'd just finished the Dakar despite injury to be my water carrier – the lowest rank in any team – was a daunting prospect.

I thought a racer like Simon would turn a novice like me down flat. After a few minutes' small talk, I made my pitch. 'I don't suppose you'd be interested, but I'm looking for someone who can help me with the Dakar,' I said.

I hadn't asked Simon directly. And Simon didn't respond immediately – he later told me that he'd decided that he'd had enough after the pain of the 2005 rally – but he also hadn't turned me down.

I told him about our plan to film a documentary about the privateers on the Dakar. 'Suppose that'd be interesting to see,' Simon said. 'You only ever see the guys at the front on telly – such a small part of the rally. Good story to be told.'

Simon talked about what I'd be letting myself in for. 'There's so much involved in getting to the start line,' he said. 'You have to enter in June and at that time the route's not even announced. You're paying seven grand to enter something, but you don't know where it's going or what the rules are.'

I soon learned that Simon had a never-ending stream of Dakar anecdotes. 'In 1998, my first year, the road-book dropped through my letterbox in December. It was eighteen days that year and the first day was just short of a thousand kilometres. The second day was nearly twelve hundred kilometres. And I'm thinking, hang on, I've never ridden more four hundred ks in a day in my life! I just shat myself.'

Again I asked myself why I wanted to put myself through such torture. 'Do you think I could do it?' I said.

'It's not technical ability you need,' he said. 'It's stamina. They grind you down. Huge distances day after day after day. You want to get to Dakar – you've got to want to crawl on your hands and knees across broken glass. It's such a long way. Such a long, long way.'

I told Simon a bit more about my plans. 'If you know of anyone who'd be interested, just let me know,' I said. Then I left Simon to think it over. I knew it would be a very difficult decision. Nursing someone else through the Dakar was a completely different proposition to doing it yourself. But for the last five years Simon had been running an off-road biking school. What better advertising for him, I thought, than getting a complete novice to the finish?

A few days later Simon rang. 'About the Dakar,' he said. 'Yeah, might be interested.'

I punched the air.

'You need to start training straight away.'

'Yeah, of course. We'll get straight down to it.'

*

On 12 April, more than two months later, I started training. I'd simply not got on with it before then. The night before, I met with Simon. He wasn't happy.

'Thing is, Charley, I could go to the start line of the Dakar *right now* and be ready for it. Could you, Charley?' he said.

'Er no,' I answered.

Simon had me bang to rights. I'd had no training on sand. I hadn't ridden a bike with aggression and speed for a very long time – and never fast off-road. And I certainly had never ridden a bike full of fuel through a desert day after day for a fortnight. I had a lot to learn and Simon's concerns were very valid.

'The Dakar's not like Long Way Round, Charley, stopping each day when *you* want. On the Dakar, you can't stop until you get to the end of the stage. You gotta get there before nightfall. From the moment the sun goes up, it's already setting.'

I winced.

'People don't realise it when they watch it on the telly, but when you come out at the end of the special section you've got maybe three hundred ks of liaison to the bivouac. And you probably had two hundred ks of liaison first thing in the morning, before the special. Never see those bits on the box, do you? You finish the special at four, five in the afternoon. It's dusk and you're setting out to ride from London to Paris. Only it's not a nice motorway. It's not even tarmac. If you're lucky it's a sandy track. But it could be dunes. And dunes in daylight are a nightmare. In the dark they're impossible.'

I knew I had a lot to learn and I feared I'd taken on too much. But I also knew I had a big advantage in having persuaded Simon to join the team. When Ewan and I set off from London for New York neither of us had any idea what to expect. We were blown away by the state of the roads in Kazakhstan. This time, I'd be with someone who knew the tracks of the Sahara like his back garden.

We started our first training session in typical Welsh drizzle, Simon watching as I reacquainted myself with riding a bike off-road. After an hour on a dirt bike, only part of it off-road, I had terrible arm pump. Shocked by the battering from my handle-bars, the muscles in my arms were seizing up. It was obvious I had a lot of work to do on my physical fitness. Other than running a few miles, I'd not done a thing since speaking to Simon in early February.

By the end of the first day off-road, I think I'd left Simon pleasantly surprised. I knew he didn't have high expectations of my ability, but I'd got through some of the hardest tracks; one of which was christened 'Oh Fuck Hill' by local riders. I could see what Simon was thinking. It was just what I would have thought – can an effete actor cut it with proper dirt riders? – so I knew I had to prove to him straight away that I had the guts to keep going. Time and time again, when Simon was waiting at the top of a rise while I lay in the dirt at the bottom, I picked up my bike and got back on it or pushed it up the hill. Simon had dropped me in at the deep end, but I'd survived and shown him I was prepared to put in the effort.

For the first month of training we rode eight or nine hours a day for three or four days a week. It was intense, slog-it-out, carry-the-bike, pick-yourself-up-again-and-again riding, but I kept up.

Shirty, the British Gas Gas distributor, had lent me two EC300 dirt bikes. These nifty two-stroke bikes were ideal for training. I could whack them around with relative ease and control them with greater sensitivity than larger bikes. I could ride them faster, thereby sharpening my reflexes. And if I fell off, I could pick them up without difficulty and carry on. The light bikes gave me lots of confidence and, as I gained confidence, the technical skills became instinctive.

In the early days I made classic mistakes. We'd be trying to climb a really rutty uphill track and my instinct was to sit right on the back of the bike to put my weight over the rear tyre in order to get some grip. But it was the wrong approach. Dirt riders press down on the front wheel because they need their weight over the wheel that steers. Sitting at the back with arms out straight, it's impossible to control the front wheel properly.

'Make the front go where you want it to go and the bike follows,' Simon would shout. 'Momentum. It's all about momentum. Momentum is our friend.'

I was learning to ride in a totally new way. Most of my experience had been on road or track bikes, and it took a lot of concentration to undo the habits of a road rider. On the track, riding sports bikes, I'd learned to tuck in my elbows into an aerodynamic position. But on a dirt track you need to ride with your elbows sticking out wide. It's the only way you can absorb the bumps and maintain leverage on the handlebars.

There were three elements to off-road riding: throttle control, clutch control and foot pegs. You had much more control and balance of the bike if you stood on the pegs, but it was difficult to get out of the habit of sitting on the seat. As soon as I sat down, I discovered, the bike was carrying me. On the pegs, I was controlling the bike.

The second new thing was to learn to avoid using the brakes. Dirt bike riding involved using the throttle and clutch to maintain momentum. Moving off from a standstill and then trying to build momentum is very difficult on dirt. It was vital to keep going, particularly when going uphill. On a very technical or steep climb, there is a world of difference between complete standstill and a little bit of movement that could be built upon to maintain momentum. Keep pushing – a little bit more, a little bit more, a little bit more – that was the key. Another vital skill was to look ahead, so that I saw things early and could plan my route. I had to spot obstacles, such as boulders or narrow ruts, as early as possible, then I had to find an alternative route and commit to it, even if it was a tiny gap, and use my momentum to carry me through it.

There were no great secrets to off-road riding. It was about courage, commitment, confidence and keeping a cool head.

Nevertheless, the learning curve was as steep and hard as the trails that Simon forced me to master. I fell off a lot and picked up a lot of injuries in the early days. Some weeks I'd be covered in cuts. I gained scars I'll have for the rest of my life. I picked up a hairline fracture in my spine and crushed two vertebrae. I cracked ribs, recovered, then fell and cracked the same ribs again.

After a few weeks I rode a really hard seven-hour training session with Simon and some local lads, including Lee Walters, a Welsh enduro legend who carved most of the trails through the mountains. All of them were expert riders with an intimate knowledge of the mountains. As soon as we set off I realised what was going on. They were out to break me. We rode up, across and through some of the nuttiest places I'd ever seen. We ascended banks as high as four-storey houses and almost as vertical. I had to ride with my chest pressing against the handlebars to keep the front wheel down – otherwise I would have cartwheeled backwards down the hill.

I took a lot of hits. Screaming along a gravel road, doing around 50mph, the back end drifting out as I cornered, a branch caught my arm. Whipping me off the bike, it dumped me on the ground in a cloud of dust while my bike ran on. 'Fucking hell, Charley,' said Simon. 'We thought you'd had it.'

Lee was laughing. 'Ten out of ten for that,' he guffawed.

Ten minutes later another branch hit me square in the face and knocked me off my bike. For the next five minutes I couldn't see for stars circling my head. Another hour or so later, I took a big fall and could hear Lee and Simon speeding towards me, shouting to find out if I was still conscious. The next day I had black bruises running from my shoulder to my knee down one side of my body. Simon and his mates didn't let up the next day, or the day after. I returned to London barely able to walk, but I'd survived. In the eyes of the Welsh lads I'd been beaten but I felt proud. I'd kept up with them and everything they'd thrown at me.

My only worry was that I'd started to make mistakes and take stupid falls in the last hour and a half simply because of exhaustion. And that worried me. At the same stage on a Dakar day – four to five hours after starting – I'd be passing the halfway mark at best.

The only solution was to put in the hours, building bike fitness and stamina so that I would take longer to tire and so that when I was exhausted I could fall back on a sound technical skill base.

When I wasn't in Wales training on the bike, I would train at a gym in London. I could tell by the size of my stomach that I needed to lose weight. When slouched in front of the television, I'd recently taken to balancing a dish on the top of my belly like Homer Simpson. It was ideal for dipping chips in ketchup.

Thinking I'd been clever in starting my gym training early, in May I met for the first time with Natalie, a personal trainer who would let me know just how much work I still needed to do.

Stripped to my shorts, I stood in front of Natalie's unflinching and rather bemused gaze as she ran a tape measure around my vitals.

'Weight doesn't really matter,' she said.

That sounded good.

'It's more the size of your body,' Natalie said, 'to see whether you're putting on or losing fat. This is where I'm going to catch you out if you're not doing what I ask you to do. OK?'

That didn't sound so good.

'Just relax and look up,' Natalie said as she took the last of her measurements before consulting some tables and calculating my body mass index.

'You are twenty-nine point three,' Natalie said, 'which is above the . . . erm . . . *concerned* level.'

'How embarrassing,' I said. 'I'm in the "concerned" bracket?'

'Yes.'

I could see that the table from which she was reading had been stuck over another table on her piece of paper. 'What's it covering up?' I said.

Natalie peeled back the edge of the table to show what was underneath it. It was exactly same table with the same ranges of body mass index, but the categories were labelled in more blunt terms. According to that table, I was officially obese.

Natalie giggled. 'I didn't wanted to hurt your feelings,' she said.

'But I'm absolutely healthy,' I said.

Natalie laughed again. So did I, nervously, as she led me out to the gym. 'How are you feeling?' she said.

'Depressed. I don't feel obese. You can change me, can't you? I'm only 4 per cent over the limit.'

Natalie devised a training plan to build up stamina, lose weight and increase strength and cardiovascular fitness. It involved running when I wasn't training on a bike and two to three gym sessions a week.

Fitness and well-honed bike skills were only half the Dakar formula. Just as important was a good bike. As soon as Simon came on board he put forward Gareth Edmunds, a young, recently graduated motor sport engineer. Gareth had been involved in dirt bike racing since he was five years old and had known Simon for some time. He'd raced in the British and European Enduro Championships, but retired from racing in the final year of his university course to concentrate on bike mechanics. Gareth was studying in Swansea, about forty miles from Simon's home in the Brecon Beacons. He had prepared Simon and Nick Plumb's BMW bikes for the 2005 Dakar. The bikes had performed brilliantly, even though Gareth had developed it only in his spare time, studying at university from nine to four, then toiling every day in the workshop from five to midnight for months.

No one in Britain had more up-to-date experience of preparing a BMW for the Dakar than Gareth. He'd also travelled with Simon and Nick on the Dakar as their mechanic – and even seemed to relish the bone-grinding exhaustion of spending a fortnight travelling every day in a support vehicle, then working through every night on the bike.

Gareth was totally committed; even during the 2005 Dakar he was making notes on how to improve the design of his 2006 bike and compiling spares lists, just in case someone asked him to join their team. When we asked Gareth to build our bike, he immediately said yes.

Gareth finished university at the end of June. On 20 July, after a short holiday, he set off for Germany to develop the rally bike at the Black Forest headquarters of Touratech, a name synonymous among bikers with off-road riding. Working with Herbert Schwarz, the company's founder, Jochen Schanz, his partner, Wolfgang Banholzer, a technician who had worked on the Dakar five times for BMW and Touratech, and Ian Rowley, Touratech's head of development, Gareth would spend the next four months in Germany.

BMW gave us four F650 Dakar bikes, three race bikes and one spare, which was brilliant, but these were off-the-peg off-road bikes built for general touring and trail riding, not for racing thousands of miles across a desert. Gareth stripped down each bike until it was just a heap of parts lying on the floor of the workshop. The 650cc single-cylinder four-stroke engine was taken apart. Gearbox bearings were replaced with stronger bearings. The automatic cam-chain tension was replaced with a manual equivalent, simply because it was more durable. Special clutch covers were made because the standard cover could not be removed without draining the coolant fluid. The new cover, held down by just six bolts, opened straight into the clutch basket, making it much easier to replace or repair the clutch.

With these new parts in place, Gareth rebuilt the engine, tuning it for reliability rather than performance. We could have got more horsepower out of it, but our need was for an engine that would reliably get us to Dakar, rather than going fast but not getting us there.

Wolfgang modified the wiring loom and control cables, making them more resistant to damage from chips and stones, and tying them in more closely to the frame so the bike would have a tighter turning circle. The subframe was strengthened, the exhaust system was improved and the lights were replaced with high-intensity Xenon and LED units. A more resilient Hawker battery was added. The BMW fuel tanks were replaced with larger and lighter tanks from Touratech.

We used standard swing arms and chain adjuster end caps, but strengthened them to take harder knocks. The front forks were replaced with factory Marzocchi forks, custom-tuned by Chris Hockey, a suspension specialist who was a mate of Simon's. We used custom-built Fournales rear suspension shocks and Öhlin steering dampers, GMX radiators and cooling system, a Venhill throttle, Tomaselli clutch perches and Magura handlebars.

The wheels were a work of art. The front wire-spoke wheel was made by Talon, a British company that also supplied KTM, which meant there would be plenty of spares on the rally if we exhausted our spare wheels. Gareth had the back wheel custom-built from a F650GS Dakar hub with extra-strong rims and spokes. Both wheels were fitted with Michelin desert rally tyres. Instead of being inflated with air, the tyres contained spongy race mousses which wouldn't deflate when punctured.

Nothing was overlooked. The standard switches and controls, such as the starter button and light switches, were replaced with heavy-duty rubberised controls positioned where we found them easiest to reach.

Gareth built a fake second exhaust and silencer to house the tool kit and a few spare parts. From a foot away you couldn't tell the difference between the fake and real tubes. He also designed a bash plate that ran the length of the underside of the bike and had a lockable chamber to hold three of the statutory five litres of drinking water required in the race regulations. As well as water and a tool kit, we had to find space to stow a survival pack including a mirror, strobe light, flares, lighter, glow sticks, first aid kit, survival blanket, water purification tablets, vitamin C, salt tablets, compasses, Imodium and our daily ration pack.

We added brackets for the GPS unit and all the other electronics required by the race regulations. Among these was the Sentinel, a warning system that emitted a piercing siren if a car or truck was approaching. In earlier Dakars, riders had been run over, knocked off their bikes or sent careering into a crash when the cars and trucks steamed past. The Sentinel would provide an advance warning – or so the theory went.

Starting with bikes that cost around £6,000 new, we'd spent about £25,000 on each bike by the time we had finished. And that was just for parts. It didn't include the cost of employing a full-time mechanic or Touratech's assistance and materials.

In effect, we had to put together four bikes – one bike each plus a replacement engine and a bike's worth of spare parts that would be carried by the MAN six-wheeled support truck, on which we were renting space from the Bowler Off-road team. We would carry the spare bike engine in our BMW X5 assistance vehicle, which would be used to drive Gareth and Wolfgang, our two race mechanics, between bivouacs. After working on the bikes all night, Gareth and Wolfgang, five-point strapped into bucket race seats and helmeted for ten to twelve hours a day, would try to sleep while Russ and Jim Foster, a former SAS soldier who entered the Dakar in a car in 1992 and now worked as a war zone cameraman, would navigate and drive the X5.

Meanwhile, I was continuing to train with Simon in Wales. By mid-May I was feeling much stronger. I felt like I knew what I was doing. And Simon seemed to be happier with my riding. Having realised how much I needed to load the front wheel, I could now keep up with him.

In spite of an inherent tendency to act like a bull in a china shop, I was coming to realise that dirt riding wasn't all about speed. Riding too fast just to keep up with other riders could get me into trouble. I needed to keep to my own pace, within my own boundaries and concentrate on technique, such as using my back brakes and a touch of front brake to swing out the back wheel in order to get around a corner at the bottom of a steep and narrow hill.

At last I'd started to enjoy myself and Simon was surrounded by great people who made it a joy to stay with him. Simon's wife Linley was very encouraging and supportive. His son Llewellyn was a thirteen-year-old wise guy who had an opinion about everything but would do anything to help anyone. And there was a bunch of Welsh riders who were all great characters.

Paul Green had a Welsh accent so thick I couldn't understand a lot of what he said, but he was a lovely guy, kind, generous and endlessly enthusiastic about off-road riding. He helped me fix my

Gas Gas, stocked loads of parts in his shop and provided hundreds of cups of tea and sandwiches during training. And, after a while, I could understand most things he said. Matt Hall was a south London lad who spent most weekends dirt biking in the Welsh mountains or at enduro races, either competing or filming them.

Tony Woodhams was a zany guy into yoga, Buddhism and motorbikes. A bit of an old hippy, Tony had been nicknamed Rubber Band on account of the contortions he could put his body through and would disappear for months on epic bike journeys through North Africa or Asia or South America.

But best of all was the feeling that I was living the dream. In one week in May I spent two days at Donington racetrack with Ron Haslam, learning how to ride a sports bike fast. I did a Donington lap in one minute fifty-five seconds (and boy was I chuffed with that), then I jumped on the back of Ron's bike and he took me round in one minute fifty-one, which was even cooler. From Donington I drove down to Wales in an X5 – supplied by BMW – and when I got there I opened the boot on a biker's wet dream: race boots, a back protector, full leathers, a motocross helmet, a filthy motocross jacket, a racing helmet with a dark visor, and a pair of motocross boots. I stood back and stared at the treasures. It was a beautiful sight and I was so proud of it.

Everything felt fantastic. The team was coming together; my first rally bike was being built for me in Germany and I hadn't had to lay a finger on it; I was feeling fitter and my riding was getting better.

The next day we got up at dawn and rode until dusk. A whole day out on the bikes – a dream – and I was loving it. It didn't seem difficult any more. I thought I'd found my niche: the harder the slog, the steeper the hill, the deeper the mud, the wetter the bog, the more I loved it.

After a few days in London dealing with the boring paperwork and logistics that surrounded the Dakar, or the tedium of a team meeting, I'd be busting to get down to Wales to pull on my bike kit and get dirty. I'd be yearning to get stuck in some mud, to fall to the ground as I tried to paddle the bike through a rut with my feet. Or to take my helmet off and watch the steam rise off me, my clothes soaking wet from the sweaty effort of pushing my bike through a bog. It was a great antidote to stress and frustration. On some days, Simon and I would set off with a pack of other riders. Some of them would hate it. They couldn't handle it when it got tough. But the harder it was, the more fun it seemed to me.

I was impressed with how much I'd improved. I had pace and I was picking up the skills. I was really happy and everything was going great at home. Life felt sweet.

Then Simon made a suggestion. 'Time for your first enduro,' he said. 'Lose your race cherry.'

That spoilt everything.

Chapter 3

MAY TO AUGUST 2005

'We can go out play riding or training – call it what you like – but you will never push yourself like you will when you're racing,' Simon said. 'That's why you need to enter some races.'

Play riding? I thought I was riding hard, but obviously Simon didn't agree. He said even a three-hour club-level event would be tougher than anything I'd encountered so far.

'What do you mean, I won't push myself?' I said.

'Go out fun riding and as soon as you start to get a little bit tired someone in the group will stop for a cigarette,' Simon said. 'You just stop. You don't just push and push and push.'

On 29 May, I drove up the M1 to Yorkshire for the True Grit Hare and Hounds race, held at Driffield army barracks. It was a simple format: packs of about twelve or fifteen riders started at one-minute intervals, chasing the pack ahead of them. Whoever completed the most laps in three hours was the winner.

At first it was a shock to find that there were some two hundred other riders hacking around the bumpy, jumpy, dusty track, but I did well, finishing towards the bottom of the middle of the pack.

I'd lost my 'race cherry' as Simon called it and I'd not disgraced myself.

'How'd it go?' Simon asked, straight after the race.

'OK. I fell over a few times and I was near the back, but I made it.'

Simon threw his arms around me and gave me a big pat on the back. No matter what happened, Simon was always very positive.

'Great. Hope you learned from it. Made you realise that it ain't easy. And when it gets hard is when you've got to really dig deep.'

A week later I was at Cwm Canol in Wales for the Wirral Off Road, another Hare and Hounds, nursing a sore and bruised left arm that I'd injured while training that week. Halfway through the race I gave up. My arm was so puffed up with blood it wobbled like a blancmange every time I went over a bump on the crowded track. It was so painful I feared I wouldn't be able to hold the handlebars for much longer. Riding through a forested section of the course, my arm becoming weaker as I clipped trees, I fell off the bike. I got up, moved off, then clipped some more trees. Fuck this, I thought. Feeling I'd given my best, I threw in the towel.

Simon wasn't happy. He put a brave face on it, but I could see he was disappointed. At first he said maybe it was the right decision not to push myself too hard. There was no point in injuring myself, he said, and then being unable to ride for a month. But I knew what he was thinking. If he was being honest, he would have said finishing is everything – no matter what happens – because that's what the Dakar is all about.

And if I was honest with myself, I had to admit I'd talked myself out of the race. I'd spent most of the three hours trying to come up with an excuse to stop. Eventually I did. I just pulled over and gave up. I was in pain and exhausted, but, more than that, I ran out of willpower.

A month later I had a chance to prove to Simon that I wasn't a quitter. Round three of the European Enduro Championship at Hafren in Wales was one of the toughest races held in Britain. On 16 July, I lined up with 160 of the best riders in Europe, including Simon and Nick Plumb. Simon didn't tell me it was a two-day race until three days before the start and I didn't even dare think about whether I was ready for it.

The night before the race, Simon explained the rules. There were time checks and checkpoints, and you had time limits for certain stages. I panicked, but Simon assured me I'd be fine. I wasn't convinced.

The race started, the crème de la crème of Europe shot off, and who was the slowest of all? Me – that's who. My spirits plummeted as everyone flew past me and disappeared into the distance.

Simon stuck with me for most of the day, egging me on and shouting encouragement. 'Doing well,' he shouted at one of the checkpoints. 'Really well! Keep going!'

It felt good to be mixing with the big boys. On the second lap, Simon pulled alongside. 'You're cruising. It's great,' he shouted. I waved Simon on. 'Just go!' I shouted. 'I'm OK.' Simon raced ahead and I didn't see him until the finish. We'd done two three-hour laps and, despite being completely outclassed, I was only about eight minutes behind the frontrunner at the end of the first day. I felt great.

'In fairness, Charley, we did chuck you in at the deep end,' Simon said afterwards, 'but you were awesome. Lucky it was a sunny day. Everyone's crying if it's wet at Hafren.'

That night I stayed in a bed and breakfast and went to bed early. 'It's all about getting through the first day,' Simon said before I turned in, 'and being really sore and waking up the next morning feeling like shit and getting back on the bike. Sleep tight.'

I woke up hardly able to move. I was fucked. Completely knackered.

A few hours later I lined up with the rest of the field for the start, but from the moment an official shouted 'go', I felt beaten. The laps had been lengthened to four hours each with seven or eight checkpoints on each lap, a couple of fuel stops and some short special technical stages. Each lap was thirty-six miles through forest and bogs. So many riders passed me that I was soon riding on my own, getting steadily more depressed. I started falling off a lot. I rode up a little goat path, fell off, climbed back on to my bike, rode down into a small valley and slipped over again. It took me about ten minutes to pick up my bike and get it moving.

By the time I got round to the special section, where a lot of spectators were standing, I was in the last five. I felt a fool, wobbling like a muppet in front of everyone. I thought a lot of the spectators would know who I was and be willing me to fall over or give up, but they were all cheering me on. Maybe they knew how difficult it was.

However, the crowd's cheers didn't help much. I rode a bit further, hating every minute. Everyone had passed me and the marshals were starting to walk away from the course to have their lunch. It was awful. Depressed, tired and really hurting, I stopped shortly before I finished the first lap. I'd shot my load on the first day and left nothing in reserve.

I made my way back to my car and was getting ready to leave when Linley, Simon's wife, appeared and persuaded me to wait until Simon had finished. With great reluctance, I hung around. When I saw him striding towards me, I wished I'd already left. It was coming off him in waves. He was pissed off and I was going to have to face his wrath.

'I'm really sorry but I was getting really tired,' I said, feeling a bit pathetic. 'I was falling off a lot . . . and I fell down this sort of valley . . . right at the bottom . . . it took me fifteen minutes to get out . . . and I was potentially going to . . .'

'If you'd run out of time and *had* to stop – no problem,' Simon said. 'But you proved yesterday that you can do it. You've got the technical ability.'

Simon went on: 'There's nothing on the Dakar to match the worst of Hafren. But what you need is mental strength. And in those terms, the leap between Hafren and the Dakar is *huge*. Today was a failure and you can't afford to fail even once on the Dakar.'

Although I could understand Simon's disappointment, I felt he was being very hard on me. Hang on a minute, I wanted to say. This is the first proper race I've ever done and you failed to tell me it was fucking two days, then you fucking failed to tell me about any of the rules and then you failed to say, 'listen, save a bit for the second day'. Instead I bit my lip. I felt that although finishing a race might be important for Simon, it wasn't for me. I knew that when I needed to finish, I would finish. I'd managed it on the Long Way Round. We'd ridden every day for 113 days and we'd finished every single one of them. We arrived at Magadan in Siberia and at New York precisely on schedule.

I couldn't see why Simon was being so negative. I'd done a day and a half of one of the toughest events on the enduro calendar and he wasn't satisfied.

But instead of building bridges, I made things much worse. I packed my things into the boot of my car, got in it, waved to Simon and drove off to go on holiday with my family. I knew it would leave Simon really questioning my commitment, but it was what I wanted to do right then. I knew Simon would see me as a quitter and I could see from the disappointed look on his face that I wasn't what he expected of a Dakar finisher. But right then I didn't care. I wanted to be with my family and away from Simon's critical gaze.

While I was on holiday I thought back over the last year. It was exactly a year since Ewan and I rolled into New York at the end of Long Way Round and here I was preparing for the Dakar with a TV deal from Sky. It was hard to believe my dreams had come true.

The week before the holiday I'd been to the Mongolian embassy, where the ambassador told us that because of Long Way Round the number of British tourists visiting Mongolia had increased by 25 per cent, something that made me feel very proud.

The day after visiting the Mongolian embassy we flew to Germany for a meeting with Touratech. Carrying a long and comprehensive list of requirements, Simon, Gareth, Russ and I were expecting a difficult meeting, but Touratech bent over backwards to accommodate all our wishes. They wanted to build the bikes exactly to our specification, they said. Then, midway through the meeting, Herbert, the owner of Touratech, said he wanted to sell the *Long Way Round* DVD and book in the Touratech catalogue. I was stunned. The catalogue was the Bible for anybody setting out to do any kind of long-distance journey on a bike. For Ewan and me, appearing in the Touratech catalogue would be the ultimate accolade.

As we were sitting in the meeting room at Touratech, talking things over, it suddenly hit me like a ton of bricks. I was having a pukka rally bike built for me on which I wouldn't even have turned a screw. The thought of how fortunate I was totally blew me away, but it also raised the hairs on the back of my neck. It brought home the stark fact that the deeper I got into the project, the less easily I could back out of it. The responsibility was enormous.

When I considered that of the three races I'd entered, I'd finished only one – and that race was by far the easiest of the three – I felt slightly foolish. Twice I'd talked myself out of finishing. I'd bottled out of the Wirral and the European Enduro races when I should have finished. I needed to prove to myself that I wouldn't buckle when things got tough on the Dakar. I needed greater mental strength. And, more than anything, I needed to do another two-day event and finish it. A lot of people had put their faith in me and the time had come to stop letting people down.

Life felt good – apart from the fact that I couldn't seem to finish a fucking enduro race.

While I was on holiday, Simon was plotting. Thinking – quite rightly – that I would have spent the three weeks in Spain larding it by the pool, not doing any riding and very little training, Simon entered me into the British Enduro Championship at Crychan in Wales on a weekend soon after I returned from holiday.

And other things had been afoot while I'd been sunning myself. Since the European Enduro, Russ and I had been searching for a third rider to join the Race to Dakar team.

Nick Plumb, who'd partnered Simon three times previously, was an obvious choice. He finished in 2003, even though he'd injured his ankle. In 2004, Nick crashed out with an injury and was reported officially lost after he was left stranded in the desert. And, in 2005, he dropped out after the sixth stage due to a technical problem.

Nick had a score to settle with the Dakar and he was undoubtedly highly motivated to finish. He was an out-and-out racer, one of the best enduro riders in Britain, but we needed someone who was prepared to let their bike be cannibalised for spare parts if mine or Simon's failed. Nick was probably too much of a competitor to dawdle with me.

We also considered an American rider, thinking it might be fun to have three riders from three different continents, and a female German rider who might provide some welcome relief from the relentless machismo of our all-male team.

But the more we thought about it, the more we kept coming back to Matt Hall. Matt had never attempted the Dakar, but he was a very experienced dirt biker. He first straddled a bike when he was only eight years old and started racing when he was eleven. In his mid-teens Matt got distracted by the usual temptations of adolescence and stopped racing, but he'd taken it up again four years ago, riding at weekends with Simon and Nick Plumb. Matt was a solid rider, and he was carrying a trump card that put him ahead of the other contenders: he was an experienced cameraman who produced his own enduro race videos. If anything happened to us, as surely it would, we needed one of our riders to film it. With a great sense of humour and no problem with playing third fiddle to Simon and me, Matt became the obvious choice.

Matt and I met as official Dakar teammates at the British Enduro. The team was complete and the bikes were nearly finished. Relieved that things were at last falling into place, I now had a new challenge. From now on I needed to impress Matt as well as Simon.

The night before the race, Simon drummed into me that a huge leap in performance was required for me to compete in the Dakar and that I'd need to start proving myself in the next few races.

'Before my first Dakar, I did the Atlas Rally, my first African enduro. Eight days in May and the biggest, hardest race I'd ever done, but I finished,' he said. 'The next January I did the Dakar and finished. A few months later, I got an offer to ride in the Tunisia

45

Rally – almost the same as the Atlas. Eight days and similar distances. They're both World Cup rounds but, after Dakar, the Tunisia Rally was like a holiday. Just unreal. A walk in the park.'

Simon made it clear he wasn't worried about my bike skills. It was the determination and mental strength that concerned him. 'When I entered the Dakar the first time, I believed I could get there,' he said. 'Probably only because I didn't know how hard it was. Blind faith and ignorance. But I did it also because it cost so much that I thought it was my one and only chance. Riding in convoy back into the centre of Dakar after the finish, I was crying my eyes out. Tears running down my face. An unbelievable feeling. I'd got what I really wanted. Do you want it that badly, Charley?'

I felt I did, but before then I had a lot to prove. On a rainy morning at 8 a.m. I joined the start line for the first day of the British Enduro. The rain didn't let up the whole day. It was carnage, a mammoth mud bath. Stuck in deep, mile-long ruts, there was nothing to do but paddle with my feet to keep the bike moving. The mud turned to swamp, but I gritted my teeth as I hacked around a course more like the Somme than a racetrack. Covered in crap from head to foot, it took ages to get anywhere. My trousers were caked with a quarter of an inch of muck and I felt twice my usual weight just because of the mud I was carrying. At one point, I stopped to scoop water from a stream to wash the mud off my gloves and handlebars because the mud had become so thick and slippery I couldn't control the throttle.

A little further on I got stuck again, my bike sinking beneath its axles in a muddy bog near a group of riders also unable to get moving and shouting at me to help them. I got off my bike and squelched over to the other bikers, pushed them out of the mud, then watched them ride out of sight, leaving me staring at their tail-lights.

Unable to free my bike because of the suction of the mud, I waited until another rider got stuck nearby. 'Help me! Can you help me?' he shouted. 'I can't get out.'

I'd fallen for that ploy already. 'You get off your bike and help me first,' I yelled. 'Then I'll help you. Otherwise you can fuck off!'

The rider helped me drag my bike out of the quagmire. I assisted him and we rode off, but the delay put me out of the race. I arrived at the next checkpoint too late to be allowed to continue on to the next stage. I was forced to retire.

At the end of a long, hard day, I was proud to have survived. My timings were dreadful, but that didn't matter. I'd had a right old laugh, skidding around the course and, most importantly, I'd not given up. I'd *finished*.

I went to bed thinking I'd cracked it. Surely no single day on the Dakar would be as hard, I reckoned. No one could do fifteen days like that.

The next day started brilliantly. The rain had stopped and the mud had caked overnight into a hard surface with fewer deep, sticky ruts. And, after the mud-sodden mayhem of the previous day, the organisers had shortened and reversed the course.

I was doing fantastically, riding confidently and enjoying every minute of it, when I put my foot down in a muddy rut. Moving off, I left my boot behind in the mud. Fuck! Just when everything was going so well.

The bike stopped on the side of the track, I pulled my boot out of the gunk and fell over. Shit! Now I was as wet and muddy as the previous day. I put my boot on and noticed I'd lost the shin guard. There was absolutely no protection above my ankle. Knowing it was a sure thing that I would fall again, I had to retire. I couldn't risk getting my foot caught under the bike without proper protection. After one and a half days' good riding I was gutted.

I felt confident I could have finished and consoled myself with the thought that if I'd been going any faster and got stuck I might have torn tendons in my foot, dislocated my ankle or broken my leg. It was lucky I'd noticed the damage to my boot when I was moving slowly.

Simon wasn't at the race, but when I saw him for training the next week I could see before he spoke that he wasn't satisfied. There was no hiding his frustration. 'You could have taped around it or borrowed someone else's boot . . .' he said, '. . . or something . . . just to keep going.'

Once again, I'd failed in Simon's eyes. He thought I wasn't a finisher, whereas I thought he was becoming ridiculously hardline. I didn't want to risk breaking my leg and jeopardising my Dakar entry by finishing a British enduro at all costs.

Simon sat me down on a sunny strip of mountainside grass for a pep talk. 'I'm going to do it scientifically rather than having a rant and a rave,' he said, 'because there was a load of good stuff in the last couple of months, but I think there is definitely stuff we've still got to sort out.

'One of them is your mental attitude. The Dakar is all about mental strength. I've seen some awesome enduro riders get out there and fail because they haven't the mental strength and determination. I've also seen average riders go out there and make a name for themselves because they just don't give up.

'We've still got a couple of months to improve and we've got nine days in Dubai coming up. We'll all get loads from training in the Dubai dunes, but the one thing – the hardest thing – is to get a hunger in your heart so strong that you don't listen to the voice in your head shouting that it wants to stop.'

'Mental attitude . . .' I said, feeling rather small.

'Yup, mental attitude,' Simon said. 'If you want that finisher's medal . . .'

'Yeah, absolutely . . .'

'. . . it's important we put you in a few more events,' Simon said. 'And it's important for you to . . .'

'. . . finish a few.' I completed Simon's sentence.

'It's for your mental strength and confidence. You don't want to go to Dakar saying I've done four races and finished one. You need to be going to Dakar thinking: the last four races I finished well. I felt good. You need those positives in your head.'

I didn't quite agree. I couldn't see myself out in the desert, thinking that because I hadn't finished the British Enduro I wouldn't now finish the Dakar. Simon's criticism had become a bit much. If it was meant to motivate me, it wasn't working. He was pushing the wrong buttons.

The British Enduro was only my fourth race ever and it had been extremely demoralising to watch every other rider pass me at twice the speed. It made me look a complete knobber. And I would have finished if it hadn't been for the boot. I was confident and riding well. I'd been totally committed, driving down to Wales almost every week, spending three or four days a week and a lot of weekends away from my family. I'd bust ribs, hairline-fractured my spine and covered myself in bruises and cuts that would scar me for life. But I knew I had to let Simon say his piece and point out my faults.

'It's just a little thing,' he said. 'It's where your hands are. Put them really square on the grips. Get your elbows right up. OK?' He showed me the correct stance and how it would enable me to control the throttle more easily.

'It's difficult because I know your race results don't reflect how well you can ride,' Simon conceded. 'But I'm worried. And I've got people calling me up and saying "Charley? I've watched him and he's all over the place. Are you sure he can do the Dakar? Because his riding position is . . .".'

I hated hearing that. I knew there were many people expecting me to fail. But *people* didn't know. *People* used to say Ewan and I didn't have a chance on Long Way Round, but we proved them all wrong.

At the end of the pep talk, Simon said: 'Right, on the bikes. We're going up the top of that mountain.' Then he pointed at three mountain bikes, one for each of us and one for Matt. As I swung my leg over the crossbar, I knew exactly what this was about. It was the time for the excuses to end. No more flabby, sore, blood-filled arms. No more shooting my load too soon. No more loose boots. It didn't matter how many miles it was to the top of that mountain and it didn't matter how I did it, I had to prove I could get to the summit.

Simon, Matt and I rode up together, pedalling and pushing for almost an hour until we'd conquered the mountain. It was a tough ride, one that I wouldn't have been able to finish a few months earlier, but I did it. In front of Simon.

Chapter 4

AUGUST TO SEPTEMBER 2005

Ten days after Simon, Matt and I forced our mountain bikes to the top of the mountain, we met up on the Sunday of the August bank holiday for Dawn to Dusk, an annual enduro race organised by Simon and Nick Plumb. The twelve-hour race around a sixteen-mile course near Glyneath could be raced either as a solo 'ironman' competitor or as a member of a team of two, three or four riders. Determined to prove to Simon that I could hack it with the best enduro riders, I'd teamed up with my old training partner Lee Walters, calling our team Tweedle Dumb and Tweedle Dumber.

Although the course was very muddy, the weather was kind and from the moment I stepped on the bike something clicked. I'd always been the rider near the back, the rider that all the other bikes would pass. But now I was the one shouting at other riders to 'get the fuck out of the way'.

Gareth turned up with the rally bike. It was the first time I'd seen the finished article. It was still missing some parts, such as the custom-painted fairing, but it was still a beauty.

'How do you feel about handing the bike over to Charley with his reputation?' Russ asked Gareth.

'Obviously it's something that I'm not that happy about,' Gareth said.

I could understand exactly why Gareth felt that way. For more than three months, the bike had been all his and he'd produced a work of art. Now there was every chance I was going to trash it. For my part, I was again overwhelmed that I was being given a £25,000 rally bike.

Lee started the race for the Tweedle Dumb and Tweedle Dumber team, riding the first two laps shortly after the sun rose on the Welsh hills. Gareth followed him out on the rally bike, riding carefully for three-quarters of the lap to test the bike, while I watched enviously from a distance.

'Very slippery out there, Charley,' said Gareth, returning to the pits. 'And a lot of rocks.'

'Which bits are slippery?' I shouted.

'All of it.'

Olly, my daughters and Russ were all watching as Lee finished his first two laps in a very good time of less than two hours before sending me out on to the track. Expecting me to take twice as long, they were all shocked when I did my first lap only nine minutes slower than Lee and my second lap faster than Lee had ridden his first lap.

With two steep hills and a large boggy stretch, the course had just about every type of terrain that the Welsh hills could throw at a rider, but I was taking it all in my stride and not getting ground down. When I first started riding off-road I crawled along the gravel road sections of courses, using them to get my breath back because I was so exhausted. But now I was pegging it along the gravel at 50 or 60mph, power-sliding around corners.

Steep hills that previously would have had me paddling with my feet, dragging the bike up the slope or hanging on for dear life, while better riders danced their bikes past me, weren't such a challenge any more. Now I was the one sailing up inclines, popping the bike from bump to bump, lifting a hand to wave at other riders as I passed them.

Part of the secret of my success was that I'd taken note of Simon's instructions. I was standing on the pegs for most of each lap instead of sitting down, and I had my elbows jutting out above the grips instead of tucked in by my sides.

But most of my improvement was simply the result of greater confidence. Riding dirt bikes, I'd discovered, was like skiing. I'd gone from being the equivalent of a novice skier, exhausted from constantly having to turn and brake my descent, to an expert, whooshing down the slopes, using less energy and showing more style simply because I wasn't scared of it. It meant I could go faster for longer and with greater ease. It was a great feeling and even when I found myself tiring I had enough stamina for an internal voice to kick in, urging me to keep going. *Come on*, it would say, *keep going*. And I would carry on through the tougher sections, feeling it was all worthwhile.

'Fucking hell!' Lee shouted as I entered the pits, passing him on his way out. 'I better get moving if I'm going to keep ahead of your time.'

All day, Lee and I pushed each other to post steadily faster times. By the end of the race, I was lapping in forty-seven minutes and twenty-four seconds, while Lee was down to forty-three minutes and one second. We came twenty-fourth out of more than two hundred individual competitors and teams.

It was great to see Simon's face as I finished our final lap. I could see relief written all across it. A team ride was not quite the same as a solo ride, but it was a finish nevertheless. And not only had I finished, I'd posted consistently faster times for each lap.

'Woo-hoo!' Simon shouted as I pulled into the finish. 'That was a bloody awesome ride, eh? *Awesome* ride.'

'Well, I'm pleased,' I said, almost lost for words for once in my life. I threw one arm around Simon's shoulder and pulled him towards me.

'I'm pleased for myself, but I'm especially pleased for Simon!' I shouted as Olly, Doone, Kinvara and Russ encircled me.

'Awwww!' Simon said.

'Because I did it for him on this one. I did it for him.'

For the first time I felt I able to do the Dakar. It was the end of August and ostensibly I had four more months to prepare for the rally, but when I looked at my diary I was shocked to see how little time for training still remained.

Immediately after the Dawn to Dusk race I had to fly out to Spain for the launch of the BMW HP2, an off-road enduro bike with a whopping 1200cc engine. After Spain, I'd spend two days at home, then fly to Dubai for twelve days' training in the dunes.

After Dubai, I'd have one day at home before flying to South Africa for another BMW event, a three-day off-road bonanza called the GS Challenge. I'd then have three weeks back home for training, culminating in another round of the British Enduro Championship in mid-October, probably the last race I could safely enter without risking an injury that might put me out of the Dakar. In mid-October I was scheduled to fly to Cannes for a few days to promote *Long Way Round* at a trade fair, then from there directly on to Dubai for a few more days of dune training, if it was needed, then back to Birmingham for the Bike Show. After that, I was spending the best part of a month in New Zealand, Australia and Canada promoting *Long Way Round*, leaving just a couple of weeks before Christmas to brush up my bike fitness before the Dakar.

The Road to Lisbon

It was a backbreaking schedule, but it was a lot better than painting and decoration, even with the added pressure on Russ and me to make sure all the logistical aspects of our Dakar entry were sorted out, including the support vehicles.

Under the Dakar rules, we were allowed any number of assistance vehicles and personnel as long as we paid for their entry and ensured they were up to FIA (Fédération Internationale de l'Automobile) rally standards. Assistance vehicles would travel on separate routes to the racing vehicles that were often longer than the race route, but wherever possible on tarmac rather than off-road. The rules prohibited assistance vehicles from supporting race vehicles on the special section (the timed off-road portion) of each stage. But assistance vehicles were allowed to support race vehicles on the liaison sections, which ran from the bivouac to the start of the special section and from the end of the special section to the next bivouac. The factory teams got around these rules by entering four-wheel-drive assistance trucks into the race because any race vehicle could assist any other race vehicle.

Our principal requirement was to transport our two mechanics – Gareth and Wolfgang – between bivouacs. Although we could have used a Toyota, Mitsubishi or Nissan 4x4 almost off the peg for the Dakar, Russ thought we ought to use a BMW vehicle if possible, and I agreed. Our only option was a BMW X5, but even BMW would concede that a production X5 was a townie car better suited to the streets of Chelsea or towing a horsebox across a Home Counties field than entering the Dakar. It would need extensive modification.

We knew several modified BMW X5s had been entered into previous Dakar rallies, but when we contacted the teams that had run them to ask for their assistance and advice, we were quoted ridiculous sums of money to make our X5 Dakar-proof.

With time running out – it was now September, only four months to the race – and a tight budget, we stumbled on Scorpion Racing, a 4x4 off-road specialist in north London. When Russ and I met with Colin Aldred, the company's owner, he immediately said he'd be interested in preparing the X5 for the Dakar and reckoned he could do it within our budget.

'When will you want the finished car?' Colin said towards the end of the meeting.

'In December of course,' Russ said. 'A week or so before the Dakar.'

'Not until then? Won't you want it earlier in the year?' said Colin.

'What?' said Russ. 'We thought you'd need all the time you could get. It's only a couple of months until then.'

'You're entering Dakar 2006?' said Colin. I could hear the disbelief in his voice. 'You want it by *this* December?'

'Correct,' said Russ.

'I'll have to get back to you on that.'

Colin's wife Roz called Russ a few days later. Had we wanted to use a Land Rover, Scorpion Racing could have prepared it in a month, she said. All the necessary parts were available off the shelf and Scorpion Racing were Land Rover experts. But preparing an X5 was a completely different matter. Every modification would have to be individually custom-engineered. It would take weeks just to prepare the drawings. In our time-frame, it was impossible.

Russ and I were stumped. We'd committed to using a BMW X5 and now we couldn't find anyone to prepare it within budget and in time. In desperation, Russ called Phil Burthem, a mate who knew Colin. With Phil's persuasion, Colin agreed to prepare the X5 with the proviso that he would only do as much as was possible in the time available and with the warning that it might not be up to Scorpion's usual standards. It wasn't ideal, but it would have to do.

We finally got the X5 to Scorpion Racing on 11 November,

fully living up to Colin's nickname for the Race to Dakar team: Lastminute.com. Russ wanted to convert the X5 back to a normal car after the Dakar, but Colin made it clear to him that the X5 would never return to normality.

His team started by stripping out all the parts they thought were unnecessary, including the interior trim, the dashboard, parcel shelves, the standard seats and the airbags, which would most likely explode the first time the X5 hit a sizeable bump. For a similar reason, two batteries were moved from the underside of the car to the boot and the exhaust silencers were removed (bumpy tracks would rip them off), leaving the X5 with a gloriously throaty and only-just-street-legal eighty-four decibel roar.

Unessential electrics were also removed, including the CD player and radio, much to the horror of Russ who would be driving Gareth and Wolfgang between bivouacs. Nevertheless, compared with other Dakar vehicles, the remaining electrical controls still looked like the Blackpool illuminations. Colin also wanted to strip out the air-conditioning, arguing that it would waste precious fuel, but Russ wisely insisted that it would be essential in the desert heat.

As for the 3.0 litre turbocharged diesel engine, Colin left it unchanged, with the catalytic converter still in place, because he did not want to leave himself open to criticism that the customised X5's exhaust was any more damaging to the environment than a standard X5. And wanting easy-cruising reliability rather than land-speed-record capability, we didn't bother retuning it.

With only the carcass of the X5 remaining, Scorpion started their modifications. The first addition was an eighty-litre auxiliary fuel tank. Foam-filled to reduce the risk of explosion and to prevent fuel surges, the auxiliary tank had a fuel pickup box with trap-doors, which would ensure fuel always flowed even if the car was upside down. Given that Russ had upturned a Mitsubishi 4x4 in Mongolia during the Long Way Round trip, it seemed a very wise modification.

With the standard one hundred-litre tank and the auxiliary tank, we estimated the X5 would have a five-hundred-mile range. Dakar rules prohibited jerrycans because of the risk they'd explode if the car turned over. With some stages longer than five hundred miles, fuel consumption would be critical. Colin warned Russ he should not run the air-conditioning on every stage.

A roll cage was custom-built from 50mm tubes with 38mm braces, each tube having to be bent, offered up to see if it fitted, adapted and tack-welded in place to protect four occupants. The X5 is a monocoque construction. It had no chassis so the roll cage had to be welded and bolted on to load spread plates, which, in turn, were welded on to the shell. Four Kevlar and fibreglass Cobra Suzuka seats and TRS four-point harnesses were bolted into the cabin.

A conventional X5 is relatively low on the ground, so the suspension was lifted by two inches. However, the X5 has independent suspension, so lifting the car caused the bottom of the wheels to point inwards. This effect is called positive camber and can usually be counteracted, but the X5 had camber adjustment only on its rear wheels so Colin's team had to create a method of compensating on the front wheels. They also put pro spacers on the wheels to widen the X5's track for more stability. We asked Scorpion to replace the alloy wheels with steel wheels so that, if necessary, we could knock out any dents.

Colin replaced the X5's air suspension (which couldn't take the increased load of the extra fuel tank, a spare motorbike engine in the boot and the two-inch lift) with Reiger coil suspension. This modification put strain on the drive shafts, so Scorpion Racing had to reset the Reiger springs by heating them in a furnace and adjusting their lift from 100mm to 50mm.

Skidding panels were fitted as protection for the bottom of the car, but this blocked vital ventilation of the transmission system. To ensure the transmission did not overheat, a new ventilation shaft had to be built and trunking installed to suck air from the front of the car to the transmission.

Although the Dakar regulations required only that fire extinguishers were carried and easily accessible, Colin built in a full plumbed-in FIA-approved fire system. At the press of a dashboard button, four litres of foam would be pumped into the engine bay and cockpit. A second fire-system button was fixed to the outside of the X5 in case the vehicle crashed upside down and was on fire. Colin also replaced the outdoor steps of the car with aluminium boxes along each side and replaced the plastic mesh on the front fascia with metal wiring to prevent stones entering the engine bay.

While Scorpion Racing was adapting the X5, Russ was tying up a deal with Bowler Racing to carry spare parts for the bikes and X5 at the exorbitant rates all Dakar assistance vehicles charged per kilogram.

In early September, the core team of Russ, Matt, Gareth and I flew out to Dubai for desert training. Simon, who had insisted to Russ that we make the Dubai trip, would join us a few days later.

Russ thought twelve days in Dubai was too long, but I knew I needed every day I could get. Matt and I had already tried training on sand on a beach in Wales and we'd struggled, even though heavy, wet British beach sand was nothing like as treacherous as soft, dry desert sand.

I was shitting myself before the beach training session, especially because it was the first time I'd ridden the rally bike.

'What d'you think about riding the rally bike on the beach, Charley?' asked Simon.

'Can't we get a Jeep?' I replied.

'C'mon, it'll be all right.'

'As long as I don't fall over, it will be all right,' I said. 'Funny that.'

Even with only ten litres of fuel on the rally bike, one quarter the amount we'd be carrying in the Dakar, I was slipping all over the place. The front wheel seemed to have a mind of its own, making the bike buck like a bronco.

Except for the difficulty of riding on sand, the bike felt wonderful. Because the Dakar organisers had changed the rules, introducing an extra petrol stop for each stage, Gareth had been able to use smaller tanks on the bike. He'd mounted them slightly forward, giving the bike a narrower and more comfortable ride than the previous year's bike, but it would still be going to the start weighing a considerable amount – about 250 kilograms fully laden with fuel, water, spares and tools. We'd be riding some of the heaviest bikes in the race. Their greater power and strength would be a boon on mountain passes and open plains, but we all knew it meant we'd have a much tougher time in the dunes than the lighter KTMs and Yamahas.

We discovered during the beach training session that Gareth had made several other welcome improvements to the bike. The steering lock was much tighter and the bike even had heated grips. We would often be setting off from the bivouac at 3 or 4 o'clock in the morning, when conditions under the clear desert skies would be close to freezing, so heated grips were a necessity, not a luxury.

In Dubai, however, there'd be no need to use the heated grips. We arrived in the early hours of the morning, but even at that time the heat was intense. Outside the airport terminal, waiting for a taxi, the sweat was dripping off me.

'It's only 4 a.m. and the temperature is already in the mid-30s,' said Matt, pointing to a plume of air condensing into vapour as it curled out of a ventilation duct. 'You know it's hot when they put air-conditioning in the street.'

The next day, after we'd ventured out for a swim under an oppressive sun, Sean Linton, a World Rally rider and desert-riding expert who trained army motorcyclists, told us what to expect when we headed out into the desert the next day: 'The first stage has a lot of camel grass and some small dunes. A lot of bumps and a lot of abuse on your body. The second part is high dunes. A lot of straight edges and drop-offs. We'll show you how to ride through them, tipping the bike on the sides of the dunes. After that, the return will be high-speed tracks – some of them winding – so you can get a good feel for the bike. Three stages and about 100ks.'

Just the thought of having to ride over a hundred kilometres of dunes and sandy tracks had me coming out in a sweat. And, to make matters worse, Simon would be arriving a few days later to put even more pressure on me.

I needn't have worried so much. Riding on sand for the first time the next day, I was surprised at how easy it could be. Moving off was difficult, but as soon as I built up speed and the wheels lifted on to the surface of the sand, it was like piloting a speedboat across waves. At low speeds it was difficult to turn or gain any sense of control, but above a certain speed the bike felt sharp and responsive as it planed across the sand. The trick was to lean back and use my foot pegs to manipulate the bike, swinging and power-sliding the back of the bike around corners, rather than using the front wheel to turn, which was completely counterproductive – when twisted, the front wheel became a bulldozer.

I tumbled off the bike several times. Much to my surprise – I'd been expecting a cushioned landing in the sand – it really hurt. A couple of times, the front wheel sunk deep into the sand as I descended a dune, sending me flying straight over the top of the handlebars, but otherwise the morning passed without serious harm to me. I couldn't say the same about the bike.

'These bikes should be unbreakable,' said Sean, shaking his head. 'How did you do it, Charley?'

I got on another enduro bike and rode off into the desert. By the end of the morning, I'd broken that bike too.

After lunch, we rode out further into the desert. It was amazing, like a perfect motocross track that, instead of being a short loop, went on for as long as I wanted.

I was riding the rally bike and finding it far easier to control than the little 450cc bike I'd been riding before lunch, maybe because I was used to a big 1150cc bike from Long Way Round. It was brilliant. I felt I understood how to ride the dunes and in the heat of the sun my fear of the sand evaporated.

Matt, meanwhile, was having a tough time. His initial reaction on riding on sand was to think: Oh shit, what the hell have I done? It felt completely alien to any riding he'd done before and, unused to big bikes, he was struggling with the rally bike. Although he'd picked up huge purple-blue bruises across his stomach and over one thigh, by the end of the day Matt was more optimistic. 'It's coming together,' he said, 'but I couldn't ride across dunes for a whole day.'

At least I now had licence to feel I wasn't the weakest link in the team, although Matt warned me that he thought I was going for it too hard. We'd see.

On the morning of the second day we headed for some larger sand dunes. I was cruising along, riding brilliantly on the rally bike, discovering for myself how to ride in large dunes and trying to remember Simon's advice, given to me in Wales, on how to cope when I got to Dubai.

'Throttle control, mate,' he'd said. 'You need momentum and a bit of angle so you can look along the dune at its crest. The main thing is to look ahead. Don't ride straight over. Take the crest at an oblique, so you've got more time to choose your route. A bit of clutch control on the top to take the speed away and then momentum going down so you don't sink in the sand . . . basics really.'

After an hour on the rally bike, I switched to the 450cc, then followed David Bright, one of Sean's instructors, out into the dunes. Gareth was following behind me. I stuck to David's back wheel, following him over one sand dune after another instead of finding my own course. It felt fine.

I watched as David climbed a sand dune, riding fast, and saw him glance back at me as he disappeared over the other side. I should have slowed down and ridden at my own speed, but I felt in control. When I got to the top of the dune, the path ahead disappeared to nothing. It was a sheer drop. I was moving too fast to turn back down the dune or to spot an escape route.

As I crested the dune into nothingness, I realised why David had glanced back at me as he went over the top. He'd been warning me, the last glance back a way of saying, 'Fucking hell! Watch out!' But it was too late.

I was in the air for long enough to realise I was in trouble and to think, Oh shit! I dropped sixty to eighty feet – a big fall – before the front wheel hit the deck and buried itself deep in the sand, sending me sailing over the handlebars. That's when I must have hit my shoulder. The pain was immediate.

Sliding down the dune, I spotted a flash of red. It was my bike cartwheeling towards me. Moments later, it landed on top of me, squeezing the wind from my lungs, making me feel like my insides had been sucked out by a vacuum cleaner. Trapped beneath the bike, I slid and bumped down the rest of the sand dune until I reached the bottom, where the bike slid just that little bit further than I did. It was enough to enable me to escape from beneath it.

As soon as I stood up I felt like vomiting. I knew I had done something bad. I tried to lift my arm. I could. It was all right. Maybe I'd escaped injury, I thought. Then the pain struck for the second time, only much, much worse. I crumpled to my knees and screamed. I tried to stand up, but the pain in my shoulder got worse, making me collapse again.

Gareth was beside me as I removed my top. 'Does it look broken?' I shouted. 'Does it look the same?'

I don't know why I asked. Anyone could see what was wrong. A bone in my shoulder was sticking up into the air.

'I don't know, Charley, I . . .'

'Just tell me it's not broken!' I begged Gareth.

'It's not broken . . . it's fine.'

But quite clearly it wasn't.

We looked around: emptiness as far as we could see and no one in sight. David had continued riding, probably oblivious to my accident and injury. Matt and Sean would be a couple of miles away by now.

Luckily, David soon returned and instinct took over. I pulled out my mobile phone and rang Olly in London. We'd been riding for about four hours and it was about 10.30 a.m. in Dubai.

'Hey, Olly.'

'What's wrong?' Her voice switched instantly from the groggy slur of a 6.30 a.m. wake-up call to the wide-awake sound of worry and concern.

'Listen, it's nothing, it's fine. I think I've broken my collarbone but it's all right. I'm fine.'

Olly was really cool about it. 'OK, what do you want me to do?'

'Can you ring Russ?'

Olly put the phone down. About ten minutes later, having spoken to Russ, she rang back, just for a chat. She was completely fine about my accident. She asked if it would affect the rally and if I was

OK, but she didn't make any kind of fuss. She was quite amazing.

While I was speaking to Olly, Gareth tried to contact the others, but couldn't get hold of them.

'Fuck it,' I said. 'Let's get to the garage.'

I jumped on the back of David's bike, threw my uninjured arm around him and tried to support my injured shoulder by grabbing the collar of my shirt.

For twenty long minutes, each of them more painful than the last, we bumped over the sand dunes towards the road and a garage at which we'd filled up the bikes earlier. With no foot pegs to support my weight, it was agony. Every tiny bump and dip jolted my arm, sending daggers of pain into my shoulder.

To cope with the pain, I tried to focus on other things. But there's little to distract your attention in a bare dune landscape and the only thing I could think about – besides the pain – was that I had really fucked up big time. This was only the second training day and we had scheduled five more days in the dunes. Out of everyone, I needed the training most, but my continued participation looked unlikely. And to make matters much worse, Simon would be arriving that evening.

Shortly after we arrived at the garage, Russ turned up. He wasn't pleased.

'In the back of my mind there was always this reservation that we were pushing you guys quite hard,' he said. 'And I was right. We were taking the same risks in training that you'd experience in the race itself.'

'It could have happened at any time, to anyone,' I said. But stripped to my waist in the midday heat, leaning against the shady garage wall with my collarbone jutting at an awkward angle, I realised my excuses wouldn't convince Russ.

'You had another seven days of this. You should have taken it nice and steady. Instead Sean took you over the biggest bumps on day two. I can't help feeling Simon shares responsibility for this and he's not even here. He's our expert, so where is he?'

Russ phoned Simon, who said it was just bad luck. 'It's the nature of the beast. It's no different to slipping over in the shower and tearing a hamstring,' Simon said. 'You can't train or prepare for bad luck. It's just unfortunate.'

'Hmm,' said Russ, unconvinced. 'Sean is a very experienced guy, but I still feel that you went too fast, too soon.'

While Russ was pondering the wisdom of our dune training regime, I was looking for someone to blame for my injury or, at the very least, a plausible excuse for my predicament.

In truth, one reason why it happened was that I was more comfortable on the heavy 650cc Dakar rally bike than on the lighter 450cc enduro bikes that I'd been riding. However, it was Matt's turn to practise on the Dakar bike. The rally bike was much faster than the smaller bikes and Matt had taken off without looking back for us, unfortunately in the wrong direction. Hoping to stop Matt before he got lost, David, Gareth and I had set off in pursuit of him, but once someone got away in the desert it was very difficult to catch up with them. When we were at the top of a dune, Matt would, more often than not, be in a dip or below the horizon. It was like bobbing up and down on large waves, trying to spot another ship also being thrown about by the sea.

So, if Matt hadn't been riding the rally bike and if he hadn't taken off without checking we were following him closely, we wouldn't have been chasing after him and I wouldn't have crashed. It was all his fault, I decided, relieved that I'd found someone down the line I could blame. It ought to be my personal motto – 'not my fault, guv; it were cos of 'im'. At least it kept me happy. Poor Matt – he had no idea how I was building him up as the scapegoat in my mind. My only excuse was that I was tired, disappointed and in a lot of pain.

Russ drove me to a hospital, where a doctor and an X-ray confirmed what I had feared. I had broken my collarbone. Badly.

Fearing that I would be the butt of everyone's jokes for the rest of the time in Dubai and not wanting to face Simon, I left that night, scuttling out of town before Simon arrived.

I knew that over the next few days the rest of the team would be having great fun. When they weren't training in the desert they'd be whacking golf balls, racing go-karts or swimming in the warm waters of the Gulf. I felt left out, but I didn't want to hang around the hotel, hearing at the end of the day what they'd been doing. I just wanted out.

I felt lower than at any time for years. Ever since Ewan and I had embarked on Long Way Round, I'd been on an upward path. I'd faced challenges, there had been hills to climb and hindrances to circumvent, but I hadn't ever felt that my bid for a new future was threatened. Now I did.

Waiting for a flight to London, I hung around at the airport for hours, the pain getting steadily worse. The bone had cut through a lot of muscle and I could feel blood dripping down into my chest. The tendons in my neck and shoulder were agony; they'd been stretched to the full and most probably damaged.

By the time the flight left, it was nearly 1 a.m. Fortunately I was so exhausted that even the pain couldn't keep me awake.

Olly met me at Heathrow, our dog Ziggy wagging his tail and peering out of the car window. Returning to the bosom of my family was just what I needed when I thought I'd fucked everything up. Sitting in my kitchen in London, I felt miserable at the thought of the rest of the team together in Dubai. The irony was I'd broken my collarbone because I'd failed to read the dunes and the fracture meant I now wasn't going to get the experience I'd need to learn how to read the dunes that would be so crucial for the Dakar. It was my only chance to master the sand and now I'd screwed up.

Chapter 5

SEPTEMBER TO DECEMBER 2005

Two days after returning from Dubai, I was on my way to a specialist bike injury clinic in Ipswich, a nervous emptiness rumbling in the pit of my stomach as I contemplated the very real prospect that my broken collarbone could put me out of action for several months and maybe even end my Dakar hopes.

'When you see somebody in slow motion breaking their collarbone, you are surprised they don't break their necks,' said the doctor, pushing my arm up to see how high he could lift it before I winced with pain. 'Their head goes right the way over as their shoulder comes forward. Now what we need to do is to stop your shoulder from coming forward.'

To allow my collarbone to heal, the doctor fitted a brace that would hold back my shoulders and envelop most of my torso. I'd also have several treatments of laser and pulse magnetic field therapies, which would induce a current through the bone to attract the bone cells necessary for healing the fracture.

'We should get you back on your bike in ten days, two weeks, something like that,' the doctor said.

'Oh really, that quick?'

'Yeah.'

'That'll be nice,' I said. 'I've got this little safari in South Africa at the end of September.'

'Oh you'll do that,' the doctor promised.

More importantly it meant I could resume training when I returned from South Africa and, hopefully, still compete in the Dakar. Within a few days I could lift my arm above my head. Other people who had broken their collarbones told me it had taken them months to get to the same stage of recovery. After a fortnight, I started taking regular treatment at a chiropractor. Meanwhile, Russ embarked on an X5 off-road training programme, something we all wound him up about, insisting it was essential after he'd rolled the Mitsubishi support vehicle in Mongolia.

Desperately needing to regain my bike fitness, by late October I was back in Wales, hacking around the mountains with Simon. Suddenly everything seemed to click into place, a relief after the disappointments of Dubai and some of the enduro races.

Quite why my riding ability had made a quantum leap in the time I was off the bike, I don't know. Maybe it was simply a result of my confidence having been bolstered by finishing the Dawn to Dusk race. Or maybe it was because I'd watched a lot of track races on television while I'd been recuperating at home, feeling miserable and sorry for myself. The one thing I'd noticed about most of the best riders – Chris Walker, Chris Vermeulen and Valentino Rossi in World Superbikes and MotoGP – was that they made sure their elbows were out at their sides, not tucked into their ribs, so that they could absorb the shock of their bikes' movements. It was what Simon had been trying to teach me, but seeing it on television in race after race drummed it into me. The first time I got back on any bike after breaking my collarbone, I made sure I stuck my elbows up in the air so noticeably it looked like I was doing press-ups on the handlebars. It was just a little thing, but it worked.

On the Saturday – my first day dirt biking for more than six weeks – I managed to ride for about five hours before my shoulder felt as if it was seizing up. The next day, I spent eight hours riding really hard. It was pissing with rain, I was filthy and there was so much mud on the seat I couldn't sit on it without sliding all over it, but I loved the ride. I rode really well – the best ever – and felt fantastic. Afterwards, I had to wash down all my motocross gear with a power hose to remove the quarter-inch of mud stuck to it.

Until then, I'd always ridden near the back of the pack, usually because I was worried that if I rode at the front I'd be pressurised by people behind me who were faster. Lee Walters, who knew the area better than anyone, had always been the fastest and usually led the way. But now I was leading. And whenever I looked back, I couldn't see anyone following me. I'd left them for dust. They were all miles away. It was a huge step for me and a great relief for Simon, who was struggling to get up some of the hills I had flown up with ease. That felt good.

At last it felt like I was living the dream. I'd turned up in my BMW car and gone riding with a bunch of six or seven guys. Previously, I was the person who was always last, always falling and never quite getting up the hill while everyone waited for me – the dreary 'knobber' – to catch up. Now I was the one at the top of the hill waiting impatiently and looking back at the beginners crashing behind me.

It was a great feeling and it got even better the following weekend at the Bike Show at the NEC in Birmingham. On the first day we unveiled the Race to Dakar team and I launched the new BMW 1200 Adventurer, a world premiere. BMW was also displaying my Long Way Round bike with my suit and my helmet. I hadn't seen the bike for a couple of months. Looking at it, I realised how much I missed it and the simple pleasures of an adventure along proper roads and through wildernesses, riding as far each day as I wanted rather than having to reach a prescribed finish line each evening. It felt like a reliable friend with whom I'd shared some of the best times of my life and, like I would with an old mate, I felt like hugging it.

All four days at the Bike Show were madness with two book and DVD signings a day. In the evenings, I met several of my bike heroes – race bike champions such as Jamie Whitham, Neil Hodgson and Chris Vermeulen, who had just got a MotoGP ride with Suzuki. I was completely star-struck by Vermeulen, but he and his girlfriend were big fans of *Long Way Round*, so the feeling was mutual. On one evening there was a dinner and party with James Toseland, another hero of mine. I found it hard to believe I was hanging out with these people.

While all the team was at the Bike Show, we had a meeting about team orders. Prompted by Simon, we talked through all the different scenarios that might occur during the rally.

'It's really easy to be analytical and cool-headed about it here,' Simon warned. 'But it will be different when the pressure point comes on the rally. It'll come because one of us is mentally on his last legs. Then decisions don't get made in the same way.'

We were a strange team. I was certainly the least experienced and maybe the weakest rider, but I was the linchpin simply because I was the guy putting the team together. I would always have precedence over Matt and Simon: if my bike broke down, they'd give their parts to me. I felt a bit overwhelmed about this and had to remind myself that it was only because I had people backing our team that we were going in the first place. In some ways it was easier for Simon because he'd got to Dakar three times before and wouldn't have entered again without the challenge of training a relative novice and making a documentary about the privateer's Dakar experience.

For Matt, it was a tougher proposition. This was his first – and quite likely his last – attempt at the Dakar. Yet he knew that if his bike needed to be cannibalised to repair mine, he would have to make the sacrifice. Even if Simon and Matt had dragged me through the last few days, and even if they were sure I wouldn't survive the next day, I would take precedence. I didn't envy Matt his role in the team.

After the Bike Show I departed on promotional tours of Australia, New Zealand and Canada. They'd been arranged months and months ago, and while in some ways I wanted to do more training, Russ pointed out to me that it could be almost as dangerous to carry on racing too hard at this point, and risk further injury. Meanwhile, Simon and Matt continued training. Matt went down to Wales every weekend. His biggest concern was riding on roads. He'd only ever ridden off-road, so BMW lent him an 1150GS Adventure to ride around London and down to Wales as much as possible. Determined to go to the Dakar start line feeling totally bike fit and mentally prepared, Matt entered as many races as he could find and finished every single one of them. By the end of the year, he had completed nearly thirty races. In the same time, I'd entered five races and finished two.

Fretting that I had not done enough training, I returned from the promotional trip to face the press for the final time before the Dakar. On 14 December, at BMW's Park Lane showroom, Russ introduced the team then handed over to Ewan, who said a few words of encouragement and introduced me. Feeling very nervous, I blathered on for far too long, not knowing quite what to say and wishing I'd shut up. Then I asked the pack of journalists if they had any questions.

'Er, Charley,' came the first question. 'Everyone who's done the Dakar says it doesn't matter how good your bike is or how much training you've done. What really separates the finishers from the rest, they say, is mental attitude. It's the one thing for which it's really difficult to train. What have you been doing to prepare yourself mentally?'

I wasn't going to let this journalist catch me out. I had just the right answer up my sleeve.

'Wanking,' I said. 'I've done a lot of wanking.'

Maybe that glib attempt at humour wasn't the best answer. For a few seconds the room was silent. No one, it seemed, could quite believe what I'd said. Half the people in the room were staring at me wide-eyed before sucking in their breath between their teeth. The remainder burst into laughter.

'Er . . .' I said. 'Er, as you said, mental strength is the one thing for which you can't really prepare, so we'll find out when we're out there . . .'

I kept talking, silently cursing my habit of saying the first thing that came into my head. I'm not sure I gave a proper answer, but, by the time I'd finished talking, most of the room was probably relieved that I'd shut up, and wanted to see the X5, which had just drawn up with a roar outside the showroom, bringing traffic to a standstill.

The last few days before Christmas were spent in chaotic panic, making last-minute preparations. Passports, tickets, documents, spare parts, vaccination certificates and everything else required for the Dakar were double-checked, then checked again.

Gradually, it was all coming together – everything, that is, except the X5. Colin at Scorpion Racing didn't have time to convert the X5 to rally standards but had worked hard within a short time-span.

Simon and Colin met at the Fleet service station on the M3 on 22 December to exchange the car, documents and instructions. Simon had volunteered to drive his van containing the rally bikes and the X5 to Lisbon with Linley and Llewellyn and was booked on a ferry to France the same day. Boxes and bags from the office were lobbed on top of the bikes in the back of Simon's van, while Colin ran around the X5, explaining its various features.

Time was running out but they just made it and the X5 and Simon's van were the last two vehicles on the ferry, getting on board just as the ferry doors clanged shut

The next morning, exhausted after not having slept properly on the ferry, Simon, Linley and Llewellyn drove the X5 and van off the ferry and began the long journey south. With huge Race to Dakar logos on either side and sponsors' stickers emblazoned all over it, the car looked great and attracted attention on every street corner.

By the end of the first day's drive, Simon, Linley and Llewellyn were still two hundred kilometres north of the Spanish border. With a long way still to go, they got up early on Christmas Eve and drove all day. By late that night, as they were nearing Salamanca, Simon received a text message from someone we'd met at the Bike Show, to whom I'd promised but failed to send some signed posters. In the weeks since the Bike Show, he'd continued to hassle us for the posters, sending increasingly desperate texts saying 'still no posters', then 'no sex from my missus until she gets posters of Charley' and eventually 'still no posters . . . thanks a lot . . . still celibate'. As Simon, Llewellyn and Linley pulled into a closed service area to consult their maps and find a hotel at which to spend Christmas Day, the latest text arrived: 'No posters . . . I put a jinx on your Dakar . . . hope you have a rotten time.'

Simon turned off the engine for less than a minute. When he tried to start it, it wouldn't fire up. It looked like the jinx had struck. All the electrics were working and the engine turned over, but the ignition was immobilised.

Shortly before midnight, just as I was about to go to bed, I received a cryptic text message from Simon. 'Just broken down – see text below.'

Scrolling down, I read the text threatening a jinx and phoned Simon. 'Is this serious or a joke?'

'X5's not moving,' Simon said. 'And we're in the middle of nowhere.'

At home in London, surrounded by Christmas presents, I located a hotel in a former monastery for Simon and his family and managed to call out a recovery truck to transport the X5 to somewhere safe. Russ called on Christmas Day, mildly panicked that no one now knew the exact location of the X5, but by Boxing Day it was in the capable hands of a BMW dealership in Lisbon.

Christmas was good, a relaxed weekend with Olly's parents. But, try as I might, I couldn't prevent thoughts of the Dakar intruding. I felt like one of the toys that my daughters were given for Christmas. Called Time Bomb, it looked like an old-fashioned bomb with a fuse. Wound up, the bomb started to tick slowly. The object of the game was to pass the ticking bomb round the table; the closer it was to exploding, the faster it ticked. Whoever was holding it when it exploded was the loser. My life felt just like that – a ticking bomb that might explode at any moment.

The pressure was also starting to affect Olly, who had asked Simon what the rally would be like in Africa. He'd told her that riding through the dunes was like being in separate dinghies in an ocean, trying to stick together until a humungous wave splits you up, sweeping one of you out of sight.

'You try and follow the person who's been swept away,' said Simon, 'but by the time you get over the next wave, they've been swept further away. And you never get back to them.'

'I'm frightened,' Olly said to me one night over Christmas. There was nothing I could say to allay her fears, other than I was in good hands.

My reputation, my family's future and a lot of money were riding on my performance over the next two weeks. I felt sick when I thought about it. But I'd been talking about it for too long, and too many people were watching, for me to pull out now. Just before Christmas, Russ had taken to calling me the million-dollar man. Taking into account the value of the sponsored bikes, the X5, the investment in the television production, the salaries for the office staff and production crew, that's how much I was in it for. Every night I'd wake in the early hours and spend a long time staring at the ceiling, thinking things over and trying not to let the panic take over. The enormity of what I had taken on began to scare me.

There was no time to deal with these feelings. The day after Boxing Day the rest of the team flew with their families to Lisbon and the countdown to the start of the race began in earnest.

Our first full day in Lisbon – 28 December – was a mad rush to get everything sorted before the official scrutineering for the race started that evening. Russ and Jim attended to the X5. If for any reason it didn't run, we would not be able to transport Gareth and Wolfgang between bivouacs and would have no mechanical assistance for the duration of the rally.

Working with five BMW technicians from Baveria BMW Lisbon, Jim replaced the EWS unit, an electronic watchdog system that prevented the car starting if a code stored inside the X5's key did not match one of six codes in the EWS. They installed a BMW black box called a GT1, a very delicate box of tricks that cost £8,000. Russ persuaded BMW to send out a GT1 computer and a technician, John Beckley, who was prepared to give up his New Year's Eve party and face the wrath of his girlfriend to come and help with the car.

Simon, Matt and I went down to the rally's administrative zone near the Lisbon docks to pack our emergency trunks. Each rider was allowed a white metal trunk, which would be carried by aeroplane between bivouacs and within which we could carry up to fifty kilograms of emergency kit in case our support vehicles and mechanics dropped out. The most extreme privateers, those on the tightest budgets, would have nothing to rely upon but those white metal trunks.

After that, we headed for where the Bowler trucks were parked, waiting for truck scrutineering to start the next day. With every kilogram on the trucks costing a lot of money, we rationalised our spares and removed anything unessential, including a bike engine and my cereal bars. Just taking my cereal bars off saved us £1,000.

Perched on the top of one of the trucks, repacking some essential spares, I looked around me. Gareth was sticking labels on to his toolboxes and spare-part stores. Matt and Simon were going through their kit. Russ and Jim were working on the X5 nearby. And I was blown away by the thought that all these people were working in such a concentrated and concerted fashion because of my dream.

Tired after another night of fitful sleep and grumpy with a snivelling cold, I headed with the rest of the team down to the scrutineering area. The next few hours, Simon had warned, would be among the most tense and fraught of the whole rally. Plenty of entrants in previous years had managed to raise the many tens of thousands of pounds needed to enter the Dakar, built and prepared their vehicle, done all the paperwork, got themselves fit and done the training, received the vaccinations and got themselves to the start only to be disqualified during scrutineering.

Seven columns of four-wheel-drive cars, three columns of six-wheel-drive trucks and a single column of bikes greeted us at the parc d'attente, the holding area for scrutineering. We parked our three bikes, with fluorescent green, orange and yellow mudguards for Simon, Matt and me respectively, then ambled through the vehicles, marvelling at the stranger ones. Someone had entered in a Renault 4 and an American team was riding one customised Harley-Davidson sidecar combination.

It was shortly before 9 a.m. We had until 7.30 p.m. to pass through the administrative checks and until 11 p.m. to satisfy the scrutineering officials that our bikes and the X5 matched the exacting standards laid out in the rally regulations.

'Better get a move on if we don't want to come back and start the whole lengthy process tomorrow,' Simon warned us and promptly disappeared through the door of a complex of portable pavilions that housed the administrative checking staff.

Inside the pavilions we were confronted by a series of some twenty booths, each staffed with officious-looking rally staff armed with clipboards and rubber stamps. To pass the administrative checks, we'd have to be interviewed at each booth, answer a series of questions correctly, prove we had the correct documentation and sit through tutorials on first aid, navigation and safety. To prove we'd satisfied the officials at each of the booths, we'd have to collect thirteen stamps in our rally books, each of which signified months of work and a lot of money.

We had a few hairy moments – the aerials for our on-bike communications units had been sent to the wrong address when the officials were insistent we'd received them, so we had to buy replacements – but by midday we'd finished inching our way from booth to booth. We'd handed over receipts to prove we'd paid our entry fee and settled our hotel bills. We'd confirmed to officials that we had booked our ferry tickets and taken out medical insurance. We'd sat through tutorials on how to use the GPS navigation equipment, the Sentinel collision alarm system and the Iritraq satellite-tracking device.

Best of all, we'd met some other biker rally entrants and started to feel part of the circus. All the privateer riders were aiding each other, lending tools, passing on advice and helping in frantic searches for the relevant documentation.

After the administrative checks, we had thirty minutes to get our bikes into the technical scrutineering hall, but first a scrutineer steward dressed in the standard uniform of the Dakar official – heavily branded polo shirt, waterproof jacket, baseball cap and trousers – with a jumble of passes around his neck allowing him access to all areas, gave the bikes and the X5 a preliminary check. Satisfied that the car was carrying sand ladders and crash helmets, and that a kill switch and a bracket to house the GPS navigation unit had been fitted, he waved us into the hall.

At first, everything proceeded in textbook fashion. The stewards examined the critical safety components of the bike and dabbed spots of paint on those parts, such as the frame, that we were forbidden to swap. Strangely, one of the stewards painted the exhaust on Simon's bike, a part the regulations allowed us to replace. It didn't matter anyway, we thought, as he'd just painted the false exhaust that housed the toolbox.

Moving on to my bike, the steward realised what he'd done. Seeing the funny side of it, he walked over to his colleague, who had just daubed paint on Matt's false exhaust, and had a laugh about it. Everything seemed fine and I knew the best thing was to keep smiling.

The stewards then took a look at the cameras fitted on our

helmets, which were stuck with Velcro to the outside. In the event of a crash, they'd fall off immediately, we insisted.

One of the stewards, a Frenchman, wasn't convinced. Russ dragged the head scrutineer over to adjudicate. He agreed with us and overruled the steward. That's when the trouble started.

We were minutes away from passing out of the scrutineering hall to deposit our bikes in the parc fermé, the guarded enclosure where the bikes would be impounded until the morning of the start, when the steward who had been overruled stopped us.

'Where's your water?' he said.

The regulations stipulated that every rider must carry five litres of water, at least three litres of which must be secured on the bike. We were going to put our three litres in a plastic bladder that we'd squeeze into a compartment that Gareth had built behind the front of the bash plate.

I unlocked the compartment on my bike to show the official.

'You will not fit three litres in there!' the official said with typically Gallic incredulity.

I looked at it and knew he was right. It was obvious a bladder would soon be punctured if wedged into that tiny sharp-edged space.

Facing what was undoubtedly a fair cop, I had visions of being disqualified before we'd even reached the start. The ultimate ignominy.

Russ, Simon, Matt and Gareth moved in, pouring water into the bladder in the forlorn hope of proving to the official it could be done. They succeeded in squeezing two and a half litres into the space, but by then the official wasn't going to be persuaded.

'Move to the side,' he said. 'Sort it out and you can go. If you can't sort it out . . .' Another Gallic shrug.

What should have been a short day was now turning into a very long one. Russ, as usual, had the solution. 'Put the tools in the water compartment,' he said, 'and the water in the false exhaust.'

Another steward came over. 'BMW, huh?' he said. I thought he was going to be one of the officials biased against any bike but a KTM. 'I did the Dakar in 1991 on a BMW,' he said. 'An 1150GS.' It was the same bike Ewan and I had used on Long Way Round. The steward walked off, returning a few minutes later with a piece of sponge. 'Here,' he said. It was just what we needed to line the fake exhaust pipe. The water bladder fitted a treat and the steward waved us through.

We'd made it into the race. Nothing and no one could stop us now.

Chapter 6

Our last free day before the race was spent trying to get some sleep, sorting out last-minute jobs and having a team meeting. Holed up in Matt's room, Simon made sure we had all of the documents we'd need to get us into the rally.

'You got your ferry tickets, motorway toll passes, passports and vaccination letter?' Simon said, leafing through a 6-inch pile of papers and stuffing them into the pockets of his rally jacket. Our jackets were already so heavily laden I struggled to lift mine.

'You'll need your road-book – that'll be your Bible for the next fortnight – bike insurance certificate, bike registration document . . .' Simon continued, '. . . your permission-to-have-bike letter from BMW, the Iritraq info and the piece of paper with the GPS codes.'

This year, the rally was introducing new navigation procedures. In previous years, the GPS satellite navigation display on every bike, vehicle and truck gave a rough heading to the next checkpoint. This year, we'd be riding blind.

In normal operation, the GPS would show neither the route

ahead nor a track of where we'd been. The only time it would come to life was when we were within three kilometres of a waypoint. It would then point in the general direction of the waypoint, but it would give us no indication of how to get to the three-kilometre zone around the waypoint. For that, we'd have to follow the road-book, a six-inch-wide roll of paper with several hundred graphical direction maps that looked like hieroglyphics to me.

If we missed the waypoint, we'd receive a time penalty. Too many time penalties on any one stage and we risked disqualification. If we got really lost, we were allowed to contact the organiser's head office in Paris to request a four-digit PIN code that we could type into the GPS unit to reveal all the waypoints for that day's stage and lead us back to the rally route. However, we'd incur a three-hour time penalty for each occasion we used it. If we requested the PIN code more than three times during the rally, we'd be ejected from the race.

Simon was not impressed with the new GPS arrangement. 'It's typical of the Dakar,' he said. 'You're in real trouble. You've lost hours already. And the organisers add further time penalties because you missed a checkpoint.'

Maybe Simon was in a bad mood. After all, he was nursing a hangover picked up after he stayed up drinking until 4 a.m. with those Scottish bikers at the party the previous night. It was the same party at which Kaz, my oldest friend, had told me bluntly why he'd come to see me off – because 'I thought I might not see you again'.

At the party, I'd been seated next to Pieter de Waal at dinner. As the head of BMW motorbikes and a former rally racer, he made me feel he really knew what we were facing.

'You sit there trying to tell people what it's like,' he said, 'and really they'll never know unless they've gone out there themselves.'

Already racked by nerves, I was just about to reply when Pieter stopped me talking. 'I'm here, Charley,' he said, 'not because you're doing this on a BMW bike but just because I want to be here. Just take it day by day and remember to enjoy it. Remember you wanted to do this. That's why you're here.

'Of course we would love to see you in Dakar, but that's not why we're here. Don't take unnecessary risks because of us. We're not in it for that. We are in it to support you. However far you get is however far you get. It doesn't matter.'

Pieter's words reminded me of when we were fixing Claudio's bike on Long Way Round. Claudio, our cameraman who had never ridden anything larger than a scooter, but bluffed his way on to the Long Way Round team, then had to fly back from Prague to take his bike licence while Ewan and I rode on to Kiev. He turned out to be an instinctive rider, who repeatedly managed to steer his bike across terrain on which Ewan and I struggled. But Claudio's determination came at a price. He damaged his bike far more often than us and we even had to buy Claudio a crude Russian bike when his BMW conked out in Mongolia after a succession of incidents that began when Claudio broke his BMW's frame while descending a Mongolian mountain. I'd phoned Howard Godolphin at BMW in England to ask his help. Attempting to fix the bike in the middle of nowhere, I listened to Howard on our satellite phone.

'Now, Charley, you're sitting down aren't you?' he said.

'Yeah.'

'OK, now look around. Just remember to smile because you are somewhere that you'll never forget,' he said.

Those were wise words. When Simon, Matt and I were in some shitty situation somewhere in the desert, I needed to remember them. I'd waited all my life to do the Dakar. If I wasn't careful I'd let my nerves ruin the experience.

January 2005, on our reconnaissance trip a year before Dakar 2006. Russ and I were checking out the rally to see if it could be possible for us . . . at least I think it's Russ!

Our kit would never look this clean again . . . from left to right: our brilliant mechanic Gareth Edmunds, Charley, Simon, Matt and cameraman Claudio von Planta.

I finally managed to finish an enduro race – Dawn to Dusk – in Wales.

Waiting for our official bike numbers in scrutineering . . . we hope!

Russ Malkin, the X5 and the unlikely lads.

Trying to fit a road-book to the bike. They were to become the bane of my existence.

Crashing out in the bivouac, exhausted after a day's racing. I hate to think how bad those shoes must smell. Probably helped to keep the insects away.

A typical service area. This shows the colour coding we used on the bikes – mine was yellow, Simon's orange and Matt's green. The same colour code was repeated on our helmets.

I was so focused on the road ahead, navigation and trying to stay safe, that most of the time I didn't notice the beautiful scenery around me.

To me the rally was all about Africa. It was a relief to be finally in the desert.

The Race to Dakar team in Africa . . . so far, so good.

Five minutes after coming out of the medical tent. With both hands broken, my Dakar dream was over, but I was adamant that I wanted to stay with my team until the end.

Simon pushes through another difficult stage of the rally.

Simon and Matt navigating dunes – the first day without me.

Many local people came out to cheer us on our way throughout the rally. This photo was taken in Mali.

Local law enforcement keeping an eye out at the bivouac.

Meanwhile, at our team meeting, Simon was still going through instructions. He was worried the officials would be keeping an extra-close eye on us because we'd be surrounded by cameras at times.

'If you arrive late at the bivouac, having ridden through the night, and you're there just before next stage is due to start, keep going. Don't make a fanfare. We need to do it low key. Otherwise they'll realise we haven't had our statutory six hours' break. They'll take us to the medics and turn it into a big drama. If you keep a low profile, you'll be back in the rally before anyone realises and then no one can stop you.'

We'd need guile as much as stamina to survive until Dakar, Simon warned us. 'One morning I had no lights. Technically you can't start without bike lights, but I'd arrived too late to sort them. The FIA guy on the start shouted, "No lights, no lights." I just put it in gear and started. Just rode off. And for sure, he was there at the finish. He pulled me over and said, "Sort it out or you're out", but I'd survived the day because I didn't stop. Just get away from the officials. Once you're on the rally again they can't do anything until the end of the stage.'

Simon was full of other tips:

– 'Every night. Bedtime reading: The road-book. That's the key to it.'

– 'And the GPS, guys, just piss about with it on the first stage when the riding's easy. Flick between the screens so you know how everything works.'

– 'Take a map and have an idea where you're going. You might think you're in a bike race, but actually you are alone in Africa. It's more than just a race.'

– 'Only buy fuel from the locals when there's no other choice. I bought fuel off a local guy with a barrel behind his house. My bike ceased the next day.'

– 'Don't be scared of stopping to rethink the road-book. If you're just a few hundred metres off track at one point, you can miss a turning point further on, get on the wrong heading and end up miles off course.'

– 'Don't get too worked up navigating in Portugal; it's very different to Africa.'

– 'And, oh yeah, the scrutineers told me they're going to check our water at the end of the first day. Because they think we're troublemakers.'

'We're not troublemakers,' I said.

'We are in the eyes of the French stewards.'

'They were charming to me . . .'

'Just accept it,' Simon said. 'They're going to be on our case for a bit.'

With less than twelve hours to the start, my nerves felt stretched taut and my heart was like a sledgehammer in my chest. Although Simon had every confidence in me, I was sure he wished I'd had more time to build up my bike fitness. I hadn't raced since August. Matt, I could tell, was nervous about his responsibilities as a cameraman as much as about riding the rally itself. And I was terrified of everything.

Simon and Matt had superstitious rituals to ease their nerves, but I had nothing of the type. Simon always put his left knee brace on first when he was racing. Matt had a lucky Buddha sticker that a friend had brought back from Thailand.

'I rubbed its belly when I stuck it on my bike yesterday,' Matt said, 'so I'm now going to have to rub its belly before I get on my bike every day.'

'I haven't got anything like that . . .' I said.

'You could rub my belly every day for good luck.'

'I'll do that if it helps,' I offered. 'I'll do fucking anything!'

As well as my fear of the rally, I was concerned about the documentary. It was difficult enough to compete, I thought, without also having to shoot a television programme. If we concentrated on the riding, surely the programme would suffer.

Simon told me to stop worrying. 'Once we start, I'm just interested in the three of us getting to the finish. That's a huge task on its own,' he said. 'But we've got a good team, good assistance, good mechanics. We're in with a good support truck. All that side of things should be fine. As for the TV, once we're out there, Russ and Claudio will take care of it. If we worry about it we'll go wrong and then there'll be nothing. No finisher's medal and no TV programme.'

Simon went on: 'All you've got to think about every day is looking after yourself. You've got to get through that race. Eat enough, drink enough and sleep enough. Otherwise you won't make it. Those are your priorities. Soon as you think about the bike or the TV or anything else, you get run down.

'Just think about getting to the bivouac, getting cleaned up, sorting your road-book, preparing your riding kit, throwing some food down your neck, rehydrating, then sleep. That's all.

'You need to prepare yourself for that. Because once the race starts, by the end of each day your brain-power will be gone. It's left in the desert.'

That evening we took a taxi to the competitors' briefing. We knew it was in a building near the start, but that was all.

'Do you know where we are going?' I asked Russ in the taxi.

'No.'

'Well, I don't know where we are fucking going. Can someone please find out where the fuck we are meant to be? This doesn't bode well for tomorrow.'

My nervous outburst was interrupted by a phone call. It was Julian Broad, one of the riders with whom I'd trained in Wales.

He was also a photographer who'd taken some of the pictures for Long Way Round.

'Hey, Charley. Where are you now?'

'Just on our way to the drivers' briefing.'

'You looking forward to it?'

'No. Shitting it,' I said. 'I've got to remember to enjoy myself, but at the moment I'm shitting my pants.'

'Listen, mate. I want you to ride safe. And I want you to make it to Dakar. Look after yourself.'

It was kind of him and lots of other friends to call to wish me good luck, and I really appreciated the call, but inevitably it added to the weight of expectation on my shoulders.

Russ, meanwhile, was trying to direct the taxi driver to the race briefing in a mixture of French, English and Spanish. '*Monsieur!*' he said at one point. 'Over there, *por favor!*' Unfortunately the driver spoke only Portuguese.

As we drove through Lisbon's Christmas decorations, I realised I'd already forgotten some of the items Simon had warned me to take. I got on the phone to Olly at the hotel, without whom I'd have been an even bigger bag of nerves.

'Can you remind me to get my wallet out of my jeans . . . it is very important . . . Oh . . . and my passport. Better still, you put them in my bike jacket . . . oh shit . . . love you, bubs.'

Matt was convinced he would drop his bike on the podium at the start. 'At least it will get me noticed,' he said. 'No one has ever done it before.'

'My experience,' said Russ, referring to the time he rolled the support truck in Mongolia, 'is that if you do something stupid, no one *ever* lets you forget it.'

'In fairness,' I had to tell Russ, 'what you did was kind of memorable.'

Russ groaned, not for the first or the last time.

Eventually we got to the start area, which was bustling with people looking at the bikes, cars and trucks parked in the parc fermé. A huge video screen was showing footage from previous rallies, the shots of motorbikes skimming across dunes like jet skis on a lake both exciting and terrifying.

Searching for the drivers' briefing, we bumped into an English couple who had ridden their Royal Enfield from Ely through blizzards in France and northern Spain. Having taken two days to get to Lisbon, they were looking for directions to the start of the special stage and had recognised me from watching *Long Way Round*. While we were talking, Russ approached from a nearby café, where he'd bought all of us cheese rolls and cans of lemonade. 'This is Russ,' I said to the couple. 'Remember him? He rolled the Mitsubishi.' Russ groaned again.

Spotting a large crowd, mainly men, lingering by the doorway of a building, we realised we'd found the drivers' briefing. Once inside, I was handed a roll of paper about the size of the rollers with which I'd spent years painting kitchen cupboard doors. As soon as I had it in my hand, my anxiety level ratcheted up another notch. It was the dreaded road-book. Inching towards the hall where around 1,500 competitors and assistance crew would be briefed, we were handed half a dozen pages of photocopied paper – the changes to the road-book. The route would have been devised about six months ago, but since then some of the features, particularly in the desert, would have moved, so we'd be given the amendments for the next day's stage each evening and have to sketch in the changes to the road-book before bed.

With all the seats in the hall taken, we squeezed into a box to watch a video about the rally, but the shots of racing vehicles didn't ease my nerves; they made me even more scared.

After the video, Etienne Lavigne, the chief executive of the rally, stepped up to a podium to explain the alert system on every vehicle. It had three buttons.

'Press the red button if you are the victim,' Etienne said. 'Press the green one if you are a witness. And press the blue one to speak to headquarters.'

Competitors would carry communications equipment that linked them directly to the organisers and pinpointed their position to within a few feet. As well as finding us in an emergency, this location tracking system would be used to check we didn't break the speed limits. In villages, we had to keep below 50kph (31mph). Outside villages, motorcycles and racing trucks were limited to 150kph (93mph), and assistance vehicles to 100kph (69mph). Press and organisers' vehicles could travel at up to 140kph (88mph), while rally cars were allowed to go as fast as they damn well pleased.

'There will be no tolerance for speeding,' Etienne warned. 'We will make daily checks of your GPS when you arrive at the bivouac. Anyone who exceeds limits will face financial and time penalties.'

After the briefing, we returned to the hotel where I joined my wife, children and some friends for a very tense last supper. Hardly able to eat, my cutlery was trembling in my hands. I also didn't feel like talking, but everyone wanted to know what lay ahead. A year earlier, Olly had known nothing about the Dakar except that Mark Thatcher once got lost on it. Now, with the start just hours away, she told me she was worried I would lose contact with Matt and Simon, get lost in the desert and follow Thatcher's dreadful example.

Unable to face talking to anyone but Olly, I made my excuses and went up to my room. A few days earlier, I'd envisaged a last night of sex with my wife before the rally, but now the thought couldn't have been further from my mind. Olly gave me a back rub and a couple of herbal sleeping tablets, but before I got into bed I needed to add the route modifications to my road-book.

Returning to my room, I had bumped into one of the female factory riders and we'd shared our anxieties about the road-book. She was going to stick the new directions over the old ones, but when I tried the same method, it didn't work. It was 11 p.m., my alarm was set for 4.30 a.m., our start time was 6.55 a.m. and we needed to start the special stage by 8.05 a.m., but right now, trying to update the road-book, I was in a blind panic. With the roll of paper unfurling in my hands, spilling over the desk, bed and floor, I didn't know where to start. I couldn't make sense of it. I called Simon. Five minutes later there was a knock on the door of my room.

'All right, mate?'

'. . . look, this whole page takes me to 326, which is . . .' I said as Simon walked in. 'You see, that's where . . . the 326 . . . everything changes. Whereas before it said go straight out . . . and here . . . now it says go along this bit of river and turn left . . .'

'Just a *minor* panic going on here,' Simon said.

'. . . And this . . . on this last little bit of the first stage, there's just a little bit of . . .'

'Look, Charley, probably the best thing is if I . . .' Simon tried to calm me.

'. . . it changes here . . . and here . . .'

'. . . just do my thing and you can copy my style,' Simon continued.

'Yeah, yeah . . . good idea . . . what about *that*?' I pointed to another change that confused me.

'Everyone's got their own way of doing it. I'm sure you'll develop yours, but right now, why not copy mine? Have you got a black marker?'

Simon took over, patiently leading me through the road-book.

Eventually he, too, conceded defeat. 'There's so many changes it's not worth bothering,' he said.

Fifteen minutes later, just after midnight, I was in bed.

In the foyer at 5 a.m., Olly and the kids were in Race to Dakar baseball caps and T-shirts while I was in my full race kit. Simon was running late, as usual, but after the panic of the previous night I was calm. Even Simon's tardiness hadn't started me fretting.

Approaching the start area and the parc fermé in the taxi, my nerves kicked in. I already had a sweat on and I hadn't done anything yet. I started to shiver – partly the cold and partly a sense of doom.

While Simon chattered away as if it were any other morning, I felt like crying. The little black cloud that had been following me around for the previous few days had started to thunder.

Pulling the road-book out of my jacket's inside pocket, I attempted to feed it on to its spool on the bike's road-book holder. It had to be fed in absolutely correctly otherwise it would crumple. And it had to be kept tight on the spool, or it wouldn't fit into the holder. Inevitably, I fucked it up badly. It was all over the place. I couldn't help laughing: here I was, about to start the world's longest and toughest desert rally, and my road-book was a mess. I'm already losing time, and I haven't even started.

With so much sweat pouring down my back that my clothes were sticking to my skin, I jumped as a hand touched me and two familiar voices shouted: 'Hey, Daddy! Hi!'

It was lovely to see Olly and the kids, but turning around to hug them only made things worse. Now I could see Simon, who had finished fitting his road-book with ease and was standing by his bike, looking calm and relaxed. At least Matt was also in a flap.

Sitting on a bollard beside my bike, my mind started to race. We shouldn't have come down to the start so early. We had too much time to think. People were taking pictures. I just wanted to get going.

Russ came over to tell me the X5 had started without a problem, with the BMW technician on board and the GP1 box of tricks in the back.

Shivering in the cold and dark, I prayed it wouldn't rain. A nice dry stage would be a good start to our nine-thousand-kilometre quest.

'Twelve months on from when we last stood at the start, watching the riders go off, and we are here,' Russ said as I prepared to get on my bike. 'A lot of pain and organisation and money behind us and, in front of us, thirty-five minutes away, the start of the Dakar. Well done and good luck. Take it easy and make it good. There's no rush.'

'Thanks, Russ,' I said.

'Remember: we are not trying to win. We're not trying to push boundaries. We just want to be part of it. It will be a miracle if we get three bikes and the car to Dakar. Just look after yourself.'

'I've waited all my life for this moment,' I said, 'and now I really don't know why I'm here.'

'I don't know either,' said Russ. 'I still haven't worked out why all these people are here, but all I can think is there's a small amount of craziness left in an increasingly sanitised world and they want to be part of it.'

At 6.50 a.m. it started to rain as the first competitor, number 252, a quadbike, moved off to the start, followed by several other quads that appeared to be little more than fortified gardening kit.

Every thirty seconds or so, another pair of competitors was waved up on to the podium by an official. A short interview was relayed over loudspeakers to the crowd of several thousand, some of the competitors did a bit of grandstanding, waving national flags and urging the crowd to cheer them on, then the start official sent them on their way.

At 6.55 a.m., it was our turn. Etienne Lavigne waved us on to the podium as I pressed the button to switch on my helmet camera and glanced down to see if the red light on my bike display had lit up to indicate the camera was filming. With Simon and Matt either side of me, I gunned the throttle and skipped slightly ahead to get a grip on the rain-splattered metal ramp. And then I was there, on the start line, thirty years of ambition and dreams flashing before my eyes as I scanned the crowd for a sight of Olly and the kids.

I looked down at the controls of my bike. The little red light wasn't on. Russ and Claudio had implored me to shoot the ride up to the podium and the start line, and now my camera wasn't working.

I tried to pull on my gloves. My hands were so sweaty I couldn't get my fingers into the correct holes. Squeezing the clutch and tapping into first gear, cramp set into my fingers. Sweat poured down my legs. Standing on the Dakar start line should have been a highlight in my life, but I was finding it a deeply unpleasant experience.

Nearly two years earlier, Ewan and I had set off from Shepherd's Bush in west London on Long Way Round. We'd had a similarly fraught lead-up to the start, but that morning was perfect. We'd whooped and shouted to each other, giddy with the feeling of escape. Two mates on the road together for the next three months, and just 244 miles ahead of us before we stopped in Brussels. It was a beautiful late spring day, the kind you dream about, the sky a brilliant cloudless blue, the air warm and soft.

On a cold, dark mid-winter morning in Lisbon, things felt very different as we faced 231 miles, including a 51-mile off-road special, before we reached Portimão.

The start official gave us the nod to prepare to move off. 'Go!' he yelled. We gunned the engines, rolled down the podium and roared out on to the open road.

Well, almost.

Not wanting to slip, we rode gingerly down the wet ramp. Standing at the bottom with a camera, Russ implored us to stop so he could take some photos, while I desperately wanted to get going, away from the crowds and out on to the road. Eventually, a steward insisted that Russ let us go and we moved off. At the end of the first straight, about 150 yards further on, we stopped to fix the cameras.

Everything sorted, Simon, who was slightly ahead and looking back over his shoulder at me, gave me a nod. 'Everything OK, Charley?'

I returned the nod.

'You lead then,' he said. At last, we were off.

PART TWO

Lisbon to Nouakchott

Chapter 7

31 DECEMBER AND 1 JANUARY
Lisbon to Málaga

Cursing Simon all the way for making me ride in front, I led the team out of Lisbon through the docks and up on to the Tagus River Bridge, at one time the longest suspension bridge in Europe. But I didn't want to be leading. I wanted to be at the back, following Matt and Simon and getting used to the road-book. Five minutes into the rally and all I wanted was to go home. I didn't want to do it any more, I thought. It wasn't fun.

Still freaked out about navigating, I was spending more time peering at my road-book than where I was going. It took several more miles before I realised our route was lined by a continuous bank of spectators either side of the road, making the damned road-book redundant. What a relief.

I started to relax, but was immediately shaken out of my short-lived respite when Simon came thundering up alongside me.

'Charley!' he shouted. 'Pull over! Pull over!'

'What?'

'Fucking back brake is on fire!'

'On fire?'

'Red-hot! You got your foot on it?'

I looked down at the disc. It was glowing bright red. For fuck's sake, I thought, I've done seven kilometres and I've fucked the back brake already. Not good.

'I can smell the brake dust!' Simon shouted.

We pulled over and checked the brake. I must have been resting my toe on the brake pedal, but it looked OK. I'd been dragging on it only lightly, so the damage was minor. I put on my helmet, we moved off and at last I managed to shut out the world. The bullshit stopped and freedom lay ahead. Just me and my thoughts. No one and nothing else intruding . . . until all of a sudden Matt pulled over.

Parked by the side of the road, Matt's bike was roaring loudly. Oh God, what the fuck now? I thought.

'My throttle's stuck,' Matt yelled.

We were twenty kilometres into a nine-thousand-kilometre race. I'd almost burnt out my back brake. Now Matt's throttle was broken. What was going to happen next? These things usually went in threes.

Crouching at the side of the road, we removed Matt's fully laden petrol tank to get at the throttle cables. In the dark we could smell petrol dribbling from the tank, but we couldn't distinguish it from the water on the road.

Cursing the bikes and thinking what a miserable start we'd had to the Dakar, I traced the cable along the bike, seeking an explanation for Matt's jammed throttle. Inside my rally suit I was wet with sweat; we hadn't ridden long enough to cool down.

And then I spotted the cause. A cable from the Iritraq satellite tracker had slipped into the gap between the throttle spring and its holder. We tied the cable down, then set off again, riding comfortably to the start of the special stage, 186 kilometres from Lisbon.

Every stage followed the same formula. After the competitors' briefing at about 7 p.m. every evening, each rider or driver would check a notice board to find out their two start times. The first would be their stage start time, the time when they had to leave the bivouac or, in the case of the first stage, depart from the start. From the start they'd travel on the first part of the stage, called the first liaison, which could be as short as one kilometre or as long as 336 kilometres. It would usually be a public road, either tarmac or compacted dirt track. After the first liaison, they'd ride the special section, which they were required to start by the second time printed on their time-cards. Entirely off-road, the special section would be timed and would range from 31 kilometres, on the final day, to 599 kilometres, which was on the ninth day. It would have up to three checkpoints. Once we reached Africa, at least one of the checkpoints each day would have petrol for the bikes, which had a range of only 250 kilometres. At these, we'd be compelled to stop for at least fifteen minutes.

All vehicles had to pass through the end of the special section within a time specified in their road-books. The second liaison section then followed and could be as short as 12 kilometres or as long as 424 kilometres. Like the first liaison, it would usually be on public roads and again there was a time limit. Any competitor failing to finish the special section or the second liaison each day by the times in the road-book would be disqualified.

As we approached the end of the inaugural liaison of the rally and the start of its first special section, Simon's van, driven by his mate Dave, was waiting for us so that we could change from road to enduro treads.

We'd swapped the tyres and were feeling good, relieved things were shaking into place, when Simon suggested we check our start time for the special section of the stage. With fourteen kilometres left to ride to the start, it transpired we had only ten minutes to get there. Oh fuck!

The panic returned and my stomach churned as we leapt on to our bikes, the fear of what might lie ahead increasing with every kilometre we rode, slipping all over the tarmac on our enduro tyres.

Matt and Simon started on the special as soon as the three of us arrived, leaving me behind, staring at a huge mud bath in a dip at the bottom of a long slope. Seated on one of the largest and heaviest bikes in the rally, my nerves subsided while I waited five minutes for the start official to wave me off. It was too late for fretting; I just needed to get on with it.

The start official's voice counting down brought me to my

senses with a thrill. I'm in a proper rally, I thought, being counted off in just the same way I'd seen it on television.

'. . . three, two, one . . . go!' the starter shouted and I was off. I raced down the hill, sweeping through the mud bath and ruts. The special was easy compared to the tracks on which I'd trained with Simon. Hurtling along the dirt tracks, I even had time to think about Olly, the kids and everything I'd been through over the last few months and to wave to people in the huge crowds lining the length of the special section. Many of them had spent the night there and were cooking on barbecues. The bike felt great; it was the first time I'd ridden it with its suspension set up properly and I even gave it a little extra gas over the bumps to lift the bike into the air – get some air, we called it – and showboat in front of the crowds.

Although the special was relatively easy, I was also aware that I could just as easily slip on a tricky or stony part of the track in Portugal as on a dune in Africa. I had a few small instances of what bikers call 'moments'. The last thing I needed was a big moment, like dropping the bike, on the first day of the race. Reminding myself the rally was all about getting to Dakar and not about posting a good position, I slowed down and rode more cautiously. All too soon, however, I'd finished the special section and was changing the treads back to road tyres before comfortably riding the final 101 kilometres to Portimão with Simon and Matt.

A few kilometres into the second liaison, Simon waved me out in front. The wily dog was pushing me ahead again to ensure that my mind was so occupied by navigating the stage I wouldn't think about anything else. Matt, meanwhile, was riding very erratically, repeatedly screaming off ahead then slowing down – a sure sign of nerves.

By mid-afternoon we had dropped the bikes off in the parc

fermé in Portimão, sorted out some minor teething problems and were ready to find our hotel. Matt and I were looking at each other, finding it difficult to believe we'd finished our first Dakar stage. The riding hadn't been difficult but we were still relieved to have survived the day. Anyone who looked into my eyes that day would have seen I was still rigid with the fear of what lay ahead. When I wasn't worrying about myself, I fretted about everyone else on the team. The pressures to succeed and to make a decent documentary still weighed heavily on my shoulders.

I walked up to Simon, who was in his usual chirpy mood. 'How do you think we did today?' I said.

'Good,' he replied. 'But way too slow. Need to get a move on tomorrow.'

I thought we'd ridden relatively fast.

As we left the parc fermé we picked up the next day's road-book. With it, the nightmare and the panic began all over again.

Walking back to the hotel, a couple of people in the crowd shouted out to me. 'Charley! Long Way Round! Yeah! Go for Dakar!'

I should have been flattered and excited by the attention, but it only increased the pressure to succeed. I felt my boots dragging as if lead had been injected into my legs. I was so tired of talking about the Dakar, I was worried I'd punch the next person who asked me about it.

'Charley!' shouted another voice in the crowd. 'How're you feeling? How do you think you're going?'

I knew what I wanted to yell back at them: How the *fuck* do you think I'm feeling? Just step inside my fucking brain at the moment and you'll see total panic.

Instead I kept walking and kept my mouth shut. But as we walked to the hotel, having a giggle about some of the things that had happened on the stage, I could feel the heavy road-book in my pocket sapping my energy like Superman's stick of kryptonite. The mere thought of the road-book was enough to reawaken feelings of panic and helplessness about how I was going to cope with the navigation over the next few days.

At the hotel, I picked up my key and trudged upstairs. Sweaty in my thermal leggings, knee braces and motocross kit, and desperate for a shower, I dragged all my kit up to the eighth floor, flung open the door to my room and collapsed on the bed. A quick wash and I was on my way to dinner at a pizza restaurant, thinking, God, another fucking day tomorrow, and not looking forward to making polite conversation with a big table of people. All I wanted to do was swallow as many calories as possible and go to bed.

As soon as we'd eaten, Matt and I made our excuses and left. We chatted briefly on the way back to the hotel about how we both felt like startled rabbits caught in headlights, then went to bed. Back in my room, I discovered a New Year's Eve party was in full swing in the room directly above mine. Drunken singing, badly played guitars, shouting and dancing reverberated through the bare stone floors, but I knew it was the one night in the year I couldn't complain, so I pulled my mattress into the bathroom, plugged in my iPod and attempted to drown out the partying while I worked through the road-book, highlighting almost everything with my marker pens.

Sitting on the floor of my bathroom, trying to devise a method to help me quickly distinguish the various obstacles forewarned in the road-book, the panic took over, just like it had done in the Lisbon hotel room. Only this time, Olly wasn't there to calm my nerves and I didn't want to bother Simon again with what, to him, was surely a trifling concern. The more I looked at the road-book, the more it seemed that everything was dangerous. It used a system of exclamation marks to warn bikers to ride cautiously, but it was all relative. One exclamation mark indicated danger, two indicated severe danger and three exclamation marks warned of acute danger. Sitting on the tiled floor of the bathroom, it all looked too much. I felt sick, like I was trapped on a rollercoaster that never stopped.

Eventually, my road-book was so heavily marked it had become meaningless. I gave up and pushed the earplugs of my iPod into my ears as far as they would go, selected a playlist called 'Charley Go To Sleep' compiled by Paul, a mate from home, turned up the music to drown out the noise of the party and fell asleep. I was so tired from the riding and so exhausted by my state of heightened anxiety that very little could have kept me awake.

While the rest of the team had been eating at the pizzeria and, in my case at least, sleeping through the New Year's celebrations, Jim and John were working on the X5. Starting the car was still unreliable, but by the time I left my hotel room at 5.30 a.m. on New Year's Day they had more or less fixed it.

Unable to eat a proper breakfast, I forced down a couple of bananas just so that I could take all the pills that Natalie, my trainer in London, had given me. She'd explained what each little tablet was meant to do for me – there were pills for my joints and capsules for my muscles; there were tablets that would replace lost salts and replenish vitamins and minerals – but, typically, I'd not paid much attention. I didn't really care what they did to me as long as they made me feel better. I'd glazed over when she'd explained them all to me and it was no different now. Down the hatch and on to the next thing was my only thought. But it wasn't that easy. Retching as I tried to swallow the banana, I realised the stupidity of my predicament. I couldn't even eat a banana because I was so stressed out about taking part in a rally that I thought I'd always wanted to do. And I didn't even want to eat the banana. Its only purpose was to line my stomach so that I could swallow Natalie's supplements, which I wouldn't have to take if I wasn't riding the rally. It seemed ridiculous. It was meant to be fun but I was beginning to fear that fun wasn't going to be any part of it.

With the cursed road-book burning a hole in my pocket, I took a taxi to the parc fermé with Matt. It was the second successive morning that we'd started our day in darkness, driving through an alien city, my stress levels rising steadily as the time of our departure on the bikes approached.

Again we were surrounded by spectators as we prepared for the stage to Málaga. 'Gladiators!' shouted one member of the crowd. It might have seemed that way to them, after all it's rare in today's age of excessive health and safety precautions for people to court extreme danger in quite such a foolhardy and conspicuous way, but I felt more like one of the hapless Christians about to be fed to the lions for the amusement of the crowds.

It was cold in the mid-winter pre-dawn darkness and the windchill would make it feel even colder once we moved off, so I'd wrapped up well. With even more clothes on than the previous day, I was soon building up a sweat while we waited to be allowed to get on our bikes, thirty minutes before our official start times. As usual, Simon was late. As usual, he seemed to be able to guess just what I was thinking when he turned up. And, as usual, I was fretting about the road-book. After such an easy special section the previous day, I was convinced this would be the day the road-book would fail me.

'Don't worry, Charley,' said Simon. 'Going to be like yesterday. Just a trail ride with lovely little green arrows telling you where to go.'

Simon might have been right about the stage ahead, but my

prediction about the road-book came true as soon as I tried to feed it into its holder. I managed to run the first part of it between the spools without creasing it too much, but it was a mess by the time I'd fed in the part that gave directions through the special section of the stage.

'Matt, I can't fucking get it in,' I yelled. 'I can't get it all in.'

'Just tear it off,' he advised. 'I'm sure Simon's got all of it.'

I ripped off the remainder of the roll and looked around at the crowd. 'Anyone want this?'

Immediately about a dozen people stuck their arms out and screamed for it. In too much of a panic to enjoy giving my road-book to the crowd, I tossed it in their general direction, thinking it was sad that it had come to this. I'd fantasised about being in this situation – a rally rider with an adoring crowd wanting autographs and trinkets from me – and now I couldn't enjoy it.

With ten minutes remaining before my scheduled departure time, I rode up towards the start line, wet with sweat under my heavy protective clothing. Simon and Matt followed me to the official who was handing out the time-cards. These carried details of our start times and the route ahead: 65-kilometre first liaison, 115-kilometre special section and a 387-kilometre second liaison to the ferry port at Málaga.

Pulling off my outer protective gloves and inner enduro gloves to be able to open the zip to one of the pockets on my jacket in which I hoped to stuff my time-card, I discovered I'd filled every pocket. It was no wonder my jacket was so heavy and hot. In the end I stowed the time-card in a pocket on my tank bag and waited for the countdown.

A few minutes before my start time, I pushed through the crush of riders congregating around the starting gate. The start steward waved me on. I shoved again and, almost before I'd registered it, I was riding the second stage of the rally.

Again all the anxieties disappeared as soon as I had my helmet on and was moving. The riding was a joy; it was everything that surrounded it – the road-book, my anxiety about sleeping and eating arrangements, my concerns about the X5 and the documentary – that was a misery.

Simon was true to his word. The liaison was straightforward and the special was as easy as the previous day. Although the track was lined by a few sheer drops and had some tight corners with exceptionally slippery rocks, it was the kind of riding that came very naturally to me. Ploughing through fields and up hillsides, it felt no more difficult than a nice, easy Sunday morning hack, passing lots of riders, shouting at them to get out of the way and enjoying myself at last.

Suffering considerable arm pump by halfway through the special section, I slowed down for Simon, who had told Matt and me to 'keep going, don't faff around' as soon as we got to the special. Matt rode ahead, skipping through the other riders. I'd kept up with him for a long section of the slippery, narrow course, but after a while I realised there was no point in trying to match Matt's speed. Matt was so completely charged by the rally he was riding almost flat out, making great progress but with little regard for looking after the bike on which Gareth had done such a fantastic job.

We finished the special section with nearly 400 kilometres to ride to Málaga. With little time to spare, we loaded our bikes into the van, which was allowed on this liaison, threw in all our kit behind it, then jumped into a spare car and raced off towards the port. Stopping on the outskirts of Málaga, we hosed down the bikes, filled them with petrol and rode the final twenty kilometres to the finish.

With two stages behind me, I was at last feeling more confident about my abilities and what lay ahead. Without riding beyond my ability, I'd finished eightieth that day out of what remained of the 252 riders that had departed from Lisbon and I felt good. Riding into Málaga, I had tears in my eyes and a lump in my throat at the sight of the crowds cheering us on. All the rally cars and trucks were beeping their horns, the police were waving the rally bikes through the traffic and the crowds were stretching out their hands to pat us on the back.

Approaching the port, the road narrowed and the crowds swelled until we were riding through a narrow canyon of outstretched hands to the boat, shaking hands with spectators, acknowledging their cheers and marvelling at the pretty girls who wanted our photos. Spotting a group waving a Race to Dakar poster and shouting 'Go, Charley! Go, Simon! Go, Matt!', I stopped. Throwing their arms around us, they said they were Brits living in Spain who had travelled hundreds of miles to see us leave for Africa. I was touched by their good wishes.

We rode on to the boat expecting a scene of chaos, but it was beautifully organised. Stevedores wrapped our bikes in bubblewrap and strapped them to the inside of the boat's cargo hold. Inside the ferry, every chair and bench was occupied by men and women in motorcycle kit, many of them watching coverage of the last two Dakar stages and other enduro races. Every table carried a stack of road-books next to a pile of coloured highlighter pens, a reminder of what had to be done before any of us could go to sleep.

Matt, Simon and I clambered downstairs to our four-bunk cabin, stripped off, showered, ate the packed dinner we'd been given and got on with the dreaded task of tackling the road-book, three exhausted men sitting on cramped bunks in their underpants, colouring in hundreds of squares on rolls of paper.

'Don't it feel good being on the boat?' said Simon.

'Yeah, great, it's just the problems we've had along the way . . .' I replied.

'Never mind,' Simon said. 'Now we're on the boat, we're in the rally proper. That's the thing, isn't it? Exciting.'

'I just want to get tomorrow over,' I said. 'The first in Africa. It would be nice to have that behind me.'

'It would be *nice* to get to *Dakar*.'

'That would be nice,' I conceded.

I worked on my road-book for a while. The stage ahead, 672 kilometres through Morocco from Nador to Er Rachidia, looked very technical. With many bumps, river-beds or wadis, some sandy sections and a few small dunes, it was going to be a rough ride.

Now that we were entering Africa, there were many more changes to the road-book than on the European stages. The course had been devised more than a year before by a team led by David Castera, who had done the Dakar five times, coming third in 1997. They drove the entire course, working out the best and most challenging routes, devising the road-books for each stage by noting down thousands of topographical features and landmarks. More recently, the course had been driven over by another team who checked the road-books provided sufficiently robust guidance. Then, a day or so before the rally arrived, each stage was again navigated by rally officials who would note any changes to the topography, landmarks or features in the road-book. It might be something as small as a tree that was previously standing now having been knocked down. Or a landslide or flood might have made a previously viable route impassable. These changes were posted every night and, like some irksome homework assignment, had to be added manually by each competitor before they started the next stage the following morning.

Of course my dyslexia didn't help. I read a warning of 'ascent with ruts' as 'ascent with rust' and 'watch out for tracks in the oued' – an oued was a dry river-bed, or wadi – became 'watch out for trucks in the road'. Fortunately I had Simon, the rally equivalent of the swotty boy at the top of the class, to help me as we lay in the cramped cabin and this night it took much less time than usual.

Having finished my road-book homework and feeling nervous about what it had told me lay ahead, I left the cabin and climbed the stairs to the top deck to watch the ferry leaving the harbour. The ferry would dock at about 4 a.m., we'd be straight off the boat and on to the stage by 6.30 a.m. But now, watching the lights of Málaga slip behind the boat, I was a mess of emotions. Suddenly my wife, children and home seemed a long way away, and I felt very alone. The next day the rally would take us into the wilds of Morocco; I was worried and frightened about what might happen. However, with two stages under my belt, I was also coming to realise there was little my worrying and fear would achieve. I just needed to get on with it and deal with any trouble as it happened. In the meantime, it was time to sleep. By the time I got back to the cabin Simon and Matt were asleep, but not even their loud snoring kept me awake as I drifted off to the sound of *Winter Wonderland* playing over the ship's tannoy.

Chapter 8

2 AND 3 JANUARY
Nador to Ouarzazate

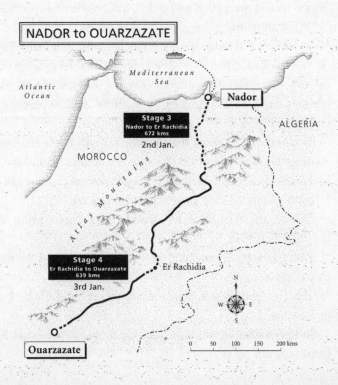

NADOR to OUARZAZATE

Atlantic Ocean

Mediterranean Sea

Nador

ALGERIA

Stage 3
Nador to Er Rachidia
672 kms
2nd Jan.

MOROCCO

Atlas Mountains

Stage 4
Er Rachidia to Ouarzazate
639 kms
3rd Jan.

Er Rachidia

Ouarzazate

0   50   100   150   200 kms

Bing Crosby was crooning *White Christmas* over the tannoy and Matt was chirruping to Simon as I struggled to shake myself on our first day in Africa. It was 2.55 a.m.

'You looking forward to today, Si?'

'Gonna be an interesting one, I reckon. Gonna be a long day, eh?'

'Yep,' said Matt.

I'd prepared all my kit beside my bunk. My boots, which stank of sweaty feet, had been stuffed with my socks, gloves and knee braces. I'd filled any empty pocket I could find with cereal bars to keep me going through the day. Everything else was in a pile at the foot of my bed.

'Biggest thing today is not making any silly little mistakes,' Simon said as we pulled on our kit. 'Just not crashing, really.'

'What about not getting lost?' asked Matt.

'If you get lost today it's not going to be for long,' said Simon. 'It's all tracks and there's still two hundred and forty riders on the rally. You're going to find your way for sure and we should be home in daylight. The only worry is it'll be the first time the cars catch up with us.'

By Simon's reckoning the cars, the fastest of which would be starting the special section less than two hours behind the first bike, would overtake us at CP2, the second checkpoint and first refuelling stop, 234 kilometres into the special.

'What's the technique for dealing with cars coming from behind?' said Matt.

'Shit yourself.' Simon laughed. 'And then get out of the way as quick as you can!'

'But I've got too much gear in my jacket,' said Matt. 'I can't turn round.'

Simon laughed again. 'You got a big problem. Not good, Matt. Definitely not good.'

'There's no general rule that they pass on the left or right or . . . ?' I said.

'No,' said Simon.

'What? They don't stick to some kind of rule?' said Matt.

'They go wherever they can get through quickly,' said Simon. 'Just get out of their way.'

'Or what?' said Matt.

'Or they'll have you off your bike,' said Simon. 'That Sentinel system makes it better than it used to be. At least you get a warning. The cars tend to be about two hundred metres behind you when it goes off, so you've got a few seconds to look over your shoulder and work out where they are and find an escape route. Make sure you're always aware what's at the side of the piste, which side you can get off without hitting a boulder or ending up in a ditch when the cars come through.'

Simon paused. 'So how does that make you feel, Charley?' he said.

'Er . . . not good,' I said.

'It's fucking shitting us up even more,' said Matt.

The prospect of the cars catching us up and cutting mercilessly through the bikes added a further dimension of danger to the day's already risky proceedings. It was an incentive to ride a little harder and faster to keep ahead of them for as long as possible. But there was a very fine line between pushing hard enough to stay out in front and pushing so hard that we came a cropper.

'Once the cars come past your pace is set,' said Simon. 'You've got to ride slow enough to give yourself time to pull aside without coming off.'

At 5 a.m. we were on African soil, the sound of drums and dancing from a welcoming party almost drowning out the roar of our bikes. As soon as we rolled off the ferry, it smelled of Africa. A whiff of drains and sewage mingling with the dust of the desert, the damp fragrance of fecund vegetation and smoke from wood fires. Russ, Jim, Wolfgang and Gareth were waiting for us, flapping about on the quayside when I needed peace and quiet to attend to my road-book, which again had me floored. I've never been someone who's found it difficult to wake up in the morning. But that morning, with my first day in Africa to worry about, the road-book felt as if it was zapping all my energy. That darned stick of kryptonite again left me desperately wanting to go back to bed.

As I tried to feed the road-book into its holder, the bottom half rolled on very slowly, while the top spool spun very fast. After a few seconds the chief sprung out of the motor, the cogs on the spools disengaged and, try as hard as I did, I couldn't get either spool to turn.

Great, I thought, my first day in Africa and I haven't got a road-book. I'm riding blind into Africa. My big nightmare had come true.

'Tuck in behind Matt,' suggested Simon before we rode off to the start of the stage. It was a relief in a way. A silver lining to the cloud cast by my broken road-book. Don't complain at all, Charley, I thought. Keep quiet and Matt will lead you all the way to Er Rachidia.

After picking up our packed lunches and struggling to find an empty pocket somewhere on our rally jackets for them, we were waved through the start. Despite a strip of tarmac covering the entire 237 kilometres of the liaison, somehow it felt totally different in Africa. Maybe it was because my road-book wasn't working, so I had more time to take in the countryside and the road than previously, but everything felt more vivid and more acute. Maybe it was also the relief of having survived the rally as far as Africa that enabled me to relax more than on the previous days, but somehow I felt at home and I was enjoying it more than in Portugal and Spain.

It didn't last long. Approaching the end of the 237-kilometre liaison, which culminated in a long climb up to a plateau to Ain-Benimathar, I spotted the flags that marked the start of the special section and my heart sank. We waited our turn, then Matt started, followed at thirty-second intervals by me, then Simon.

We'd planned to ride together, Matt at the front, navigating because I didn't have a road-book, me in the middle and Simon at the rear, from where he'd be able to come to our aid if anything went wrong. But the first African special was quite different to the two European specials. The big change was the dust. It blew slowly across the track, hanging in the air because there was very little wind. It forced each of us to hang back on our predecessor just so that we could see where we were riding.

Long plumes of dust made overtaking anyone very difficult. And if Matt overtook anyone he immediately forced Simon and me to follow suit, simply because he was doing the map-reading and we needed to ensure there was no bike in between, kicking up a dust cloud that would obscure our view of the route he was taking.

So what did Matt do? He flew off the start line, riding flat out, bouncing all over the place, throttle wide open with no thought of Simon or me. I was livid, but was vindicated when Matt came off soon after the start.

'Just relax,' I yelled to Matt. But he got on his bike and raced off again. I needed him to hang back. We were on a wide, flat plain of sand and gravel, criss-crossed by tracks. The air was heavy with dust and without Matt's lead I was struggling to find the correct route.

Riding much faster than I wanted, I stuck behind Matt. His navigation was excellent; using a mix of the road-book and guidance from other bikers, he led us up a stony track to the top of a mountain. On a hairpin turn near the top, the organisers had positioned a cameraman, which meant one of two things: either it was a particularly hazardous section, where competitors were most likely to come unstuck, or it was a location with a particularly beautiful backdrop. In this case, it appeared to be for the latter reason. The view from the tabletop of the mountain was absolutely stunning. But we couldn't afford the time to take in the scenery. The track ahead was a mess. Other bikes were heading left and right but Matt insisted on following the heading on his compass. For a while we rode by faith, not knowing if we were on the right track. Then we spotted a fast-moving dust cloud ahead to our right. Knowing what the dust cloud meant, Matt and I pulled up beside each other – Simon had dropped back for some reason – and looked carefully all around us. The cloud meant one thing: cars – the reason Matt had been riding like a bat out of hell.

Matt took off again, really flying this time in a forlorn attempt to keep ahead of the cars. With Simon's warning ringing in my ears – the faster you ride, the bigger the moments – I tried slowing down in a bid to force Matt to cut his speed. He was bouncing all over the place, nailing it so much that I thought a moment was inevitable. We should have been riding at about 80 per cent of our abilities, but this was 95 per cent riding and I was struggling to keep up as he passed a string of riders. Navigating brilliantly, Matt was very impressive but there was little margin for error.

Following in Matt's wake was a relatively comfortable way to complete the stage, but the way Matt was riding I couldn't afford to relax. I still needed to know our exact position and precise route ahead. If I had to stop for any reason Matt was unlikely to notice. He checked behind him only every five or ten minutes. By the time he would realise I'd stopped, he'd be miles away and, without a road-book, I'd be completely lost.

We arrived at the first refuelling point. One of the officials took our time-cards while we topped up the petrol in our tanks which, having ridden 236 kilometres into the special, was getting very low. After the mandatory fifteen-minute rest another official returned our cards. With still no sign of Simon, we were just about to start the next part of the special when the first car came screeching through the checkpoint, flat out and clearly taking no prisoners.

It was an amazing sight and noise, a high-pitched whine like a jet engine. Travelling far in excess of 140kph, the car's suspension was absorbing the kind of bumps that would have thrown bikers clean off their seats. With five-foot springs and industrial-strength shock absorbers, the wheels were vibrating so much they blurred.

'Fucking hell!' Matt screamed. 'We can't wait for Simon. We've got to go.'

'. . . Oh my God,' I said, '. . . oh my God.'

We rode on, placing all our hopes in the Sentinel warning system. It relied on the car drivers being bothered to use it – and quite a few drivers simply couldn't be arsed – but, even if every driver used the Sentinel to warn us they were approaching, it was still a hair-raising experience when they passed by.

In some ways, the Sentinel made the cars' behaviour even worse. It gave them licence to give riders a last-minute alert that they were nearby and then to blast past without giving them much room to get out of the way. Many car drivers used the Sentinel simply as an excuse to barge through motorcyclists. We didn't want to hold them up. We weren't interested in racing, we just wanted to be given a chance to get out of the way safely. But it was like expecting a Formula One racing car to make its way gently through traffic in a small-town high street. The factory rally cars made it clear that they would quite happily drive over the top of us if we didn't vaporise from their view the instant they warned us with the Sentinel.

What made the behaviour of some of the cars even more unreasonable was the fact that every now and then a car team would pass through the motorcycle field without endangering any of the riders. If they could do it, why couldn't everyone else? It would take a car killing a motorcyclist before the car drivers or the organisers would do anything about it.

Another sixty kilometres on, we stopped at CP3, the third checkpoint of the special section. While Matt and I were drinking water and trying to get some food down, Simon turned up and we decided to ride as a threesome again. Before we set off, I took Simon aside.

'Matt's really riding too fast and is all over the place,' I said. 'He's had some right old moments.'

'Right, guys,' Simon said. 'Been a nice easy stage so far. We've got rid of a lot of miles, so let's take it calm here.'

Matt brought the pace down a notch or two. Nevertheless, there were still times when he'd do 80mph if the terrain allowed it.

The organisers liked to mix up each special section as much as possible. At times we'd be down to a few miles an hour, chugging up a slippery, windy, boulder-strewn track to a mountain top. But they'd also make sure there were enough fast gravel tracks on each stage to allow us to get the kilometres under our belts. After all, we had nearly seven and a half thousand kilometres ahead of us and only twelve more days in which to complete it.

'Doing really well!' Simon shouted when we stopped briefly. 'Riding's spot on. No problems.'

It felt good to get Simon's praise, but I also didn't need him to tell me I was managing very well. I'd not encountered anything yet that was technically more difficult than hacking around the Welsh hills. There were moments that were sublime and moments which were just awful – mainly when the cars came through. It was just the extreme distances that were a fright.

In spite of his best intentions and Simon's instructions, it didn't take long for Matt to push the pace again. About half a kilometre after he moved away from us, we saw him slip, then tumble. His bike banged along the road. By the time we caught up with him, petrol was flowing everywhere. I wanted to tell him I thought he was a fucking prick and that I'd warned him to slow down, but I knew the priority was to fix his bike.

I parked my bike. Matt was all right, but there was a massive hole in his left petrol tank. Fortunately there were less than twenty kilometres to the end of the special section and we'd be able to find a petrol station on the liaison.

'That's a good hole, Matt,' Simon said, inspecting the side of Matt's bike. 'I've never seen someone punch a hole in a petrol tank like that.'

Matt's bike was a mess. The front fairing had fallen off, the tank was broken, the handlebar guards were poking up at an odd angle and it was only our first morning in Africa. The one thing I learned from Long Way Round was to look after your bike.

While Simon and I got down on our knees to repair Matt's petrol tank Matt stood aside, filming us. Fortunately we had another tank among the spare parts being carried in the Bowler truck and would be able to replace Matt's punctured tank that evening. In the meantime, crouched between the boulders to the side of a dusty track under a cloudless blue sky, we stuck tape over the holes.

'Just take it easy for the last twenty ks,' said Simon. 'We don't want any more damage. At least Gareth'll be pleased. Give him something to do this evening.'

Suddenly the silence of the desert was interrupted by a voice with a French accent.

'Mr Boorman?'

I looked around.

'Mr Boorman?' It was a Frenchwoman's voice, but there was no one in sight. Then I realised the voice was coming from my bike.

'Hello?' I said, walking towards my bike. 'Hello?'

'Mr Boorman?' The voice was coming from my GPS and Iritraq unit. 'You've been stopped for a while. Are you OK?'

'Er, yes?

'Are you sure?'

'Everything's fine,' I said. ''We stopped to fix something. It's fine.'

It was the Paris headquarters of ASO. Their monitoring systems must have noticed that we had been stationary for some time and alerted the staff. I gave the woman our numbers – 172, 173 and 174 – and assured her we'd be moving soon.

Damaging his petrol tank seemed to slow Matt down. The track was clear enough for me to take the lead for the last part of our ride to the end of the special, where one of the officials came over to me.

'Well done,' he said. 'Bravo. Fantastic.' He handed me some tissue. 'Nice and clean on the goggles. See you tomorrow. Well done!'

I looked round. He was congratulating every rider that finished the special. A lovely touch from a lovely man, it crowned my first proper day of the rally.

Simon was happy. We'd worked well as a team, although I was slightly disappointed in Matt. He was meant to be our cameraman, but he seemed unable to resist the urge to race off ahead, so the only time he'd filmed us as a team was when we caught up with him to repair his petrol tank. I thought we should stick to our plan of riding at 80 per cent of our capability. With twelve days left, it was important we nursed our bikes whenever possible.

The liaison was just as busy as the special section. A continuous queue of bikes rode in a long stream of dust along a road made only partially of tarmac and winding over a mountain pass. Matt fell again so I stopped to help him, dropping my own bike in the process but quietly proud that I'd not had as many offs as Matt and that I was riding well within my abilities.

We refuelled at a petrol station before reaching the bivouac, then Matt rode straight past the entrance. By the time I'd overtaken Matt and persuaded him to turn around, Simon had disappeared. Passing through the entrance gates, I found the stick of kryptonite waiting for me; we were stopped by officials who exchanged that day's time-cards for the next day's road-book. With the road-book in my breast pocket, weighing me down by much more than its actual weight, I rode through the darkness of the bivouac, looking for our mechanics' pits.

Russ and the rest of the crew had parked the X5 and pitched their tents with the lads from the Bowler trucks, who had set up a pit about the size of a tennis court, boxed in by their 4x4 and 6x6 trucks. Gareth and Wolfgang were waiting, spanners and wrenches in hand, and immediately got to work on our bikes, dropping the bars on my bike a little and fitting a new road-book holder, as well as performing a simple service on each bike, changing the oil and air filters, checking all the cables and tightening all the screws and bolts. After his many falls, Matt's bike needed more work than the other two but was soon repaired. Gareth had built a bike that was well up to all the knocks.

Simon, Matt and I shuffled over to the mess tent in the central area of the bivouac for supper. Like most of the competitors, I was managing to eat properly only once each day. Nerves and the pre-dawn starts made it difficult to swallow a decent breakfast. Lunch was usually a pack of unpalatable and indigestible survival rations handed to us by the start officials, which I rarely ate. Dinner was the only chance to restock calories and nutrients, but I was too nervous to eat as much as my body needed.

After dinner, we ambled over to a notice board at the centre of the mess area that showed our start times for the next day, the PIN code for our GPS navigators and four sheets of changes to the road-book. My heart sank yet again at the sight of our homework, but at least we were home for the night. Two other British riders who were sharing our pits were still out on the stage.

Patsy Quick and Clive Towne were making their fourth and third attempts respectively at the Dakar. Patsy was a bubbly blonde with an infectious laugh and cheeky manner, while Clive was almost her opposite – unassuming with a shy seen-it-all-before grin. Both of them had Simon Pavey to blame for putting them through years of Saharan misery. Patsy was the first British woman to complete a Tunisian rally called the Optic Rallye Tunisie and was on her way to winning the European Women's Enduro Championship and the British Women's Motocross Championship when she met Simon. Over dinner and many bottles of red wine at Patsy's kitchen table, Simon spun his usual Dakar tales. Entranced by Simon's stories of hardship, triumph, disappointment and success in the desert, by the end of the evening Patsy was determined to enter the Dakar. With her husband Clive Dredge as her mechanic and team manager, Patsy entered her first Dakar in 2003. On day twelve she came off her bike at the top of a nine-hundred-foot dune and cartwheeled to the bottom, rupturing her spleen. By chance, a medical helicopter saw the crash, landed and flew her to an Egyptian military hospital for an emergency operation.

The next year Patsy was back, this time with Clive Towne, a friend from her home town of Heathfield in East Sussex, as support rider. On stage seven they got bogged down in the dunes, then separated after darkness. Fortunately they found each other shortly before the end of the stage, but they reached the bivouac with only half an hour to spare before the next stage started. Barely fortified with a handful of peanuts and with no time to service their bikes, Patsy and Clive started the next stage on bikes that were damaged and under-powered. They spent another night battling through the dunes, but this time arrived at the bivouac too late to start the next stage. Patsy and Clive were disqualified, but determined to return in 2005. That year, they spent three days stranded in the desert after Patsy had a crash that Clive described as the biggest he'd ever seen.

Convinced that a lighter bike was the key to surviving the dunes, this year Patsy and Clive had exchanged horsepower for agility. They were riding 525cc KTMs – lighter than the monster quarter-ton KTM 660 bikes they'd previously used. With much more Dakar experience than Matt or me, Patsy and Clive were still stuck in the desert while we were clambering into a tent. I dropped off to sleep almost immediately, the drone of the generators and screech of power tools unable to stop me.

The next morning we discovered what had happened to Patsy and Clive. Congregating at the start of the special section, a fifty-six-kilometre ride from Er Rachidia into the desert, we caught up with them.

'What's been going on with Mr Towne's life?' Simon asked as we snacked on our rations, waiting for the signal to start. 'Third day of the rally and disaster strikes already.'

'Puncture,' said Clive. 'Two hundred ks from the finish.'

The tyres on all our bikes were filled with mousse instead of compressed air. It made them less likely to puncture, but if the mousse detached from the wheel rim it would shred and the tyre would collapse.

'You rode 200ks on the rim?'

'200ks on the rim.' Clive shrugged. He was one of the most laid-back people I'd met on the rally. With a quiet optimism and hangdog expression, nothing seemed to faze him. He just got on with it.

'Fair play to you,' said Simon. 'You're a fucking legend.'

Patsy explained they'd used every zip-tie and strap they had to keep the tyre on the rim for the haul to the bivouac.

'Got in this morning at quarter past four,' Patsy said. 'Late dinner, early breakfast. And here we are!'

'Excellent!' said Simon. 'We'll see you in Dakar this year, for sure. What do you reckon, Pats?'

We were not without our own troubles. That morning, shortly before leaving the bivouac, I'd attempted to feed the road-book into its holder upside down. Realising my mistake, I extracted it from its spool, which screeched and whined as I attempted to turn it backwards. On my second attempt, the spool jammed and chewed up the road-book. On the third attempt, by this time drenched with sweat inside my jacket and trousers, I got the damned stick of kryptonite fully into its holder for the first time on the rally.

Shortly after 6.30 a.m., Simon, Matt and I rode off from the start, but within a few kilometres my little kryptonite friend was up to its usual tricks. It wasn't in my pocket, so its hold on me was not as strong. But even secured in its holder, I could still feel its deadly rays boring into me. Pressing the button beside my clutch that wound the road-book on to its next page, I yelped as the road-book ripped in half. Gripped by total panic, I immediately stopped.

'Fucking hell!' I shouted to Matt. 'God! No!'

'Hey. Come on, Charley. Calm down.'

While Matt looked on, I taped the two parts of the road-book together and then we rode off. I'd beaten the curse of the kryptonite.

The road-book worked fine for a while, but a couple of kilometres later I watched with horror as the paper stretched, then snapped again. Frantic with worry that I was losing time and would soon be overtaken by the first of the cars, I called out to Simon.

'No worries, mate,' he said. 'Matt, go ahead. Charley, go in the middle. I'll stay at the back and make sure nothing happens to you.'

Matt tore off ahead as usual, but Simon stuck to my tail like glue. Trying to keep up with Matt, I had to ride at 90 per cent of my capability, clearly too fast. Matt was bouncing through the field, overtaking people, cutting them up and riding as if it was a twelve-hour enduro, not a sixteen-day rally. I needed him to keep a steady pace as I didn't have a road-book. Fortunately the route was obvious, but it still left me worrying about what I'd do if Matt rode too far ahead and I got lost.

About ten kilometres into the special, I fell off my bike. It was nothing serious. I just couldn't get into a rhythm. A few kilometres further, I fell off again on a patch of sand over a riverbed. Feeling I wasn't riding properly, I shouted at myself. It was a stupid fall and I needed to shake myself together. With such a heavy bike, I didn't want to drop it too many times. Picking it up rapidly sapped my energy. It took three movements, especially if the tanks were full. First, I lifted it on my knees. Then I got underneath it and lifted until the handlebars were level with my waist. Finally I dropped slightly, bending my knees so that I slipped beneath the handlebars and could push it upright with a straight back.

After that fall, I regained my rhythm. I was riding well, but there was no sign of Matt. He had raced ahead, oblivious to my falls.

Simon and I arrived at the first dunes about twenty kilometres into the special. Memories of breaking my collarbone in Dubai flooded back but, unfortunately, not accompanied by any recall of how to tackle the dunes. Other riders went skipping ahead, leaving me to pick my way through dozens of ruts while one bike after another overtook me.

Less than a mile into the dunes, I slipped over. Simon was immediately at my side, pulling me up and offering encouragement, but my nerves had got the better of me.

'I can't do this,' I said. 'I'm all over the place. How am I meant to find my way through this mess of tracks?'

'No worries, Charley. These are easy dunes. Not even proper ones. You can do it.'

'I can't. I'm really struggling. I can't get it and I'm going to sap my energy.'

'Just follow me.'

Simon led the way, showing me how to cross the ruts at an angle and use the sides of dunes as banked corners. It made all the difference. Knowing that Simon was riding well below his ability just because he wanted to help me gave me an enormous respect and affection for him. Simon was a master at finding nice little patches of virgin sand where our tyres could still get a grip and plane across the surface. It was beautiful and we were soon having a laugh, riding close to the crowds and showing off.

Every so often, Simon would ask me if I wanted to take the lead, but I was happy to stick behind him. At one point we spotted some cars screaming along parallel to us, a helicopter hovering just above them but, strangely, only a short plume of dust stretching behind them.

Heading over towards the cars, Simon found a hard-packed track that led around the dunes, which explained why the cars weren't kicking up much dust. We were making good time, but there was still no sign of Matt so we rode on into the next area of dunes, which were larger and flecked with clumps of camel grass, some as hard as boulders. The camel grass was a new challenge: one wrong move and it could flick a rider off their bike.

I followed Simon into the higher dunes and through the camel grass, enjoying the ride because Simon's lead was making it much easier than if I had been on my own. Unlike in Dubai, when I crashed because I'd followed David over the top of a dune, I followed Simon at my own speed and parallel to his track. Even if Simon took the top of the dune with ease, I'd shut off my throttle as I crested, have a look around and choose my own line. Occasionally I'd depart from Simon's route to find a different path down the dune so I could better maintain momentum to get up the next one.

Simon and I stopped at the first checkpoint, expecting to find Matt waiting for us. We were just about to ride off when the familiar stubby silhouette of Matt appeared. It turned out Simon's detour on to the track near the dunes had put us in front of Matt.

We rode off in high spirits, glad to be reunited. About four kilometres after the checkpoint, a huge Kamaz truck and a Gauloises car blasted past with the usual scant consideration for bikers. Another kilometre or so further on, we got the last laugh when, on turning a corner, we found the truck and car stuck in the soft sand that the locals called fesh fesh. Unfortunately, the truck had run over a motorbike in the process. The bike was on the ground and its rider was removing his helmet as we quickly veered to the left to avoid crashing into them. Leading us down into a dip, Matt hit a large clump of camel grass, swerved and lost control as his front wheel hit some fesh fesh. Matt came to a stop on his back, pinned down by his bike.

I jumped off but couldn't find ground hard enough to support the stand of my bike.

'Help me! Give me a fucking hand!' shouted Matt as I tried to get to him. Simon, meanwhile, had parked, but wasn't running to Matt's aid.

'I'm filming!' Simon yelled, holding a camcorder. At least he was obeying Russ's dictum that one of us should always get a camera out at the slightest sign of trouble.

Matt's screams for help were almost drowned out by the chaos of the Gauloises car and Kamaz truck chucking up immense clouds of dust in their efforts to liberate themselves from the fesh fesh, which was as fine as talcum powder. The truck was sinking deeper, its wheels spinning helplessly. Having gained some grip, the car had surged off with the motorcyclist in pursuit, looking as if he wanted to inflict some violence as retribution for being run over.

Meanwhile, Simon and I were in fits of laughter at the sight of Matt stuck under his bike while mayhem raged nearby. Eventually, Matt got up of his own accord. 'Let's get the fuck out of here!' he yelled. 'If another car comes through, it could be our turn to get run over!'

Matt was taking no prisoners. Freaked out by the proximity of the cars and trucks, he wasted no time in getting back on his bike and roaring off, leaving Simon and me standing in his dust cloud.

'Whoa! Slow down, Charley,' shouted Simon as I rushed to jump on to my bike and follow Matt. 'Your bumbag is hanging off. The zip's broken.'

I looked behind me. The bag containing all my documents and cash was dangling from the back of my motocross jacket. Another few kilometres and I would have lost it for ever.

Punching some holes in my jacket with a penknife and using a cable tie, I secured my bumbag. But by the time I'd finished Matt was miles ahead. Simon and I rode off, but I immediately became stuck in another fesh fesh patch, my engine whining with a high pitch as I tried to power through the sand. Petrified that it would sink up to its axles, I jumped off my bike and ran beside it, gunning the engine and pushing as hard as I could. Bit by bit I made it across the fesh fesh to where Simon was waiting for me, then tucked in behind him to race after Matt.

A few kilometres further on, we hit the largest dunes yet, most of them liberally peppered with camel grass. Weaving our way carefully through large clumps, we were surrounded by carnage. Almost every dune we crested revealed yet another vehicle stuck in the soft sand or overturned by camel grass, but with Simon leading the way we made good progress, riding steadily and safely. Towards the end of the special Matt pulled up beside Simon and me.

'My seat's come loose,' he shouted.

'Where?' said Simon.

'Halfway through the dunes.'

'No! Which bit of the seat has come loose?'

'Oh . . . the bracket's snapped. The seat went sideways. Made life a bit interesting but I got through.'

Matt had been riding with his legs squeezed together to hold the seat in place, so we all got off our bikes to fix it just as another batch of cars came steaming through.

'That's a shame,' said Simon, indicating the cars. 'We passed loads of those guys in the dunes. Now they're all in front of us again.'

Simon fastened a zip-tie around the seat, then wrapped a BMW luggage strap around the petrol tank. While Simon and I were working on Matt's bike, three locals in long flowing robes turned up and took an interest in our tools and the kit spread out around Matt's bike. We chatted to them briefly but couldn't afford the time to engage in conversation. The sun was low in the sky and we wanted to make as much progress as we could before dark.

'So how did those dunes rate?' Matt asked Simon.

'Easy. Small fry.'

'If they're the easy dunes . . .'

'Oh yeah. You better believe it. Those dunes were *tiny*.'

'But they were quite cut up,' I said.

'Not that bad. They were *easy*.'

That made me feel great. I thought I'd been doing so well, but now Simon was saying the dunes were molehills compared to what we could expect when the rally reached Mauritania.

We all buggered off as soon as we'd repaired Matt's seat. Simon sat behind me as we rode at a good pace, overtaking a lot of other riders and feeling strong. At the end of the special the same official that we'd met the previous day was congratulating each rider that passed through.

'Hero! Bravo!' he shouted to each one of us before wiping our goggles clean and patting us on our bikes. 'Only 197 kilometres to home!'

Four hours later we were in Ouarzazate, a small town built around an oasis and with nothing to offer visitors – not that any competitor would spend any time sight-seeing or looking around the towns where the rally stopped. Instead, exhausted and in need of food and water for ourselves, and mechanical assistance for our vehicles, we'd spend all our time when we were not racing at the bivuouac, where our assistance team of Russ, Jim, Wolfgang and Gareth was now waiting. The X5 had survived its second day in Africa with no major crisis. Nick Plumb had also made it back to the bivouac and was sharing our pit.

I was more hungry than I could remember having been for a very long time. We stumbled over to the central area of the bivouac, where Bedouin tents had been erected in a U-shape around a central courtyard in which a band was playing Moroccan music. Caterers had set up two counters at the top end of the tent, from which they served a never-ending succession of four-course meals. Anyone could help themselves to wine and beer from fridges, or coffee and tea from urns. Being a French event, the food was excellent. And with a full stomach everything seemed clearer. The Dakar wasn't the nightmare I'd thought it was two days earlier. I felt incredibly fortunate to be in the rare position of fulfilling my longest-held dream.

As I sat in the bivouac, finishing my dinner, listening to the music and chatting with Simon, Matt and the rest of the team, I realised I was up to the challenge ahead. I'd survived four days with honour.

I'd wrestled the road-book and the kryptonite had failed to weaken me. The Dakar had become everything I'd hoped it would be and at last I felt I was part of it, not some bit-part actor along for the ride, but a player on the main stage, united with every other rider and driver by my desire to ride on to the beach at Dakar.

Chapter 9

4 JANUARY
Ouarzazate to Tan Tan

OUARZAZATE to TAN TAN

Stage 5
Ouarzazate to Tan Tan
819 kms
4th Jan.

MOROCCO

Ouarzazate

Atlantic Ocean

Oued Sous

Atlas Mountains

Oued Drâa

ALGERIA

Tan Tan

N
W   E
S

0   80   160 kms

WESTERN SAHARA

Our third day in Africa started well. I'd relaxed about the road-book amendments at last, marking fewer obstacles and realising that many of the directions were superfluous and could be ignored. I'd evaded the grip of Lex Luther and his kryptonite, somehow managing to get my road-book into its holder without it ripping. And, feeling more confident and less exhausted, if still a bit stressed, I was able to swallow a decent breakfast. The car still had a few niggles and the assistance crew were flapping around, Russ insisting on taking photos when all I wanted to do was concentrate on preparing for the day ahead, getting to the start and escaping into that blissful state when, with my helmet pulled down over my head, the outside world would be securely shut out.

Ahead of us was our longest stage so far. If I survived it, by that evening I'd have ridden 3,067 kilometres, just over a third of the total distance. But I didn't want to tempt fate by thinking too far ahead. First we had to reach Tan Tan, 819 kilometres away. Departing shortly after 5 a.m., we had to ride 187 kilometres of tarmac in darkness to reach the start of the special section by 8.15 a.m., just after sunrise. We then faced 350 kilometres of special section across a variety of challenging terrain, including wadis (ravines that became water courses in the rainy season), chotts (lakes and marshes, which could be wet or dry), dunes, and stretches of dusty, open plains – probably the most dangerous terrain of all because of the temptation to ride them as fast as the bike would carry us. Finally, we had to ride 282 kilometres of liaison from the end of the special to the bivouac.

After two brutal days in Africa, everyone was quiet at the start of the special. My shoulder was painful and I'd taped up my hands, which were covered in blisters and sores. To combat the pre-dawn cold, Simon, Matt and I had ridden the liaison section wearing black binbags over our jackets. The bags were Nick

135

Plumb's idea and proved remarkably effective at reducing wind chill. Having refuelled at first light, we were ready and waiting to start when Simon sounded the warning.

'Gonna be a bit of a bitch today,' he said. 'Wind's kicking up a lot of dust.'

Leading our team of three, I soon discovered how right Simon's prophecy was proving to be. For most of the day we rode directly into a south-westerly wind. With a slight crosswind, the dust would have dispersed. Instead it hung in the air like fog, obscuring a particularly rocky track.

We'd been riding for about an hour when one of the organiser's helicopters pulled alongside me. Helicopters were a mixed blessing for motorcyclists. The sight of one was a welcome indication we were on the correct route, but very often the distraction of the chopper flying nearby triggered an accident. As soon as the helicopter, which had a camera fixed to its underside, dropped down low Matt came steaming past me. You show-off, I thought as I saw him race ahead, his elbows pointed out at right angles to his handlebars. You fucking showman!

But I had the last laugh as the helicopter stayed with me for about five minutes, ignoring Matt, who had raced out of shot. The disadvantage of the helicopter's attention was that it was whipping up clouds of dust that made riding even more hazardous than usual. Thanks very much, I thought as I started to climb a gravelly mountain track strewn with boulders the size of beach-balls. With the piste soon deteriorating into a mass of rocks, I slowed to little more than walking pace, gingerly picking my way up the steep slope while the camera followed me intently, making me feel conspicuously stupid as the bike twisted and bucked beneath me and I slipped on my pegs.

I spotted Matt in the distance, riding with ease while I struggled. At first it was dispiriting to see Matt steam up a mountain track that I found difficult. The usual doubts and insecurities entered my head. Sucking on the mouthpiece of the water bladder strapped to my back, I was sweaty, thirsty and fed up. I wished I'd never embarked on the rally and desperately wanted to go home. Every so often on that ten-mile climb I'd hit a rock, bounce off to one side then veer in the opposite direction as I yanked the bike to regain balance, while my legs flew all over the place. I wasn't enjoying it at all, but then the sight of Matt climbing the mountain pass with ease started to focus my mind. I knew I could ride a slope just as well as him. The secret was to get into a rhythm and to look far enough ahead to see obstacles coming, but not so far that the scale of the task became daunting.

Bit by bit it came together until I was riding as smoothly and as fast as Matt. I was enjoying it so much that somewhere along that long grind up the mountainside I'd not noticed that Matt had stopped. Once I'd crested the mountain it got even better – a joyous journey through stunning scenery as I bumped my way down into a valley where the track split in two directions. Unsure which fork to follow, I stopped. A few minutes later Matt rolled up.

'It's that way.' Pointing left, Matt barely stopped to see if I would follow him. 'Definitely.'

Tucked in behind Matt, I had my doubts but was happy to let him navigate. After a while, Matt stopped.

'I think we've taken the wrong track,' he said. 'We've missed the waypoint.'

Not wanting to incur a time penalty, we doubled back. Eventually we found the checkpoint, where a couple of ASO officials were sitting in a 4x4 beside a little tent. One of them took our time-cards and stamped them.

'Have you seen number 174 – Simon Pavey?' I asked one of the officials. He looked down his checklist.

'Yeah, he's been through. About fifteen minutes ago.'

It didn't make sense. Surely Simon was behind us? Or maybe he had passed us when we took the left track at the bottom of the mountain pass? That might be it, I thought, but then he would have waited for us. Or maybe he was pissed off because we didn't wait for him at the bottom of the hill? I didn't know what to think.

'If he comes through after us, please let him know we were asking after him,' I said.

'That won't happen. He's gone that way,' the official insisted, pointing into the distance.

I felt slightly uneasy – what if Simon had a technical fault? Or, heaven forbid, he'd had an accident? We had no choice but to trust the officials.

I spotted another British rider waiting at the checkpoint. 'Have you seen Simon?' I asked him

'Yeah, he passed me some time ago. He's a long way in front.' I told Matt.

'That's weird,' he said. 'Why has he gone on? Have we pissed him off by taking the wrong fork?'

But we both knew Simon wouldn't be bothered about our navigational mistakes. After all, we were novices at this game.

We had no choice but to keep going. After the checkpoint, Matt and I tried to track towards the route we'd taken after coming down the mountain. The dust was horrendous so I dropped back to get some clean air. In the process, Matt and I were separated. I didn't mind. For the first time in five days my road-book was working and the track ahead was obvious. After a while I bumped into Nick Plumb. We rode together along a dry wadi and through a valley until Plummy slowed down and started circling a patch of dry grass.

'Don't know where next, Charley,' he yelled.

I also didn't have a clue, then I spotted a plume of dust in the distance. 'What about that over there? I reckon it's a bike.'

He needed no encouragement. 'Come on boy!' he shouted and he set off immediately with me following close behind. I was delighted to be riding with Plummy, who was one of the few riders who would always stop to help any other competitor and who would shout encouragement to me. 'Yer doin' great, Charley,' he'd yell. Or: 'Top stuff, Charley.' Hearing his praise made me relax more and ride better. Plummy wasn't one for giving away compliments.

We passed through several sections of fesh fesh, which never ceased to frighten me. However, I'd learned, from riding behind Simon the previous day, to find my own path of unbroken sand to support my bike and crossed the fesh fesh with relative ease.

I was making good progress, but many other riders were having a much tougher time. Every ten kilometres or so we'd see a medical helicopter on the ground near a competitor being enveloped in bubblewrap for the flight back to the operating theatre at the bivouac.

We'd experienced challenging terrain over the previous two days. The dunes had been hard, but this stage had its own particular difficulties. As the road-book warned in its idiosyncratic translation, our riding would 'have to be fine-tuned to a maximum on account [of] alternate fast stretches and navigational traps.' Those navigational traps ranged from hidden wadis to a sudden, unexpected large boulder on an open plain, which could easily spell the end for a motorcyclist travelling at high speed.

I'd seen competitors dropping out with injuries or technical faults over the previous four stages, but nothing like as many as on this day. Quite clearly, the organisers had decided that this should be the day when things started to get tough.

I lost touch with Plummy and rode on my own for several hours. Maintaining momentum at the same time as navigating was difficult, but I was happy plodding along at my own pace. I hooked up with another rider for a while, working with him as the cars and trucks sped past us. More confident than me, he saved my skin a couple of times, waving me off the track when he saw a speeding vehicle approaching and urging me to slow down and let the dust settle when the visibility declined. We looked after each other but after a while it became clear that, although he was going quite fast, I was faster and needed to press on.

Hacking through a large section of camel grass, I came across Matt in some fesh fesh. I had almost passed him before I spotted the luminous green band on his helmet and mudguard. Matt was just pulling clear of the powdery sand and immediately caught up with me.

By this stage the rally cars were steaming through at an alarming rate, pushing us off the gravelly track into the rocky plains on either side of the piste. The rocks were so large and so widespread that we had to stop every time a car passed, otherwise we might have hit a large boulder in the car's dust cloud. Stopping and starting was very frustrating, breaking the rhythm of the ride in a particularly hard stretch of terrain through wadis, across dams and over shale and shingle.

Matt had already had a tumble after a fast car forced him off the track and he hit a rock. A little later, pulling out of a wadi into a relatively open plain, my Sentinel screeched into action. As usual, I almost shat myself as I swung my bike to the left. Peering over my shoulder into my dust cloud, I was immediately confronted by the sight of a Gauloises car coming straight for me. The driver must have hit his Sentinel when he was only a few metres behind my rear wheel. I'd heard people say they could see the whites of someone's eyes and always thought it was an exaggeration. Right then I discovered it wasn't. I could see the driver looking straight at me. I yanked my bike further to the left as he forced his steering wheel to the right, missing my back tyre by inches.

In any other circumstances, escaping death or injury so closely would have finished me off for the day. But the Dakar rally didn't allow for rest and recovery. I had to keep going.

To make matters worse, I was becoming very tired. I'd been riding since just after 5 a.m. and with neither food nor rest since before dawn – and accumulated sleep deprivation since Lisbon now starting to bite – I was worried that I would fall asleep on the bike. Even if I didn't drop off, any slip in reaction time when the cars were coming through could prove fatal. However, I also knew from previous stages that the first 250 kilometres were likely to be the toughest. Surely, I thought, the piste would soon open up so that we could get some kilometres under our belts before sunset.

Another sixty or so kilometres further and we'd reached CP2, which offered refuelling for bikes as the cars screamed through, trailing enormous plumes of dust.

'Has 174 – Simon Pavey – been through?' I asked one of the officials.

'*Ah oui. Certainement,*' the official said.

With the computer in front of him, there was no reason to disbelieve the official, but it still seemed strange.

We noticed that the French competitors were treated differently. We'd all seen officials take a more lenient view of transgressions by French riders and we'd all heard an English rider tell a story one night in the bivouac of how he'd got hopelessly lost with a pack of privateer riders. One of the pack was French and had used his bike's communication system to call someone. No one else spoke French so they didn't know exactly what had been said. All they knew was that after the phone call, the French rider set off on a new compass heading that led them, within two and a half miles, to a checkpoint they would otherwise have missed.

Simon and other British riders had tales from previous years of turning up at checkpoints at the end of hot, gruelling dune sections only to be told there was no water left. Five minutes later, French riders turned up and somehow some water had been found.

So when the official told us Simon had passed through the checkpoint we weren't convinced that was right. We had to assume it was the truth.

'Maybe he's got the hump with us,' said Matt. 'But that's not like Simon.'

Plummy arrived. He also hadn't seen Simon. 'You guys are riding so fast,' said Plummy, 'maybe you've left Simon behind. I'm having trouble keeping the same pace. Maybe Simon's also having a bad day.'

There was some truth in what Plummy said. I was enjoying the terrain and maybe if it didn't suit Plummy it also didn't suit Simon.

While refuelling the bikes, we discussed our strategy. With only 120 kilometres of special and then 280 kilometres of liaison on tarmac, we had plenty of time to spare. Matt suggested we calm the pace and I agreed.

We set off from the checkpoint and I zipped along, feeling that I was riding well within my capabilities and really enjoying it.

With one eye on the road ahead, I was searching for a wadi that was highlighted in my road-book with a double exclamation mark, meaning it required considerable caution. The road-book warned me not to take the direct route into the wadi. Instead, it said, I needed to go around a hump and then descend into the river-bed. Spotting the hump ahead, I was confused. A very clear track led straight past the hump – not around it – and down into the wadi. Nevertheless, believing it best to stick to the road-book, I was preparing to divert around the hump when a massive Kamaz truck thundered past me, following the track straight down into the wadi. Seeing the truck take the drop into the wadi so easily, I changed course.

Suddenly my front wheel slipped sideways, the bike dipped and I was on my side, my helmet filling with gravel as I slid along the ground.

What the fuck? What happened there? It had happened so quickly I didn't know why I had fallen.

Attempting to get up, I discovered my leg was stuck under the bike. Trying to push a quarter-ton of BMW plus recently refilled fuel tanks off my legs, searing pain shot through my hands. Aaaagh! I screamed. It was agony. The pain was too much for me to be able to push the bike off my legs.

Realising I was bang in the middle of the piste and hidden from view by the sudden drop into the wadi, I screamed to Matt, who had stopped nearby. If a car or truck came over the lip of the river-bank, it wouldn't see me until it was too late. Without a shadow of doubt I'd be killed.

'Fucking get me up!' I yelled. 'Get me up before a car comes!'

Fortunately Plummy had caught up with us.

'Stop there!' Matt shouted to Plummy.

Plummy leapt off his bike at the top of the ridge above the wadi and kept a look out while Matt dragged the bike off my legs and on to the side of the piste.

I could hardly stand up for the pain in my hands. All I wanted to do was lie down on the ground and throw up. My right hand had swollen up to fill my leather gloves like a couple of pounds of sausages. When I tried to move my fingers, I nearly passed out. I could feel the bones crunching inside my hand. Oh fuck, I thought.

'I'm gonna be sick!' I leant over. Although the vomit didn't come, I knew it was a sign that something was seriously wrong.

My left hand was no better. The thumb hurt even more than my right hand and was pointing out at an acute angle.

'Fuck, Matt, I've blown it. I've fucking blown it. The stage, the race, the TV series. It's all fucking over!'

'No!' Matt insisted. 'It's not. It's not over unless you say it is. Come on. Don't even think about that now.'

'It's not gonna look good. Is it? I've blown it. I have. Everything's a write-off. I've only done four days.'

Matt later told me that for a split second he too thought it was over, that we were about to make some tacit agreement to stop. He said he could see the despair in my eyes, but then he realised that there was only one course of action. I needed to get back on my bike and get to the end of the day.

'Come on, Charley,' he said. 'We've got to get going. We can't stay here. We're invisible to anyone coming along the piste. Get on your bike.'

He was right. Whatever I'd done to my hand, I wasn't going to make it any better by staying stock still in the middle of nowhere.

Back on my bike, I consoled myself that maybe I'd not broken anything as I was at least managing to grip the handlebars. Moving off cautiously, I immediately lost control, the front wheel again washing out in the sand. Maybe I couldn't grip them after all.

Matt was at my side immediately, helping to push up my bike. I crouched beside my bike for a few moments, trying to come to terms with the agony in my hands. Then I got back on my bike and started riding.

I could just grip the throttle with the thumb and forefinger of my right hand. By crooking the index and little fingers of my left hand I maintained a loose grip on the left side of the handlebar, but every time I squeezed the clutch I screamed and nearly passed out with pain. And with my left thumb out of action I couldn't move the road-book or hook the mouthpiece of my water bladder into my mouth.

Riding behind Plummy, I felt delirious with nausea. It told me something was seriously wrong, but I didn't want to stop to investigate in case it was no more than a bad sprain. Having come this far, I didn't want to give up on the race. I didn't want to be out of it. With my future hopes resting on success in the Dakar, I needed to continue.

The accident had happened only a few kilometres after the refuelling stop at CP2 so I had the best part of 120 kilometres to ride to the end of the special, then another 282 kilometres to the end of the stage.

Matt was a complete star. He stuck behind me, shouting whenever a car or truck approached, while I trundled on, not using the clutch or front brake, just the throttle and the back brake. The jarring and jolting of the bike sent shock waves up my arm. I felt every bump acutely and – just my luck – the final part of the special was mostly rocky tracks. It felt as if lightning bolts were shooting up my arms.

Matt later told me that he could tell by my body language that my injury was bad. The way I was slumped on my bike, unable to ride with conviction, indicated to Matt that I was seriously hurt and he started to worry that I wouldn't be able to cope with the terrain. There were sections in which I should have been standing up on my pegs, but I was able only to sit down. For more than one hundred kilometres I clung on, pressing my palms on to the handlebars in an attempt to maintain control while cushioning my fingers and thumb from the worst of the jolting. After a while, I could feel my palms and wrists beginning to swell, the tendons bruising from the hammering they were taking. It was hell.

Eventually we reached a wide, open sandy plain. I needed to crank up the speed if I didn't want to arrive at the bivouac after dark, but I could barely twist the throttle. It kept slipping through my hand and I couldn't move my hand fast enough to grab it and hoick it open. Meanwhile, cars were rocketing past us as we passed Clive and Patsy who, oblivious to my injuries, waved and shouted, 'Go! Go! Go!'

Amidst the terrible pain a vision of my sister Telsche popped into my head, smiling at me and urging me to keep moving forward. It felt like Telsche, who died of cancer in 1997, was calling out to me, saying, 'It's OK, I've been here and I'm looking after you. You'll be all right.'

With Telsche watching over me I made good progress, climbing a long mountain pass to a plateau and then descending to another plain. The long haul to the end of the special stage passed surprising quickly, although every second I was begging for it to be over. By the time we reached the end the pain in my right arm was so great I couldn't lift it. I had to use my left arm to hook my right hand around the throttle instead.

I rolled up to the finishing line of the special section relieved that the worst was behind me, but full of trepidation for the 282 kilometres of bumpy, potholed tarmac between us and the bivouac at Tan Tan. As usual, the friendly official was waiting to stamp our time-cards and wipe our goggles.

'Hero!'

'I don't know about that. I've done my hands in.'

The official looked at them and turned white. '*Merde!*'

I got off the bike, but couldn't remove my helmet. 'Aaarghh!' I yelped. The pain was getting worse. My right glove was stretched even tauter than before. I didn't dare remove it in case I couldn't get it back on.

Meanwhile, Matt was struggling with his road-book, which had jammed because the top spool was full. He ripped out a long section, borrowed some tape from an official and stuck the top of the remainder, which would direct us back to the bivouac, to the tattered remains of the route we'd just covered.

'Have you seen rider 174?' I asked one of the officials. 'Simon Pavey?'

'174? He's gone. Passed through a long time ago.'

We must have pissed Simon off something rotten, I thought. It was most unlike him not to wait for us.

I swallowed a couple of painkillers and we rode on to a petrol station a few kilometres beyond the start of the liaison. I wanted to ring Russ to warn him that I had injured my hand. It was 3 p.m.; by now Russ and Gareth ought to be at the bivouac. We had cellphone coverage but it wouldn't connect to Russ's satellite phone, so I tried Gareth's phone. It rang, but Gareth didn't answer.

'Have you tried Claudio?' said Matt. Claudio, our roving cameraman, was flying with the ASO officials from bivouac to bivouac.

'Claudio . . . good idea.'

'Mind you,' said Matt, 'he's not a lot of good to us is he?'

'He can talk to the organisers or pass on a message to Russ.'

A few moments later I heard Claudio's voicemail click into action. Typical – just when I really needed to talk to someone no one was answering. I tried Gareth again. He answered.

'How are you mate? Is Russ there?' Then I told Gareth the bad news. 'Listen . . . I've had a small off. Pretty stupid, I know, but I seem to have damaged my hands. It's fucking painful. I just thought I ought to let Russ know. It wasn't a big fall; just a small one. Just a stupid little thing. Coming around a corner, I lost the front end. So please just let them know.'

I called off and looked at my phone. A text message had arrived from Olly. 'I love you,' it said. 'Sorry I missed your call. Don't worry, you'll be fine.' If only she knew. 'Call any time, even at night if you can't sleep. Big kiss. Olly.' Fucking hell.

I read the message to Matt.

'Not want you want to hear, is it?' he said.

'Well, yes, but no,' I said. 'Shit! I've fucked up, man. What am I gonna do? *What* am I gonna do? Fuck's sake.'

I felt so angry with myself. If it had been a high-speed spill or a really tricky part of the course I would have felt better about it. But it was just a silly little fall, the type all of us had made dozens of times over the last few days. Only this time my luck had run out.

While Matt and I were deciding what to do next, Simon turned up with Plummy. He'd been behind us all along and I could see he was miffed we'd not waited for him.

I tried to explain. 'At the first checkpoint I asked if you were there and you weren't.'

'And the British guy said that you'd gone on,' Matt chipped in.

'I must look like someone else,' Simon muttered.

'I've had a small fall, Simon,' I said 'My hand is swollen and this thumb is . . . I can't hold on very well.'

'We'll go and see the medics when we get back, eh? Can we just have a coffee or something?'

I could see that Simon couldn't have been less interested in my injury. It wasn't that he didn't care about it or me, it was more a case of having space in his head for only one objective: getting to the end of the stage. Nothing else mattered.

At that moment I realised that was what it took to do the rally. You had to be so focused on reaching that beach in Dakar that absolutely nothing else got in the way. *Nothing*. Simon once told me that I needed to be prepared to crawl across broken glass on my hands and knees if I wanted to succeed. Now I understood what he meant. No pain was too great. No technical fault was too insurmountable. No obstacle was too high or too difficult. *If you wanted to get to Dakar.*

'You've been here a long time, have ya?' said Simon.

'No, about ten minutes.'

'Right. Have you fuelled up?'

'Yeah, we've fuelled up.'

'Will I fuel here then?'

'Yeah, no prob.' Looking down, I noticed something odd about Simon's front wheel. His brake calliper was missing 'Has it been like that all day?'

'Since kilometre thirty. That's when it happened.'

'The whole calliper came off?'

'Yup. I broke the carrier in half.'

Simon explained what had happened. Coming down the mountain shortly after we'd been tracked by the helicopter, a rock kicked up and flicked off his front wheel. He'd thought nothing of it; after all, we'd heard rocks pinging off the sump every few hundred metres.

'Then I came down into the next corner, pulled the front brake and went "oh shit!" as a bit of calliper flew off and went bouncing through the rocks.'

Simon had ridden all but thirty kilometres of the special without a front brake. I felt guilty we hadn't been there to help him.

'Tell you what,' said Matt. 'This is a fucking sport for madmen, isn't it?'

He was right. How else could you explain a couple of hundred people riding motorbikes so heavy you could barely lift them off-road at an average of seventy miles an hour between randomly dotted rocks the size of footballs while cars and trucks came flying past twice as fast, looking like they were on a testing ground for missiles and creating an instant whiteout of dust in areas where it was too dangerous to leave the track, so we'd hit a little bump and the back end would go flying in the air, twisting around while we kept the throttle full open. It was mad.

'Whether you finish this one or not,' Matt said as Simon rode off to refuel his bike, 'do you think you'd ever, ever do another rally again?'

'No. Definitely not. It's too dangerous.'

'It scares the shit out of me. And you're always up against time. Always thinking about getting back to the bivouac before night. And when you're back in the bivouac you're thinking about the next day.'

While Matt and I were agonising about the wisdom of doing the rally, Nick Plumb listened. Like Simon, he'd had a bad day. After I'd lost contact with him he'd followed the leading truck for several tens of kilometres, thinking it would be easier to let the truck do the navigating, but then he realised the truck was lost.

'I realised we were well off course, so I just had to hope the truck would find its way. They were going over fucking great rocks and there was a ditch in the rocks and nothing I could do. The truck bottomed and I came off. Snapped my front brake hose and damaged my mousse. So not a very successful day really.'

Nick had also cut his hand but, like Simon, he wasn't going to let anything get in the way of making it to Dakar.

'What d'ya reckon to that?' Nick pointed at his mousse. 'It's really soft.'

'Them front mousses don't come off,' said Simon. 'You'll be OK.'

'Really need to get to the end now,' said Nick.

'The end of the day or the end of the rally?' Matt said.

'End of the rally. Tick the box, do the job.'

'Then you're retiring?'

'Oh yeah. Get on with my life. Oh yes.'

With that, Nick set off for the bivouac. I tried to contact Russ again. This time he answered the phone.

'Are you together with Si and Matt?' he asked.

'Yeah.' I told him what had happened – getting separated from

Simon and Matt; Simon's damaged calliper; our close scrapes with the cars; the officials who repeatedly told us Simon was ahead of us; and, finally, my accident.

'OK. But you're OK in yourself?'

'Yeah, I'm all right. I just don't know about my hands.'

'Good.' Russ was calm as ever. 'As long as you're OK and it's only your hands. Matt and Simon are OK?'

'Yeah, they're both with me here.'

'OK. Well, take it easy, mate 'cos we're waiting here for you at the bivouac, so just ride it easy. OK?'

'OK.' Speaking to Russ made a big difference. Ever the reassuring presence.

'Have you spoken to Olly?'

'No I haven't,' I said. 'Don't, *don't* call her yet.'

I didn't need Olly worrying unnecessarily while I was still in southern Morocco, on my way back to the bivouac with two unbelievably painful hands.

A few minutes later Simon, Matt and I left the petrol station. The road to Tan Tan was fairly straight, but it was getting dark and the temperature was dropping. With my hands starting to freeze because I couldn't wiggle my fingers to keep them warm, I turned on my heated grips, but they soon became too hot to hold. If my hands hadn't been injured I would have held the heated grip between two fingers and moved my hands around to prevent cramp. But now I couldn't and it was agony.

The liaison took ages. With Simon's front brake broken we couldn't ride any faster than sixty kilometres an hour. At that rate, the ride to Tan Tan would take us nearly five hours. At one point we pulled over for a rest, but that just prolonged the torture for me. Later on we had to leave the tarmac, which was being repaired, and ride on a gravel track pitted with tiny holes that sent spasms of pain shooting up my arm.

About fifteen kilometres from the end of the stage our headlights picked out the shape of a rider bent over his bike by the side of the road. As we drew closer we realised it was Nick. We all stopped.

'What's happened, mate?' said Simon.

'What a nightmare. Everything's gone wrong today,' said Nick.

'What now?'

'I came off. Mousse exploded on the road. Spurted all over the place. I managed to swerve into the ditch, then went down the road a bit and into the sewer. Nearly took my hand off.'

'Did the mousse just go bang?' said Matt.

'Disintegrated. And the tyre came off.'

Fortunately a garage was nearby. With the assistance of about half a dozen policemen we helped Nick replace his mousse with an inner tube and force his front tyre back on to the wheel.

We set off on the last stretch of our slow trek to Tan Tan. By the end, I was crying with pain and desperate to stop. Inside my helmet I was shouting at Simon to get on with it, but he couldn't ride any faster. We found the bivouac, handed in our time-cards, and I rushed ahead of Simon in search of our pits. Russ, Gareth and Wolfgang were waiting as I rode straight in, stopped, peeled my right hand off its grip and screamed for someone to 'please grab my bike before I fall over'.

Fourteen hours after leaving Ouarzazate, I was home at last.

Chapter 10

5 JANUARY
Tan Tan to Zouérat

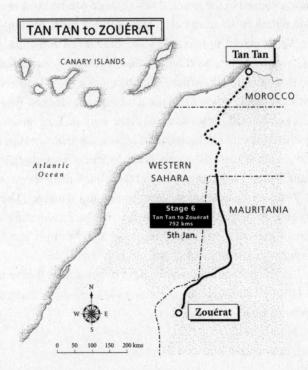

TAN TAN to ZOUÉRAT

CANARY ISLANDS

Tan Tan

MOROCCO

Atlantic
Ocean

WESTERN
SAHARA

MAURITANIA

Stage 6
Tan Tan to Zouérat
792 kms
5th Jan.

N
W E
S

Zouérat

0   50   100   150   200 kms

My hands felt as if they had frozen solid. Unable to wiggle my fingers or clench my fist, cramp had set in, turning my hands into claws.

'What do you think, mate?' said Russ as one of the pit crew held my bike so that I could swing my leg free of it.

'I don't know. I really don't.' Despite obvious signs that my hands were seriously damaged I was still hoping I could continue the rally. Part of it was pride – I didn't want to crash out on the fifth day. Another part of it was ambition – the nerves and anxiety of the first few days behind me, I'd relaxed, started to enjoy the riding and wanted to keep going. And part of it was a sense that I didn't want to let anyone down. For all those reasons I'd endured the agony of riding back to the bivouac when many riders would have chucked in the towel, thinking there was no need to continue when they could have been carted off in a medical chopper.

'I'm hoping I'm wrong,' I said, 'but I don't think this is good.'

'You'll be fine,' said Simon. 'Let's just get your jacket off.'

This was much easier said than done. My hands were so swollen that I couldn't pull them through the sleeves. We released all the zips and straps then, with the help of Russ and Simon, I feathered my hands through the sleeves. Someone cut through my gloves but it was still agony getting them off my fingers, which crunched as I tugged gingerly at their thick leather encasings.

With my hands bared, I could see the damage. They were covered in purple and black bruises, but more alarming was the size of the swelling on my right hand and the angle at which my thumb was sticking out of my left hand.

'Jeeez-sus!' said Russ. 'We have to get you to the medical.'

'OK . . . But what are we going to do if I can't carry on? It's going to be a fucking disaster!'

'No it's not.'

'Fucking hell it is.'

'Let's just see what the doctor says,' Russ insisted. 'And besides: we've had five great days. But let's see what the doctor says first of all before we decide how we go from here.'

Russ was fantastic. I'd seen him like this before when people got hurt on Long Way Round. Faced with a string of problems, he cared about nothing except the safety of whoever was hurt. He would shut out everything else and become like a parent, reassuring, protective and caring. It was just what I needed.

We arrived outside the heavy-duty white plastic airlock that kept the dust outside and the cool air inside the air-conditioned medical tent.

'Have a seat,' said a nurse as we walked in. 'You OK?

'I fell off. I've done something to my hands.'

'What's your number?'

'172.' I suspected it would be one of the last times I used it.

'Mr Boorman?' She was checking a list on a computer.

'Yep, that's me. Charley.'

'Don't worry about anything,' said Russ as we sat down, but my panic went into overdrive. I looked at my left hand, which I thought was OK but it had ballooned since I took my gloves off. It was now looking a lot worse. 'We can work anything out.'

'I'm just scared.'

'Of what?'

'Of fucking doing it. It's frightening out there.'

'Is it?'

'It's just a nightmare. You're going along and it's so dusty and the cars and the trucks are going past, you can't fucking see anything . . . the whole day in dust. Fucking hell.'

'You don't have to do it,' said Russ.

While I'd been on the bike my two broken hands had completely filled my mind. I couldn't think of anything other than the agony of it and how a stupid little fall could have such massive consequences. Now that I was in the medical tent the scale and the ramifications of those consequences were becoming clear.

A French doctor in a red T-shirt with 'Medical' printed in large white letters turned up with an interpreter. Pointing at my left thumb, the interpreter said it was 'definitely dislocated'. My right hand, he said, might be 'complicated'. He told me I'd have to wait a long time for treatment, as they were overwhelmed with injuries. When he left, I peeked through a tent flap into the next section of the medical facilities. There were bodies everywhere, many lying on stretchers. Some of them would have been among the injured I saw being packaged in bubblewrap and airlifted from the special section.

'I just want to go home.'

'No one's putting any pressure on you to continue,' said Russ.

'Everybody *is* though. Everyone's waiting for me to fail.'

'No they're not. No one is waiting for you to fail. Most people who attempt the Dakar don't succeed. We've always said this is your *attempt* on the Dakar.'

'I suppose you're right.'

'Don't put pressure on yourself,' said Russ. 'It's not worth it. We can solve most problems. You've gone a long way already. You've done a fantastic job and everyone's seen that.'

'It's just all the sponsors and all the people that have put effort into the bike and . . .'

'Whatever happens to you, Si and Matt can push on. If you have to take a role as team manager – and I'm talking about the worst-case scenario – then you can work with Si, Matt, Gareth and Wolfgang to make sure the bikes are fixed up, to advise them how to push on and to be at the bivouac to meet them. So don't worry about it.'

'I don't really want to go home.'

'You don't have to go home. We're going to get to the end. It's a hard race, mate, maybe the hardest in the world, but let's just wait and see what the doctors say. You might be on that bike tomorrow morning.'

While we were talking, a female radiologist wheeled in a portable X-ray machine and prepared to take some pictures. As she moved my arm about and manipulated my fingers I found it very hard to think of getting back on to my bike.

'Look at my arm,' I said. 'Look at that. That's my bone.'

'OK, it could be dislocated,' said Russ.

'It's all swollen underneath as well. Fucking hell.'

I started to sob, crying like I hadn't cried for ages. It was too much. A nurse came over, put her arm around me and told me I'd be all right. That made me cry even more. The nurse's sympathy made me want to curl up in my wife's arms and be engulfed in her love, away from the scene of my failure.

'I'll have to go back and face everybody,' I said after the nurse went away. 'And explain why I failed. I'll have to tell my kids I didn't finish. I'm sure my wife will be very relieved, but *God*, what a nightmare. So many people relying on me . . . the list is just endless . . . and everybody here just so that I could do what I wanted to do. And now I'm fucking . . . fucking . . .'

What made me so despondent was that I'd been riding well. I wasn't exhausted and I'd felt in control. It was just a silly little slip.

The radiologist returned. 'Any news?' I said.

'Yes. There's something.'

'Is it broken?'

'Yes.'

'Fuck,' I looked at Russ. 'Sorry.'

'Don't say sorry. There's nothing to be sorry about.'

I asked a nurse if I could go outside for a couple of minutes to where Matt and Simon were waiting. I told them the diagnosis: one dislocated thumb, four broken bones in my right hand.

'The doctor said I can't ride so I'm going to try to get on one of the ASO planes. I'll meet you at the end of every day. I'll look after you when you come in, help sort things out.'

'We're worried about you.' Simon, ever the optimist, had been convinced that I'd be able to continue. I was out of the rally but at least I had lived my dream to ride the Dakar. I felt privileged to be a part of this amazing event, and began to relax after the stress of the last few months. Although I was out, I still wanted to be part of the Dakar and to find out exactly why riders are drawn back year after year. People kept saying to me that I had unfinished business and that I'd need to come back next year, but I just couldn't comprehend it.

I could see the disappointment in his face. We'd had such a good ride the previous day and getting me to Dakar had been just as much Simon's dream as mine. We'd spent most of the last nine months living and working together. He'd devoted so much time and attention to preparing me for the race. And now, on day five, I was joining the dozens of riders who had already dropped out of the race. At least my injuries weren't as bad as those of the competitors I'd seen lying semi-conscious on stretchers in the medical tent.

'I'll be fine,' I said.

'I'm sorry about it, mate, really sorry,' said Simon. Then he turned to Matt. 'We better go and get some dinner and make a new plan.'

'Yep,' said Matt.

'Change, as ever,' said Simon. 'Always in the Dakar. Change, change, change.'

Simon and Matt walked off. I returned to the tent where the doctor was waiting to treat my hands. Chris Evans, the person who at the MotoGP race in Valencia had convinced me to have a go at the Dakar, had turned up to translate.

'He's giving you some painkillers,' Chris said. 'After he's injected the anaesthetic you'll have no feeling in your hand so you've got to be very careful about burning or cutting it because you won't feel it. Gradually sensation will come back and then you'll have quite a bit of pain.'

The doctor used an electrode on my wrist that made my fingers twitch so he could determine the right places to inject anaesthetic. He injected several shots under the nails of my broken fingers and dislocated thumb, all of which made me yell with pain. Then he manipulated the bones in my hand and tried several times to push my thumb back into its socket, but it kept popping out.

'If he can't get your thumb back in,' said Chris, 'he says he'll have to put you on a plane to Paris, where they'll operate on you.'

'He's got to do it,' I said. 'I can't leave the rally now. I've got to get on that plane tomorrow morning to Zouérat.'

Despite the anaesthetic, my thumb still seared with pain as the doctor tried to force it into place. 'Aaaaaghh!' I yelled.

'Shhh!' said Russ. 'You've got to act brave. Otherwise they'll think you're a wimp and not let you on the plane tomorrow.'

'I just drove 450 fucking kilometres with two broken hands and you're calling me a wimp?'

Eventually, with the help of an orderly holding my thumb firmly in place, the doctor encased my left forearm in a plaster cast. He squeezed my right hand between two plastic splints, bandaged it and my right arm up to my elbow, then left me sitting with both elbows resting on a table, my arms sticking straight up in the air.

'This will make wanking difficult,' I joked.

As a kid I'd always wanted a cast. Now that I had one I didn't know how I was going to manage around the camp. I wouldn't be able to dress or undress myself, let alone take my boots off, have a shower or wipe my arse. Picking through a plate of food in the medical tent while the plaster set, I discovered that even eating would be painful.

The fact that I'd made it through to the end of the stage with two injured hands was some consolation. And I'd been the fourth fastest British rider that day, the first that the rally really got tough. But I was bitterly disappointed to have gone out after such a trivial fall. In the last year I had broken my collarbone, cracked several ribs, had a hairline fracture on my spine, been bruised all over my body and picked up dozens of scars. Now I'd broken both hands. After all I'd put in so far, it seemed very unfair to go out.

When the plaster had set one of the doctors returned with a pair of scissors.

'Time to cut this off.' The doctor pointed at my competitor's wristband.

'So my race is officially over.' I watched as he snipped the thin band of plastic. 'A symbol of my failure.'

I thanked the doctor for all his help. 'How long do I have to wear this for?' I held up my arm.

'Six weeks.'

'*Six weeks?*'

'You've broken ligaments. They have to fix. It needs six weeks. The pain will last for a long time, but try to keep moving normally. If you don't, after six weeks you will find moving difficult.'

I asked the doctor and one of the nurses to sign my plaster.

'Is this your first Dakar?' the doctor said.

'Yes. My very first. Not a good way to end it.'

'Will you come back?' the nurse said after writing *Bon Voyage* up my arm.

'No. Never.'

But the doctor thought otherwise. 'I have just treated someone who has done it seven times and reached Dakar three times. After every year he vows it will be his last. And every year he comes back. Even when he is in the race he does not know why he is doing it. He does not even enjoy it, but he always comes back. Maybe you will too.'

I'd heard similar stories many times before, but as I walked away from the medical tent I was absolutely convinced this would be my last Dakar.

'I'm so relieved it's over,' I told Russ. 'I'm so glad I don't have to go out into that dust again tomorrow. It's dangerous and crazy and I was frightened. I'm so relieved.'

It was a crazy event. Two hundred and forty bikers spending tens of thousands of pounds each to pursue a dream that, for most of them, would end in disappointment. Outside the top ten riders, all of whom were professional and heavily supported by team-mates, everyone in the race knew they didn't have a chance in hell of winning. All we wanted was that finisher's medal, but the race was designed to deprive two-thirds of us of even that. And to get to Dakar wasn't just about riding up to twenty hours a day for fifteen days. The hardest part was putting up with all the bullshit that went with the riding – mastering the road-book and the constant changes to the route, finding time to eat and sleep, worrying about your bike and making sure it was ready for the next day and, all the time, the ticking clock. I'd come to realise that to succeed at the Dakar you needed to be operating at no more than three-quarters of your absolute ability. Riders who did that would have the energy to spare when they inevitably made mistakes or whenever their run of luck would inevitably falter. Like many riders, my problem was that, at times, I was operating at very close to 100 per cent of my capability, which left no room for error.

I rang Olly. 'I've had an accident.'

'Oh . . .' Olly's voice dropped.

I knew why Olly had gone so quiet. Her greatest worry was that I was going to return home in a wheelchair or worse.

'It's all right,' I said. 'It's not bad. I've done my hands in, but I'm OK otherwise.'

'*Oh no*, Charley. That's awful.'

I knew Olly was disappointed for me, but I also could hear in her voice a huge relief that I was relatively OK and that the race was over for me. No more long days watching my progress on the Dakar website, tracking the movement of my bike on the Iritraq system, worried that something had happened to me. No more sleepless nights wondering if I'd damage myself seriously the next day.

'Don't worry,' Olly said. 'It's all going to be OK.'

We chatted for a while, then I hung up. I could tell Olly was delighted. Her nightmare was over, my dream had finished. The contrast felt odd.

I walked back to our pits feeling I'd failed everybody including myself. I was out of the Dakar. I'd have to explain the reasons why to dozens of people, many of whom had spoken to Simon and told him they thought I was just some spoilt rich kid unable to ride a dirt bike, just wanting to enter the Dakar for the sake of something glamorous to do. I'd heard the same kind of things during Long Way Round when people had even suggested we had a Winnebago following us around. I knew it went with the territory. I knew I was very fortunate to be able to enter the Dakar or ride around the world and that inevitably there would people who would be jealous. After all, I'd be jealous of someone in my position. But I also knew how much work I'd put into it. And, above all, I knew I'd done it. That was the one thing no one could take away from me. Anyone could criticise me, but most of those critics would never have accomplished what I had. With Russ, I'd put a team together; we'd got the financing and support we needed; we'd recruited Simon, Matt, Gareth, Wolfgang, Jim and Claudio as well as our invaluable event managers Lucy and Asia. We'd got the whole shebang to the starting line in Lisbon; I'd survived five days of the race and ridden nearly four hundred kilometres with two broken hands; and now I was going to make sure the team got Simon and Matt to Dakar.

I almost laughed out loud when I read the road-book's assessment of the sixth stage from Tan Tan to Zouérat. 'The hours of sleep stored up from previous stages will be an asset when tackling this long road,' the road-book read. 'The long liaison to the start of the special will take place at night in conditions which require maximum vigilance.' Which hours of stored sleep? And when had we ever not been required to maintain maximum vigilance, even in daylight?

Even on paper, the sixth stage was a killer. It began at 1.40 a.m. with a 336-kilometre liaison from southern Morocco via Western Sahara into Mauritania, with the special section starting just over the border. More than one hundred kilometres of the liaison was off-road and therefore just as difficult as any special section; it even had a timed checkpoint. The special had a lot of sand, a long sixty-kilometre stretch of soft and high dunes followed by nearly thirty kilometres of camel grass. Nevertheless, I felt a deep pang of jealousy when I saw Simon and Matt ride off into the darkness that morning. I'd returned from the medical tent shortly after midnight and with less than an hour to go before Si and Matt had to get up, there had seemed little point in going to bed. Instead I took up smoking again with a vengeance. Up until then I'd allowed myself one celebratory cigarette each day at the end of the stage. Now, reasoning that I'd been inhaling dust and carcinogenic vehicle fumes for most of the last five days, I talked myself back into smoking more than twenty a day.

By the time I saw Matt and Simon's tail-lights disappear shortly before 2 a.m., I'd smoked five cigarettes and was feeling very low. Riding to Dakar had been my dream and now they were continuing it.

I also knew that the moment the doctor told me I was out the rally changed as much for Simon and Matt as it did for me. No longer charged with his primary objective of getting me to Dakar, Simon had to work out whether he should now think only of himself or watch out for Matt.

Russ and the assistance crew also had a long day ahead of them. For the first time they were following the same route as the competitors. To complicate matters, they were required to leave after the last of the competitors, but ideally needed to arrive at the bivouac before them. The X5 had so far survived with relatively few problems. The starting system was still playing up but James and Wolfgang had got to grips with the GT1 computer that reset it. However, the car had yet to be properly tested off-road. Today would change that.

Unable to sleep, I spent the rest of the night sorting out my passport and papers, organising my little rucksack, badgering people to help me cut the sleeves off all my long-sleeved tops so that I could get my injured hands through them and realising how the Dakar is essentially all about money. The Bowler team mechanics and truck drivers were pulling an all-nighter, working flat out on the car belonging to one of their clients, a Norwegian millionaire who had rolled on the way to Tan Tan. Overwhelmed by the amount of work needed to get the car rally-worthy by the start of the next stage, the Bowler mechanics woke Gareth and Wolfgang shortly before midnight. They helped out while the driver fretted and encouraged the mechanics to keep going by slipping one-hundred euro notes into their pockets every hour or so.

While the Norwegian millionaire was handing out his financial incentives, the locals had scaled the periphery fence around the bivouac and were pinching whatever they could find – a stark reminder of the vast gulf in wealth between the people inside the bivouac's fence and the local population outside it. Several times I heard a rustle of footsteps nearby and wheeled around to see one of the locals flitting through the shadows. Shortly before dawn I went in search of some fresh water. When I got back, my sleeping mat had been stolen, along with Simon's.

Just after sunrise, Russ and the assistance team set off. 'Good luck, guys!' I shouted as the X5 rolled out of the bivouac. 'See you in Zouérat!'

'Eleven days left,' said Russ from behind the steering wheel. 'It's like being in a cell scratching lines into a brick. It seems like a very long time.'

Meanwhile, I flew on to the next bivouac. When I arrived I set about securing a site for our pits and phoned Lucy to find out if she'd heard when Russ expected to reach the bivouac. Lucy told me the X5 had broken down and was stranded about 450 kilometres from Zouérat. Just what I didn't need to hear. Immediately the panic returned. After my injuries, my misgivings about being able to ride off-road in Africa and my anxieties about the road-book, the X5 breaking down was the last straw. Faced with the stress of dealing with a stranded car, I just wanted to go home.

With Jim at the wheel, speeding through the desert at around one hundred kilometres per hour, the X5 had hit a ridge, flown about twenty metres through the air, landed with an almighty thud and swerved as the rear suspension collapsed. Jim had managed to control the car, which had nearly turned over. When the X5 stopped they discovered the rear left wishbone had snapped.

Considering the X5 was running on standard suspension and was loaded with four adults, a spare motorcycle engine, spare parts for the bike and the X5, roll cages and extra goodies, perhaps it was not surprising that something would give.

Russ's immediate reaction was to pace around the car, swearing and sighing, groaning and shaking his head while Jim, Gareth and Wolfgang set about jacking up the car to have a good look at the damage. But within ten minutes Russ had calmed down, hatched a plan and got on the phone to Lucy in London.

'At least we're the right way up and we've only got one thing to solve. I've got a plan and if you and I pull this one off, I'll love you for ever . . . Lucy? . . . Luce? . . . Lucy?'

The satellite link had gone down but via three phone calls over the next fifteen minutes Russ managed to spell out his scheme.

'I need you to phone Charley and tell him what's happened. I need him to talk to Sven Quandt.' Sven was the manager of X-Raid team, which was using customised BMW X3 and X5 cars. 'See if he knows how we can fix the back of our car. Charley also needs to talk to the helicopter controllers to find out if they can chopper a spare wishbone from Zouérat to us here in the desert. And I need you to get a spare wishbone to Zouérat . . . Lucy? . . . Luce?'

Russ, by his own admission, was winging it. 'I'm just grasping at straws, chaps,' he told Jim, Wolfgang and Gareth when he came off the phone. 'I've never been stuck in the Sahara before. Let's just hope Keith isn't too far behind us.'

They'd last seen Keith Banyard, the lead driver of the Bowler team trucks, that morning at Tan Tan. Although his trucks were utterly dependable and very likely to catch up with the X5, Russ knew Keith's team had probably stopped for breakfast before leaving the bivouac.

While Lucy sourced a spare wishbone, I went in search of Sven

Quandt. However, like all rally cars, the X3 and X5 cars they were using bore little resemblance to their factory equivalents. Beneath their one-piece carbon Kevlar bodies, they had a latticed tubular space-frame chassis – a completely different construction to our X5's monocoque body, and one that didn't use the same wishbone. I realised there was no point in approaching the X-Raid team so I turned to Chris Evans, a veteran Dakar problem-fixer. After asking if we had spare rear wishbones on the truck – charged for every kilogram on the truck we'd removed many of our spare parts in Lisbon – Chris suggested welding, but the wishbone was made of an aluminium alloy that was very difficult to repair.

'Trouble is that you're not going to get an instant solution,' said Chris. 'You're going to have to sweat it a bit. Whatever happens, the organisers won't leave them out in the desert. You might not see the X5 until Nouakchott in three days's time, but you will see it again.'

The determining factors, I was learning fast, were money and imagination. Anything was possible provided we could pay enough. The worst-case scenario would be that we couldn't repair the X5 in the desert. That would mean getting the organisers involved. Maybe they'd send a helicopter out there to pick up everybody and dump them at the bivouac, but if that happened we'd have the personnel but no transport.

The alternative, Chris explained, was to get a local to drive into the desert with a pick-up to tow in the X5. It would be more expensive, but at least we'd have the car.

'For now, when you know relatively little and it's still early days, I think you've got to resist the panic,' Chris said. 'Every time something goes wrong it has its own natural life span. The organisers won't let your guys die of thirst out in the desert. It's very bad publicity.'

There were hundreds of Dakar myths about how competitors and assistance teams had solved problems that seemed insurmountable. Chris told me about a rider who broke down on a motorcycle and realised after a while that he was close to where he'd broken down the previous year.

'This nomad turns up from nowhere. He tells the rider that there's a bike just like his five kilometres away. The rider follows the nomad. And behind a stone hut he finds his old bike. He strips the part he needs from his old bike, fixes it to his new bike and gets to Dakar. Your problem is there aren't many BMW X5s abandoned in the desert.'

'Yeah. Exactly.'

'The locals tend to buy Mitsubishis.' Chris was laughing. 'Oh . . . and there's one other thing. They've broken down in a war zone.'

Western Sahara was the scene of one of those sad wars that drag on for decades, flaring up every so often and making life a misery for the local population. After the death of Franco in November 1975, the Spanish government abandoned Western Sahara, their colony since the early twentieth century, and even repatriated Spanish corpses from its cemeteries. Morocco and Mauritania immediately invaded, expelling most of the locals by force, in some cases using napalm. The Saharawi people fled to neighbouring Algeria where they declared their own republic in exile and fought a guerrilla war through the Polisario Front, a nationalist organisation that had been fighting the Spanish since 1973.

In 1979 Mauritania withdrew from Western Sahara, leaving it all under the control of Morocco which wanted access to its rich phosphorous deposits and potential offshore oil fields. By building a series of 'Moroccan Walls', three-metre-high barriers longer than the West Bank barrier or the Berlin Wall, and the heavy use of mines Morocco contained the guerrillas. The area was now officially under ceasefire and patrolled by UN peace keepers but riots and demonstrations still broke out frequently and the Polisario Front had recently been threatening to resume fighting. Not a good place to break down, it seemed.

Fortunately the Bowler trucks had caught up with the X5 by early afternoon, stopped and had a look at the damage. Unfortunately they'd then declared they were unable to repair it. Russ's solution was to leave Wolfgang and Jim, the best car mechanics on the team, with the X5 while he and Gareth hitched a lift with one of the trucks. Wearing crash helmets to protect their heads against inevitable knocks, they climbed into the pitch black of the hold of one of the trucks for the 450-kilometre journey to Zouérat, where Gareth could work on Simon and Matt's bikes when they finished the stage and Russ could try to source a wishbone.

In the meantime, I'd found a local fixer who offered to pick up the X5 on his low-loader. If Russ wasn't happy with that solution I thought that, with luck, we'd be able to get a replacement wishbone to the X5 the next day, fix it and drive the car to Nouakchott, the capital of Mauritania where the rally would take a rest day in two days' time. Russ and Gareth would have to find some way to get to Nouakchott, possibly by waiting for the X5 to pick them up or by hitching a lift with whoever delivered the wishbone from the BMW dealership in Nouakchott. If it all panned out as planned I'd be able to stop running around like a headless chicken exhausting myself when I needed to attend to Simon and Matt.

The aggravation of the X5 breakdown had made me question even more why so many people chose to return to the Dakar rally year after year. All around me there were people like Chris Evans, who had been working on the rally for years. I asked him why.

'It can't be for the money, 'cos the money's shit,' he said. 'I've got no idea why I do it, but there is something exceptional about the Dakar. Maybe it's because there's always something going on to keep me stimulated. There's lots of things to do; there's lots of toys to play with and there are solutions to be found to ridiculous problems.'

He was right. We certainly had a ridiculous problem and some extraordinary solutions for it: a broken vehicle stuck in the desert; some bloke coming from a BMW dealership in a remote town in one of the poorest countries on the planet; a local fixer in Bedouin dress offering us a low-loader; two of our team spending the night in the desert; satellite phones going off left, right and centre; and I had two broken hands wrapped in plaster and bandages. As well as my problems, Chris had several other minor dramas with which he was dealing. It was like compressing a lifetime into a couple of weeks.

'I can see the appeal to other people,' I said. 'But it's too stressful for me. I'm not good at this kind of thing.'

'The only time it's stressful is when there's no solution,' said Chris. 'As long as nobody's hurt everything can be solved. Injury is the only thing here you can't fix. Everything else is possible. And the challenges are interesting. You've got to manipulate people. It won't work if you're very stressed and aggressive with them, they'll just back off. Everyone here has dozens of other things to do instead of helping you. But if you go up to them, say hello, shake their hand and seduce them, you get the best out of them. That's a very interesting challenge. We live in a very safe and relatively dull part of the world and we get to do this and it's fantastic.'

Fortunately, Matt and Simon had a fairly uneventful day and arrived at the bivouac in good time, Matt summing up the stage as, simply, 'a fucking long way'.

Simon, as usual, was pissed off with the cars and trucks, which continued to make life a misery for motorcyclists. 'We were on the stop, doing 130kph and the cars came past as if we were not moving,' he said. 'At one point, two trucks came either side of us, all of their six wheels off the ground and flying past us at more than 150kph.'

Matt and Simon's only concern was that Gareth and Wolfgang were not waiting for them as they rode into the pits. Their bikes were in relatively good shape but they still needed a service before the next day, so Simon and Matt changed the air filters, wheels and oil themselves, then crawled into their sleeping bags while Gareth and Russ were still en route to the bivouac. At 1 a.m., I bumped into Simon stumbling around half asleep.

'. . . Gareth not here when we went to bed,' he slurred. 'Matt and I done what we could . . . but few things still to do . . .'

'It's all right, Simon. Gareth's here now. It's being done. Gareth's checking the bikes.'

'. . . Gotta get up at six . . .' Simon said, shuffling back to his sleeping bag.

Chapter 11

6 AND 7 JANUARY
Zouérat to Nouakchott

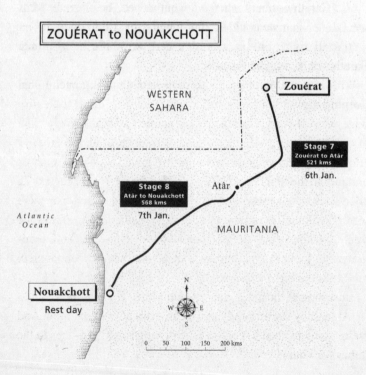

'It's gonna be carnage today,' Simon said on the morning of the seventh stage. 'They've got this mad plan to send the slowest riders out first, so the people with the least experience are going to open the piste and do the navigating. People will be going everywhere, all sorts of directions through the dunes.'

The road-book summarised the 521-kilometre stage from Zouérat to Atar as 'a tricky pass' and warned that it would be 'the major difficulty' of the first week. It was an unwritten rule that by the rest day at the midpoint of the rally about one-third of the competitors would have been weeded out. The organisers planned for a steady war of attrition all the way to Dakar, so that no more than 40 per cent of the entrants reached the end. It didn't look good if too many people succeeded in reaching Dakar. ASO had to tread a fine line between making it a dream that people would feel was achievable and making it the hardest race in the world. Stage seven was going to be one of those stages that made sure the race maintained its tough reputation.

With only a 10-kilometre initial liaison and a 12-kilometre final liaison, but 499 kilometres of special section, almost the entire stage was off-road. The road-book painted a bleak picture. The first 25 kilometres of the special was gravel. Then came 39 kilometres of camel grass and dunes, followed by 145 kilometres of dunes to the first checkpoint and refuelling station. The next 75 kilometres were a mix of gravel plains and dunes, after which there were 71 kilometres of pure dunes to CP2 and another refuel. The final 144 kilometres of the special were semi-dune and semi-gravel. It looked a nightmare, but Simon seemed undaunted. 'Today is the big one!' he said.

'Just look at those big dunes,' said Matt. 'Fucking hell.'

'At least by starting early we get an extra hour of daylight. And we're going to need it 'cos we'll be driving round in circles in the dunes for hours.'

Matt didn't look happy.

'You'll love it, Matt!' Russ was trying to encourage a despondent Matt.

'Bollocks.'

'You'll enjoy it.'

'Have you *seen* the dunes?'

'Listen,' said Russ. 'You got this far, mate, just enjoy it now. Every day's a bonus.'

As Simon and Matt pulled out of the bivouac Russ asked me if I was still jealous of them.

'I don't think so. Having seen what they're going through and having experienced what I did.'

'Really?'

'It's just so hard. And then there are the logistics and assistance headaches.'

'It hasn't held up the project so far,' said Russ. 'It's held Wolfgang back, but we got Gareth through last night.'

'But if the bikes come back in a bad way tonight, then he's going to really struggle.'

'By tonight we could have the car sorted. All I have to do is find the guy with the flat loader.'

Russ had just come off the phone to Lucy, who had spoken to BMW and been told that changing the wishbone was not complicated. To fit it we didn't need specialist equipment, just brute force to compress the suspension springs. Scorpion Racing had replaced the X5's standard springs with heavy-duty springs, which would be more difficult to compress, but Jim and Wolfgang had found a solution. Working through the night, they had used cable ties to compress the springs sufficiently to allow them to replace the wishbone. All we had to now was get the wishbone to the X5.

A couple of hours later, Russ was standing in front of a brand-new Toyota Land Cruiser negotiating with its owner Mohammed, the local fixer. With his gold-framed glasses, gold wristwatch, educated manner, clipped moustache and expensive shoes he could have been an Italian or Spanish banker; only his Bedouin robes indicated otherwise. Mohammed was a smart operator. He knew our backs were against the wall and he showed every sign of wanting to profit from it. Although he spoke only French and we were relying on Claudio to interpret, I could tell from his body language and the way that he sucked in his breath through his teeth what he was saying: this is going to cost you a lot.

'How is he going to charge us?' said Russ. 'By the hour or by the day?'

'He wants two thousand euros there and back,' said Claudio.

'Two thousand euros? About twelve hundred pounds?'

'Yes.'

Russ blinked and pursed his lips. I knew what he was thinking. Russ hated paying too much for anything but he also hated wasting time.

'He says the price will include his chauffeur, the car, the GPS to find the X5,' said Claudio. 'And he will stay there for twenty-four hours.'

'Can he do it for fifteen hundred?'

Russ's question was followed by a long exchange between Claudio and Mohammed. Eventually Claudio had an answer. 'He does not like negotiating about price, particularly as he is moving on today and cannot give you one of his own staff. He will have to use one of his local contacts instead.'

'Does he have a driver with mechanical experience? I need someone who knows how to repair it and who knows how to compress the rear end so we can fit the new wishbone.'

'All his mechanics have left today. All he can do is what he has offered: car, GPS and a driver for twenty-four hours.'

The negotiations went on for ages. Russ wanted to make sure he'd checked every angle. Would he take us to Nouakchott if we couldn't repair the X5 in the desert? Would the car provided be a four-wheel drive strong enough to tow the X5? Did he have a low-loader to transport the X5 if necessary? If he did take us to Nouakchott, could he get us there in time for the rest day, which was only two days away?

Mohammed was getting restless. He had other business to which he clearly needed to attend.

'He says he cannot guarantee anything,' said Claudio.

Ideally we wanted a low-loader and an undertaking that it would transport the X5 to Nouakchott by the evening of the following day, which would give us the following rest day to have the car repaired at the BMW dealership. Russ asked how much it would cost.

'He says ten to twelve thousand euros,' said Claudio after a long discussion and several mentions by Mohammed of '*c'est pas trop cher*'.

'No,' said Russ emphatically. 'Not doing that. I will sort it out myself if we are going to be charged that much. I could hire a plane for less. I know we are over a barrel here but I am never going to pushed into a corner, whatever happens.'

Russ's refusal immediately changed the negotiations.

'He asks how much we are able to offer for a truck.' said Claudio.

'Look,' said Russ, 'here's the thing: it's not how much we can offer. We know we are in a spot but we are not paying ten thousand euros to solve it. Finished.'

Eventually, Russ agreed a much-reduced fee to be transported in a four-wheel drive pick-up to the X5 and set off mid-morning, while I flew on to Atar. By 5 p.m. Russ had got to the X5, the wishbone had been replaced in forty-five minutes and the car was back on the road, heading for Atar. Against considerable odds, Russ's gamble had paid off.

Unfortunately, the day had not run quite so smoothly for Simon and Matt. At 6.30 p.m. I was sitting in a tent at the airfield in Atar, staring at a computer screen and worrying. According to the Iritraq display on the screen, Simon and Matt had 101 kilometres to ride to the end of the stage, which meant that as night was falling they were caught smack in the middle of a long section of dunes.

I knew just how hard this stage could be. The previous night Simon had regaled me with one of his many Dakar tales, on this occasion about the time two years previously when he and Nick Plumb almost dropped out on this same stage.

Their troubles had started on the previous day when, about one hundred kilometres into an eight-hundred-kilometre stage from Ouarzazate to Tan Tan, Simon caught up with Plummy, who was crouching by the side of the piste with a broken shock bolt. They worked together for six hours to fix the bike then rode the rest of the stage non-stop through the night, arriving at the finish at 1 a.m., just as the first bikes were leaving for the start of the following stage – a lengthened eleven-hundred-kilometre stage from Tan Tan to Atar.

Simon and Nick immediately took the start then rode back into the bivouac to fix Nick's bike properly, both of them pitching in with their mechanics to get the job done. Eventually they left at 4 a.m., three hours behind everyone else.

In spite of not having slept for more than thirty hours, they rode the special-section well. By dusk they'd reached the Chinguetti dunes, the last big obstacle before the run-in to Atar. Everything had gone well that day, but things soon turned ugly in the dunes. Both of them got stuck and had to help each other dig the bikes out over and over again. Eventually they conceded the only way to get through the dunes would be to continue on their own. Riding together was slowing them down; as soon as one of them built up momentum and a rhythm the other would get bogged down in the sand.

The going was still horrendous but as midnight passed into the early hours of the morning Simon slowly made his way through the dunes, cursing the winds that were turning clear skies into a dust storm. Relieved that, according to his roadbook, the end of the dunes would soon be in sight, Simon climbed a long, steep dune then buried his bike in the soft sand of its crest. Collapsing on the dune, gasping to regain his breath, he heard a voice.

'Help!' the voice called.

'Plummy?' shouted Simon. 'That you, Plummy?'

In the short bursts of silence that punctuated the roars of the engines of other vehicles trying to conquer the dunes, Nick and Simon shouted through the dark at each other. All around them beams of white and red lights shone into the dust cloud like searchlight beams. Nick, it turned out, was stranded five hundred metres away. His battery had packed up.

Simon removed the battery from his bike and, holding a tiny flashing light so that other vehicles would see him, trudged the through the dust cloud and across the dunes to Nick's bike. They hooked up Simon's battery and started it. From where they were standing they could see bikes, cars and trucks in a valley between the sand dunes.

'We've got to get to there,' said Simon pointing at the vehicles. 'They're all moving.'

Between the two of them they manoeuvred Nick's bike into the valley then set out to find Simon's bike. Simon had left a second flashing light on the seat of his bike but they couldn't spot it. And the wind had obscured his footprints. All they knew was that

Simon's bike was parked on a high spot. For hours they climbed to the top of dunes before they happened by chance upon the dune on which Simon had left his bike.

They put Simon's battery back in his bike then Simon rode it to where they'd left Nick's bike. For another couple of hours they tried to get a run off Simon's bike to start Nick's, but they couldn't get Nick's bike to fire up. With the first glow of dawn appearing in the eastern sky they were forced to give up. Simon rode off to finish the stage while Nick retired from the rally.

As I came out of the tent, hoping that Simon and Matt were having a better time in the dunes than they'd experienced two years previously, I bumped into Chris Evans, visibly excited by the unfolding drama.

'They've got half the field still out on the bloody piste! And we've got another very hefty day tomorrow and then traditionally another very hefty day after the rest day.'

'I'm just worried about Simon and Matt.'

I told Chris that they still had around one hundred kilometres to ride and that they appeared to have been making slow progress. 'I feel like mother hen waiting for her chicks to come home.'

'They'll be all right. And if they survive the stage after the rest day they should be able to consider themselves home and dry. If Matt and Si can get through the next few days you're laughing.'

Chris made it sound so easy. Just two more hard days to endure, then Dakar would be within their grasp.

'It's so disappointing,' I said.

'What do you mean?' Chris looked confused.

'I'm so jealous of them. I really am.'

'You'll just have to come back and do it again next year.'

'I think I might . . .' I was all over the place, one minute declaring the Dakar to be insanely dangerous and glad to be out of it then announcing I'd be returning for another attempt in 2007. In that, I suppose, I was no different to any other Dakar competitor.

I asked Chris what he reckoned a rider needed to finish the Dakar.

'Any decent clubman rider could do the Dakar. What you need is a huge amount of determination coupled with a positive attitude. Simon's probably told you that line about needing to be prepared to crawl on hands and knees across broken glass. That's one of the few intelligent things he has ever said.'

In my short time in the rally I'd seen that experience played a large part. Patsy Quick was on her fourth attempt and this year, having learned from experience, she'd come back on a lighter 525cc bike.

'As for the top riders, it is the thinking man's rally. You need to be clever to win. It's a strategic race. You might want to come second on one particular stage so that you are chasing the leader the next day rather than being the first out in the field, chased by all the rest. As well as being wily, you need a pathological lack of fear, extreme bike skills and the ability to sleep immediately anywhere.'

I'd certainly come to realise the frontrunners were a breed apart. That combination of ruthless determination, insane ambition and composed cool was rare, which maybe explained why just a handful of riders dominated the event year after year. It also explained why, out of a team of five top riders racing two years previously, two were now dead and two had abandoned bike racing for cars because it was safer.

I'd also started to see what it took for a privateer to succeed. Simon's recipe for surviving the mental pressure created by the relentless demands of the race was never to look too far ahead. The secret was to focus only on the next twenty kilometres and to break down the road-book into manageable chunks. Simon set himself targets. It could be the first one hundred kilometres of the stage, or half the distance, or the next checkpoint. By not thinking about the stage as a whole, he didn't start each morning thinking he had 750 kilometres to ride, only the challenges that lay ahead before his next landmark.

While I was pondering all this, Simon and Matt were struggling in the dunes, trying to get to the end of the toughest day so far. By about 8 p.m. I was really worried about them and had taken to checking their progress on the Iritraq every half-hour or so. All it told me was that they were hardly moving at all.

Shortly after 9 p.m., Patsy and Clive rolled in. I was overjoyed to see them and really proud of their achievement but most of all I wanted to hear news of Simon and Matt. First I had to listen to the account of their day. As soon as Patsy started talking, it was clear it had been a mammoth stage.

'There was no let up from the camel grass all day. And then those top racers came blasting past us this morning . . . how they ride that hard all day I'll never, ever know . . . I wouldn't want to have been on a big bike, but on a light bike the problem is you're conscious the whole time of not wanting to wring the bike's neck and kill the engine . . . there was no let up at all . . . and everywhere, deep tracks made by the cars.'

Clive's bike had an electrical fault that had slowed them down and they'd led a car that had no lights through the dunes. 'He couldn't do enough to thank us,' Patsy continued.

'And then we saw some poor lad lying on the side of the track after the end of the special. He'd got through the whole day and then something had happened. I don't know what. That's the thing with the Dakar. You never know what's suddenly going to come and bloody hurt you. But we're here! Yes!'

Then came news of my boys: 'Si had an off this morning . . .'

'Si did?' I felt the panic rise inside.

'Yeah, a biggie.'

'Shit. A biggie? How's the bike? Did you see? Was there any damage?'

'No, I think the bike's fine. Si was just a bit concussed.'

Shit again. This was not what I wanted to hear. 'Si? Concussed? Really?'

'Yeah. It's that camel grass. You think everything's going nicely, but it can kick you off your bike like that.' Patsy clicked her fingers. 'But Si seemed all right when I saw him later. He was fine and he took the front.'

'And how was Matt doing?'

'Very well, but I think they were struggling in the dunes a bit. Every time you've got to pick that thing up, it's bad . . . and then the panic sets in and you ride like a tit.'

After speaking to Patsy, I headed up to the airfield to take another look at the Iritraq. At twenty past ten I was sitting in the semi-darkness of a tent, staring at a computer screen, beside myself with worry. I typed in Simon's number first. A little red motorcycle appeared on the screen. It indicated that Simon had covered 485 kilometres and still had 36 to ride, of which two-thirds were the special section.

'Good,' I said. 'Let's have a look at Matt now.' I typed in Matt's number.

'Oh . . . oh . . . Fuck!' Matt still had eighty-five kilometres to ride. Fifty kilometres separated him from Simon. 'What the fuck's going on?'

According to the Iritraq, Matt had not moved in the last hour. It showed that Simon and Matt had stuck together all day, passing through all the checkpoints together. Something had obviously gone very wrong. It didn't look good.

Back at the pits, Nick Plumb had just arrived. He'd had

problems with his BMW overheating and suggested that Matt or Simon might have had similar trouble.

'Every time you stop to let your bike cool down all you think about are the minutes ticking away,' said Nick. 'I was looking at that sun every single time, thinking fuck, fuck, fuck, it's coming down. So I'd go a minute longer than I should have done with the warning light on and then stop, engine off, fan on, just leave it for a bit. At first the warning light would take a couple of minutes before it came on, but it got so bad it would come straight on again almost as soon as I rode off. I think it's something like that that's holding them up.'

'Could it be fatigue?' I said.

'No, not with Matt. He's the fittest one of all of us.'

'He doesn't look it,' I laughed.

'No, but he bloody is,' said Nick. 'There's no question about it.'

Gareth agreed. He thought either the engine was overheating or it had blown completely.

'He can't have hurt himself,' said Nick. 'Because Si would still be with him . . . I'm hoping it's maybe something so silly that Simon's left Matt there to fix it because he's so close to the end and they don't want both of them to drop out of the race.'

Nick had seen Matt have a big off immediately after the start of the special and he'd seen Matt lose touch with Simon early on in the stage.

'Just as Matt was looking over his left shoulder to check Simon was still behind him, Simon whipped past him on the right. It's that simple. I caught up with Matt who had slowed down. "Matt!" I shouted. "He's there!" It's that easy to get split up. Matt would have been riding around wondering where the fuck was Simon.'

While we were trying to work out what had happened to Matt and Simon two lights appeared in the darkness, riding towards us.

Then we heard the bikes' engines. They were Beamers. Moments later, Matt and Simon was standing in front of us.

'Fucking hell! Jesus! Matt! Well done, mate!' I yelled. 'Simon! My boys! Jesus, we were so worried because your Iritraq said Matt was eighty-five ks out and Simon was twenty-five ks from here.'

'That was the fucking hardest thing I've ever done.' Matt looked like every last ounce of strength had been squeezed out of him. By contrast, Simon looked quite fresh, the thick dust caked to his face cracking as he smiled and talked about the day they'd had in the desert.

'Really?' I said. 'That hard?'

'I did actually leave him in the desert.' Simon's eyes twinkled with delight at the telling of the story.

'What was it like, Matt?'

'Like hell, but worse.'

'I take my hat off to you, mate, I really do. Do you know how many people are stuck out there? Half the field is missing.'

'It was like riding in concrete dust that was neck-deep.'

'Jesus!' I said.

Then the stories started. Simon had crashed early on, going fast in fourth gear through the camel grass. He'd broken his mudguard, ripped his trousers, cut his lip and bruised his hand. I offered him the mudguard from my bike and he immediately asked for my motocross trousers.

'Simon Pavey crashed?' I said. 'I've never seen you crash.'

'It was big. It rang my bell big time for about the next hour or so. I was going along with a head like a buzzer.'

A little further on, as he was coming down the first big pass, about forty kilometres into the special section, Simon dropped his bike and the chain came off his rear wheel.

'Took us a while to repair that, didn't it?' said Simon.

Then they told me what had happened later on in the day. They reached the dunes after midday and by about 3 p.m. it had become obvious that Matt was struggling. Stuck in a bowl between two dunes, their bikes buried up to their axles in the soft sand, Simon thought it was about time they faced up to their difficulties.

'Fucking really in the shit here,' said Simon.

'Why?' Matt thought Simon was referring only to their current difficulties in the bowl.

'Really needed to get a move on. It's gonna be dark in a few hours, there's more dunes to come and we ain't getting through them in the dark.'

'Right,' said Matt. 'OK . . .'

But in spite of Simon's cajoling, they didn't make any faster progress. Simon was riding through the dunes with comparative ease but Matt fell or got stuck in the sand at least twenty times. Some of the time Matt managed to lift up his bike himself and get going again, but the problem with dunes is that as soon as you start falling off or becoming stuck you use up so much energy freeing the bike and getting it moving that you soon become too exhausted to ride efficiently and avoid mistakes. By the time the sun set, Matt was caught in a vicious circle of exhaustion and declining performance.

Riding in the dark, it was almost impossible to pick a good line or to navigate properly. Instead Matt and Simon were forced to follow the tracks that already been made through the dunes. Unable to find their way on fresh sand, they were covering increasingly shorter distances before they got stuck. A few times they got a little run on, but often they were managing less than fifty feet before they sank into the churned-up tracks.

Simon rode with one eye peering back over his shoulder, looking for the beam of Matt's headlights, but the dark made it more difficult for him to stop. The key to riding through dunes is keeping the gas on until you reach a ridge with a large enough patch of camel grass to support your bike – otherwise your bike will sink as soon as you stop. In the dark it was difficult to spot camel grass patches, so if Matt didn't appear over the crest of the previous dune Simon would have to turn around and ride back to him. But the air filter on Simon's bike was clogging with sand and he was finding it increasingly difficult to get back to Matt each time.

Eventually, just after they entered Chinguetti, the final thirty-kilometre stretch of dunes, Simon had taken to parking his bike at the top of a dune and walking back to wherever Matt was stuck in the sand. On one occasion, he walked for four hundred metres through sand which came up to his knees, then helped Matt pick up his bike before walking all the way back to his own.

On other occasions, Simon also got stuck so he'd have to free his bike as well as help Matt. Often Simon was having to ride back over dunes he had already crossed – not something of which you'd want to make a habit, particularly in the dark.

Matt urged Simon to continue riding on his own. 'Si, if you want to go just go.'

'No.' Simon was insistent. 'You know you can do this. Let's keep going.'

But Simon knew that he would have to set a deadline. If their progress didn't improve by 9 p.m., he'd have no choice but to set off on his own. Any later than that and he risked both of them spending the night in the desert and dropping out of the race.

At about twenty to nine Matt got caught in a bowl between several dunes. Simon could see Matt was exhausted and couldn't get out on his own. Simon parked his bike, clambered down into the bowl and started to help Matt. Pulling the bike at the front, Simon inched its front wheel forward by passing the tyre from hand to hand, while Matt pushed from behind and gunned the engine. Even with both of them working flat out, their lungs burning as they gasped for air, they couldn't get it up the slope.

'I'm finished.' Matt panted. 'I can't do it . . . I can't do it . . . you go on.'

'I'm not leaving you here in this hole,' said Simon. 'It's too dangerous. Let's get your bike out of the bowl.'

They shoved, sweated, grunted and pushed for another half-hour until they eventually manoeuvred Matt's bike on to a little rise with a patch of camel grass slightly to the side of the main track.

Simon helped Matt set up a camp for the night, using the beacon and little green luminous stick given to them by the rally organisers to warn oncoming vehicles that Matt was asleep beside his bike. As they looked back through the dunes they could see strings of twinkling green lights stretching out in every direction. Cars, bikes and trucks were stuck everywhere. Simon gave Matt his camera so that he could shoot a video diary, then got on his bike and rode off into the night.

He crossed the next dune to find only the last foot of a car sticking out of the sand, the rest of it buried at the bottom of a bowl. Its driver and navigator were staggering around, dazed and bewildered.

Over the next crest Simon dropped down into a valley that led between the dunes and took him to a waypoint about half a kilometre from where he had left Matt. The sand was still soft but he no longer needed to climb from the valley up the dunes. Looking at his road-book, he noticed the next waypoint was about ten kilometres away. Something about it seemed familiar. Then the penny dropped. I know this place, he thought, I've been here before. It was exactly the spot at which Plummy's bike had packed up two years previously. Back then, they'd tried for hours to get it working then Simon had been forced to leave Nick in the desert. He remembered crossing just one more dune then emerging on to a hard sandy piste that led to the finish. It had been 3 a.m. that time, he'd thought he was finished and that he couldn't make it to the bivouac, but when he got to the sandy piste he'd discovered the rest of the stage was straightforward.

If this is the end of the dunes, Simon thought, then Matt can do it. He turned around and rode four kilometres back into the dunes, nearly getting knocked off his bike by a car coming the other way.

Matt, meanwhile, was preparing to record his video diary. He'd filmed Simon riding away from him and had made sure his position was safe when he saw the beam of a motorcycle headlight coming back towards him.

'I thought, who the fuck is mad enough to be riding back into this shit?' And I realised, it's got to be Simon. Who else could it be?'

'You must have been pleased to see him,' I said.

'I wasn't sure whether I was glad to see him or not. I could guess what he was coming back for.'

As Simon approached, Matt could hear the distinctive engine note of his BMW. As excited as a child, Simon pulled up beside Matt and urged him to get back on his bike.

'Come on!' he yelled. 'We're getting out of here. You can do it.'

For a split second Matt thought Simon was trying to encourage him just to give it another go. Then he realised even Simon wouldn't risk his own ride to the extent of riding back through the dunes. It was enough to lift Matt's spirits. He got back on his bike and didn't fall once while crossing the last few dunes.

Once they'd got through the dunes they still faced a difficult ride. The darkness and the thick dust reduced visibility to less than ten feet. Because so many competitors were stranded in the dunes the piste was relatively free of traffic, but at one point a car cut straight through a gap between the two of them, clipping Matt and nearly knocking them both off their bikes. They arrived at the bivouac at about 11 p.m., exhausted, dirty and desperate for food and sleep.

'Man, you have done the most amazing thing,' I said. 'I know a little bit about how difficult it could be, but fuck me, Matt, you did it. You rode through the big dunes. You did the Dakar dunes, man.'

'If Simon wasn't there I would never have got through it.'

'It was mad.' Simon was shaking his head. 'Absolutely mad.'

'I'm really proud of you,' I told Matt. 'I think you're amazing, I really do. *Amazing.*'

'I think I'm stupid.'

At 568 kilometres, the next stage was even longer. The only consolation was that it ended in Nouakchott, the Atlantic coast capital of Mauritania, where we'd have a rest day before heading back east into Mauritania on a long loop leading through Mali and Guinea then on to Senegal.

'On the first part of the special the winding route crosses canyons and wadis. Competitors will feel themselves shot like a pinball against the massifs,' the road-book warned. 'After the series of zigzags, a very fast stretch will tempt the most itchy to push the speedo. But overconfidence could lead to bad surprises.'

The most worrying aspect of the stage was the heart of the 508- kilometre special, a two-hundred-kilometre stretch of dunes and soft sand. Nevertheless, as Simon and Matt departed, I couldn't help feeling a pang of jealousy. I knew they were facing a day as tough and unrelenting as the previous one but part of me still wanted to be with them, experiencing the rally first-hand.

For the first time since Lisbon I no longer felt sick with nerves. On paper, my life had become very simple: fly to the next bivouac and keep my fingers crossed – or at least those fingers I could still move, crossed – that nothing went wrong for the boys or for the X5. But that wouldn't do justice to the heightened state of anxiety that enveloped every hour of my day. I was constantly worried about Simon and Matt. I felt like their nanny. And the further we got into the race, the nearer we got to Dakar, the more terrified I became. Every little problem was magnified. I'd feel fine until about three in the afternoon, then the anxiety would start to grip. At times I thought it would be easier to be on a bike doing it myself than sentenced to hours of waiting.

Hanging around the bivouac gave me an opportunity to discover more about how the rally worked. It was an amazing operation, one that I couldn't help thinking was so successful because it was organised by the French. If we British had organised it our obsessions with health and safety would have allowed red tape to strangle the rally. The French organisers had the right mix of efficiency and laissez-faire to allow one of the largest sporting events in the world to keep rolling with the minimum of fuss. The logistics involved in moving several thousand people, a full catering operation, twenty-six aeroplanes, more than a dozen helicopters, thirty-five television editing suites and extensive medical facilities, including an operating theatre, through west Africa, across distances of up to eleven hundred kilometres a day, were jaw-dropping, so much so that armies would visit ASO to study its operations.

However, there was a potential downside to the formidable operation. Its sheer scale and the fact that it travelled through some of the most barren and impoverished parts of Africa made it a sitting duck for criticism, although ASO pointed out that, compared with resorts such as Club Med, it spread more wealth around the locals. It had also been argued that if the rally passed through a village in the middle of nowhere the locals would make enough money out of it to last them all year. We were told the locals loved it because very little ever happened where they lived. But the truth was none of us knew for sure how much the rally benefited the villages and towns through which it moved. I was determined to make sure Ewan and I spent time getting to know people, and learning more about their culture, if we managed to fulfil our dreams of riding through Africa in 2007.

My day passed relatively uneventfully. Groundhog day recommenced. I took my place in the queue of journalists, film crews, catering staff and officials waiting to fly in one of the squadron of ASO planes bound for Nouakchott. An hour or so later, I was in the Mauritanian capital, a ramshackle place designed for 15,000 people when it was chosen as the seat of government in 1957 but now home to nearly a million, many of them living in shanty towns or tents.

The X5 arrived by early afternoon, ready for a full service the next day. And then the waiting game started again. At half past six the Iritraq said Simon and Matt had only eighty-four kilometres left to ride, but it took until nearly 10 p.m. before they arrived at the bivouac. They'd averaged only twenty kilometres an hour for the last section and both of them were shattered. Matt, wide-eyed and trembling, looked like he'd had an even worse experience than the previous day.

'Well done, mate!' I threw my arms around Simon and Matt in turn, wincing each time as pain shot through my two broken hands.

'You made it!' said Russ. 'We were a bit worried because it took you a bit longer than we expected.'

'It took us a bit longer than *we* expected,' said Matt.

'Fucking dust!' Simon looked like someone had dropped a large bag of flour on him. 'Couldn't see your fucking nose. Look at my front mudguard.' It had shattered. 'I drove straight through a tree!'

'What happened?'

'Car went past. Just covered me in dust. Couldn't see a thing. I was going straight, this tree just exploded in my face.'

'You made it,' said Russ. 'That's all that matters.'

'I was all right until that last thirty ks. Then I couldn't see beyond the chinguard of my helmet. The dust was just hanging in the air. No breeze to disperse it. We were going like one mile an hour . . .'

The day had started well but Simon, still dehydrated and tired from the previous day, didn't put enough fuel in his tank at the first refuel, a mistake he'd never previously made. Realising that Simon was running out of fuel they were forced to stop twice to transfer fuel from Matt's bike to Simon's.

Dominated by rocky passes, on which Simon and Matt never got beyond second gear, the first hundred kilometres of the special section was very tricky. It took them nearly five hours to reach the first checkpoint, 165 kilometres into the special. Later in the day they got lost, which added about an hour on to their journey, but by sunset they were doing well with only seventy kilometres left to ride.

'I thought: no problem,' said Simon. 'Seventy ks on a piste. An hour or so. Easy.'

With their heads spinning from the exertion of riding all day on empty stomachs they stopped for a five-minute rest at the side of piste. As they sipped their water and ate the meagre contents of their ration packs, they looked back along the track but couldn't see any sign of approaching bike lights. The still air had turned what should have been a simple procession home into a nightmare. With no breeze, the dust thrown up by dozens of cars and trucks powering through the bikes, 'like ignorant pricks' according to Simon, just hung in the air, becoming thick as soup and severely reducing visibility.

Then Matt hit a bump and his lights went out, forcing them to slow to walking pace just as they hit a large area of fesh fesh. Not riding fast enough to avoid sinking, they pulled off-piste, riding over bushes and between boulders, passing bikes and one of the organiser's ambulances stuck in the fesh fesh, and finding it safer to ride on the rough than on the piste without lights. But, because they were travelling so slowly and because the air was thick with dust, their bikes soon overheated so they had to stop many times. And every time a car or truck passed them, they were forced to pull over and stop in case they rode into a hole.

More often than not, the car drivers failed to use their Sentinel systems. For a car to pass through a bike's dust took a second and was no big deal, but the rider would be immediately blinded by the passing car's dust, which often billowed for a couple of hundred metres behind the car. Not knowing if another car, bike or truck was following the car, the rider couldn't simply hit the brakes in case someone drove over the top of them. They had no choice but to ride blind for a few seconds.

Simon was caught in a car's dust cloud when a tree appeared directly in front of him. With no time to swerve out of the way, he gripped his handlebars tightly and rode straight through it. The African tree exploded as he hit it, its dessicated trunk and bone-dry branches shattering into tiny shards. Fortunately, the bike survived, except for some slight damage to its fairing, and Simon was no more than slightly shaken.

Matt was hit by one of the Bowler cars, which charged through his dust cloud without sounding its Sentinel or flashing its lights. It clipped his leg, ripping his trousers.

'Tell you what,' Matt told Russ afterwards. 'I am never *ever* doing this again. It's *too* dangerous. You've got to be mad to want to do it.'

*

All the next day, while the racers rested and their mechanics worked feverishly to service their vehicles, we heard more stories of carnage and misery in the desert.

Patsy Quick and Clive Towne had been doing well until, eighty kilometres from the end of the special, the nut holding the front sprocket on her bike broke off and oil poured out of her engine. Unable to repair the damage in the desert, the only solution was for Clive to tow Patsy through the soft dunes in the dark. Nursing sore wrists, a very swollen knee and other injuries caused by exhaustion and minor knocks, Patsy told us that at times they managed to move only a couple of metres before Clive's bike bogged down into the sand. It took them six hours to move across the final fifty kilometres of soft sand before they reached the harder surface of the piste. They had stopped and started so many times the electric starter failed so for the last few hours they had to kick-start Clive's bike every time it stopped.

While Matt and Simon spent the rest day attempting to replenish their reserves, stuffing pasta and cakes into their mouths whenever they weren't sleeping, Russ and Jim took the X5 for its service at Atlantic BMW in Nouakchott, where it was fitted with two new wishbones, a new air filter and various other essentials. Towards the end of the day, Russ and Jim returned from the BMW garage only to discover that as soon as it got to sand the X5 stopped moving. The wheels wouldn't turn, even when Russ pressed the accelerator to the floor.

'I just want to see the positive side of everything, but this car's sick,' said Russ. 'It just doesn't go and tomorrow morning we've got to start the second leg. I feel like we're jinxed now. Every two days something small is chucked in our path for us to deal with.'

Initially Jim and Wolfgang thought the X5's transmission management system was preventing the wheels turning, but after working on the car for most of the night Jim discovered that the turbo had failed. Like any decent Chelsea tractor, the X5 was fine cruising on tarmac at 80mph, although with a broken turbo it took a long time to build up speed. Without a turbo, however, it lacked the grunt it needed to pull away at 5mph in a couple of inches of sand. With the best part of nine hundred kilometres of off-road ahead of them, the next day was going to be interesting.

By late afternoon most of the British riders still in the race had congregated at one end of the bivouac to discuss the day ahead. I could tell from the way in which Simon was withdrawing into himself that he was worried.

'It's going to be a killer,' said Patsy, who in three previous attempts at the Dakar had never made it as far as the rest day. 'Lots of dunes. How's that make you feel Matt?'

'Not too good, actually.'

'It'll be all right,' said Simon. 'Nothing we haven't seen before.'

But I could tell he was rattled.

All day there was one question I wanted to ask Simon, but I never did directly, probably because I knew the answer. Did he think I would have made it to the rest day if I hadn't crashed out on day five? I'd seen that the rally proper started in Mauritania. Until it reached the soft sand maybe ten riders dropped out each day. But as soon as the rally entered Mauritania dozens of riders dropped out every day. I'd proved in Morocco I had the pace to ride off-road at speed confidently. But I'd not discovered if I could do it in the sand.

All I knew was that the Dakar was less about my bike skills and more about whether I could tap into that little reserve of energy that successful riders needed when they were stuck in the dunes, completely exhausted. Some people had it – Simon obviously did – but others got to the point where they couldn't pick their bike up one more time. I'd never know if I was one of those people or not.

The organisers held a meeting at 7 p.m. in which they warned the competitors that they faced a particularly hard day. When they advised privateers to request the PIN code that would unveil the entire route on their GPS displays we knew even the organisers were rattled. The last thing they needed was competitors lost in the desert with more injuries than their ambulances and helicopters could handle, or even a death. However, they warned the competitors that anyone caught cutting through to the tarmac rode that led from Nouakchott to Kiffa would be immediately disqualified.

By the time Etienne Lavigne brought the fifteen-minute meeting to a close the subtext of his briefing was obvious: a lot of you will drop out of the rally tomorrow, but if you survive it you should make it to Dakar.

Afterwards we grouped in the bivouac. Listening to Matt's reaction to the briefing, I became worried he was talking himself out of the rally. Every time I heard him speak he would make a joke about getting stuck in the dunes the next day. Although it was often funny, I suspected he was using humour to hide his nerves. I could see in his eyes that he was wondering if he was ready for another long day of torture in the desert. My worries were confirmed when Simon took me aside.

'We've been talking about tomorrow,' he said. 'It's going to be an incredibly hard stage; loads of dune crossings with six hundred ks of special. Matt was struggling in the dunes the other night. If the two of us go through the dunes together tomorrow it's going to be hard and it'll slow us up. I don't know what the tactics should be, but I'm concerned that if Matt has another bad day and I wait for him neither of us will survive it.'

The time had come to face our priorities. We needed to get at least one rider to Dakar.

'You've got to do what you've got to do,' I said. Even if that meant leaving Matt to fend for himself in the dunes. Russ called a team meeting.

'The dunes we've done up 'til now are nothing like as hard as we had last year,' said Simon. 'Hopefully if it's not too bad tomorrow . . . if it's just a case of helping each other a little bit . . . then it's no problem.'

I could tell Simon was skirting the issue.

'But if it's a case of me having to stop loads . . . then . . . ah . . . we'll have to go our own way . . . sort of thing. Yeah.'

I could see how uncomfortable Simon was with the idea of deserting Matt, possibly at a time when he needed his help most.

'The truth is, it's five hundred kilometres of dunes,' said Russ. 'And if we're going to get at least one of you to Dakar we need at least one of you to make it to Kiffa.'

'I feel really bad about it, I do,' said Simon. 'I don't want it to be like this. I want us both to go out there and have a good ride.'

'But it's got to be this way, really, doesn't it?' said Matt.

'Yep,' said Simon. ''Fraid so.'

'Then that's the way it is, mate.'

PART THREE

THE ROAD HOME

Chapter 12

9 JANUARY
Nouakchott to Kiffa

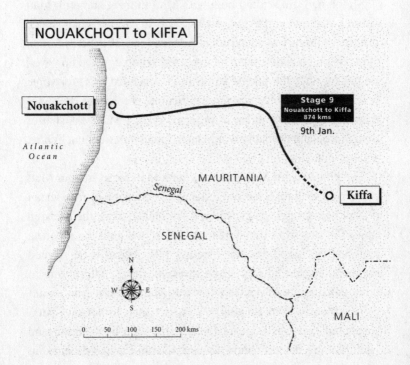

NOUAKCHOTT to KIFFA

Nouakchott

Atlantic
Ocean

Stage 9
Nouakchott to Kiffa
874 kms

9th Jan.

MAURITANIA

Senegal

Kiffa

SENEGAL

N
W E
S

MALI

0   50   100   150   200 kms

'Bits of me are hurting that have never hurt before.' Matt looked exhausted as we stood in a circle, chomping our breakfast in the dawn half-light. 'Like my fingertips. Don't know why, but they really hurt.'

It wasn't just Matt's fingertips. Everything felt different on the morning of the ninth stage. Four days after I broke my hands, the ramifications of my accident were still becoming apparent. Of all of us, I suppose Simon was now affected the most. Before the accident his role had been the quiet, dependable one at the back, supporting me and making sure we all made it to the bivouac each night. Now he was our frontrunner, the star on whom all our hopes were riding, and we had to make sure that nothing impeded his progress.

Simon had tried riding both with Matt in front and with Matt behind, following in his tracks, but it didn't make much difference. Matt was an excellent rider and just as good as Simon at picking a good line, but it all appeared to boil down to how well he got on with the bike. Even Simon conceded that, for some reason, this year's bike was more difficult to get through the dunes than any bike he'd ridden in previous rallies. Matt was shorter than Simon and probably would have found it easier on a lighter, smaller machine.

The plan was for Simon to stick with Matt for as long as Matt could ride with him, but not to delay his decision to race ahead if Matt was struggling. I suspected Simon had made the decision to go flat out from the start long before we held the meeting and that he asked for the meeting only because he wanted reassurance that he was doing the right thing. Attempting to be as considerate as possible towards Matt, Simon didn't want to say bluntly 'I'm fucking off on my own tomorrow' but I suspected that was his true feeling. I'd seen how Simon and Nick Plumb's determination, focus and ambition made them shut out anything that impeded their progress. Some people would have called them blinkered, but those were the qualities that separated Dakar finishers from the also-rans. I admired that single-mindedness, but it also left me worried for Matt on the biggest day of the rally.

In spite of the team meeting and the pressure on him, Matt was in great spirits as we ate our breakfast, taking the mickey out of Russ, who had spent most of the rest day with a phone clamped to his ear, attempting to sort out the various problems afflicting the X5.

'Suntan's coming on a treat again, eh Russ?'

'Yeah, you working on a desert look?' I chipped in.

Russ smiled and grunted, his mouth full of bread, while the rest of us laughed.

'Just barking orders every so often.' I did an impression of Russ. 'And pointing.'

'Two mobile phones. One on each ear.' Matt held imaginary cellphones either side of his head. 'Luce? You there? Who's there? What's going on?'

Russ laughed and played along. 'Sort it out!'

'Buy! Sell!' Matt continued the joke. 'Wishbones! High-rise jack!'

Buzzing with nervous energy, we all knew why we were cracking jokes and arsing around. Then Matt put it into words: 'I'm shitting myself, Russ.'

The smile had gone from his face. 'We were all sweet until about halfway through yesterday. We were all sitting down – Patsy, Clive and everybody – and we all started talking ourselves into panic mode, everybody getting hysterical.'

'Really?' Russ was looking serious too.

'Yeah. Simon provoked it, 'cos he went all quiet and when Simon goes quiet you know there's trouble in store.'

Russ looked concerned. 'So how did he bring it up?'

'He kept saying it's gonna be fucking hard – "I've seen some hard ones, but *this* one . . . ooh, fucking . . ." – and when he started talking about finding a short cut to a bit of tarmac, then I knew it would be really bad.'

'Any road work and you're out,' I warned.

'You're worried then?' said Russ.

'I'd be lying if I said I wasn't,' said Matt. 'And it just feels worse the further you come because you've made all that effort.'

'Think of it as just one more day.'

'There's only one other Beamer apart from us still left in the rally. I can't help thinking that's significant.'

'Really?' Russ looked worried now.

'Yeah, just that Spanish guy.'

'You managed OK in the dunes in Dubai,' I said.

'That's the thing. I can't believe how different it is. The sand is much deeper and softer so the bike doesn't ride on top. It just wants to go down, front or back, the whole time . . . at least that's what it seems like.'

Nick Plumb was listening in. 'How do you do it, Nick?' I said.

'I just try to be flowing. *Really* try. And I psyche myself up. As soon as I hit the sand I say to myself: Put your all into it. It's like a hill: when you get to the top, then you relax. If you relax halfway through it – and I know the dunes; you're talking hours and hours and hours – you're fucked. And I just think of all kinds of things to keep me going. I'm not religious or anything but by God, I'm praying to anybody. I'm praying to Mecca, to Buddha, to anybody for help to try and get me through it. I really do.'

'Think of me, Matt.' Russ knew it was the most unlikely suggestion. 'Think that we might see each other at the end.'

'I'm praying to Russ. The great producer in the sky.'

'You *can* do it Matt,' I said. 'You've done it before.'

'I think if you can get that power on and just stay on there.' As usual Russ was full of helpful suggestions. 'If you get into that rhythm then, you know . . .'

But Matt needed more than words.

A short while later, Russ and I watched Simon, Matt and Nick ride off.

'A sad moment,' said Russ. 'The first time I've watched the bikes go out and thought about who might come back. I've always expected them all to come back but today, that conversation with Matt, if he is struggling at the beginning, well, you can't keep going for six hundred kilometres, can you?'

'Even Simon is really worried,' I said. 'And he never flaps.'

The strange thing was that yet again I felt jealous of Matt and Simon. 'I realised this morning I never got a proper go in the sand Maybe I would have hated it. And maybe I wouldn't have made it through the day, but at least I could have said I did a day in the dunes. And that's what the Dakar is all about.'

'The race *does* start in Mauritania,' said Russ.

'Definitely. And all that talk this morning made that very clear. And it made me feel like I missed out.'

'If he said: Charley, put my lid on, you go . . .'

'Well . . . Russ . . .' I held up my bandaged hands.

'Forget the hands.'

'But if I had my hands, I would still be in the race.'

'Would *you* have taken *his* place this morning, if some miracle happened?'

'*This morning?* No!'

'Exactly. But after that big speech, you're meant to say: "Yes, I would have gone to the dunes!"'

'I don't know . . . no . . . no . . . well probably . . .'

'Matt's going to have the most miserable day of his life out there.'

'But when he gets to the end of it it'll be one of the best days of his life. You don't have the passion for bikes that he does and I don't think you get it.'

Our musings about whether or not the Dakar remained unfinished business for me were interrupted by news that three Chinese mechanics, who had been supporting two Chinese Bowler car entries and travelling in the largest of the Bowler trucks, had left the rally. It gave us the opportunity to put Gareth or Wolfgang in the truck, a nuclear-blast-proof eight-wheel-drive beast with thirty-seven gears, in case the X5 didn't survive to Kiffa.

In the meantime, I had an appointment with the ASO plane to the next bivouac. On the way to the airfield I stopped at a roped-in pen that the the riders and mechanics called the elephants' graveyard. It contained about thirty bikes, about a quarter of the number that had dropped out of the rally so far. Some had mechanical failures, such as a collapsed rear suspension; others were completely wrecked after crashing. Quite a few of the bikes had been pilfered for spare parts by privateers and their mechanics. All of them were very different from the shiny steeds I'd seen lined up in the parc fermé in Lisbon. With road-books still stuck at the point at which they went out of the race, every one of them told a story. On one bike, the road-book was frozen at kilometre 245.93 on a nasty sequence of obstacles highlighted with three exclamation marks. A dotted line indicated the track went off-piste. Three humps represented dunes and a squiggly right arrow meant the track passed through a twisty section between the dunes. Quite clearly the rider hadn't negotiated what would have been one of the most dangerous stretches of that stage. I just hoped he'd survived to tell the tale.

Another of the bikes, number 222, belonged to Darren Duesbury, one of the British riders. I'd last spoken to him the day he was penalised for speeding through a village. He was very upset because he thought the time penalty might eventually lead to his disqualification. He'd planned to visit one of the orphanages in Dakar and offer to pay for a child's education, but disqualification would mean a plane home before he reached Dakar. He was encouraging every biker to pay for one child's education, a lovely idea but one that maybe hadn't happened as, according to his road-book, he dropped out at kilometre 410.60 in a dangerous area with dunes, camel grass and two exclamation marks.

I thought back to a few days earlier, when I was sitting in the ASO plane waiting to fly to Zouérat on the morning after my accident. I looked out of the window. Below me, on the tarmac, was my bike. A fork-lift truck picked it up and was about to load it on to a nearby plane when one of the ground mechanics realised it was still full of fuel. With a big thick knife like a machete, he slit the fuel pipes. Petrol poured out everywhere. It was like blood spurting out of a slaughtered animal. As I looked on, a local in Bedouin robes ran over with some buckets to collect the petrol. At the time it felt like the closure of my rally, but now I felt I wouldn't be totally satisfied until I'd ridden at least one day in the Mauritanian dunes.

Simon, Matt and I left Nouakchott by our various routes. Russ, Jim, Wolfgang and Gareth were also about to leave on the assistance route. Nouakchott had been the last stop at which we all came together every evening. From this point on, our routes took us in very different directions. It makes sense from here on for Simon, Matt and me to tell our own stories, rather than for me to attempt to explain their experiences, which were very different from mine.

*

SIMON The day started badly for me. Already late for the start, Matt and I couldn't find our way out of the bivouac. Not the best way to start the hardest stage of the rally.

I was pretty freaked. I'd done enough Dakars to know what was coming and I was already depleted. We'd struggled on what I thought was a relatively straightforward day and, however much I wanted to be part of getting a whole team through, I still wanted to be on that finish line. Nothing was more important to me.

I'd slept really crap the night before. I didn't have my mobile phone with me in my sleeping bag. I had been using it as a clock, but Russ had taken it for charging. So whenever I woke in the night I didn't know whether it was midnight or four-thirty in the morning, just fifteen minutes before we needed to get up. Sometimes it's the tiny things that really make a difference.

I'd told everyone that the stage to Kiffa would be fine, but that was just my way of coping. Be positive. No worries. But of course there were worries. The biggest one was that I didn't have any spare air filters for the longest day of the rally. The night before, when we were getting everything ready, I'd put two spare air filters in my jacket. I didn't want to repeat the experiences of our filters clogging with sand in the dunes. But the next morning, just three minutes before the start, I was forced to swap them for a spare camera unit. Bloody hell, I thought, just what I don't need, but I had to get on with it.

I felt a total bastard as Matt and I rode the short liaison to the start of the special. There seemed to be something very symbolic about no longer riding with a brightly coloured Race to Dakar team mudguard after mine shattered when I rode through a tree. With a white mudguard and instructions to leave Matt behind if he faltered, I no longer felt part of the team. Instead I felt a right selfish shit and the last thing I needed out in the desert was to lose friends, although I couldn't help thinking that was what might happen.

At half past eight Matt and I were waiting at the start of the special. Behind us were parked some fifty 4x4 vehicles belonging to spectators, press and officials. To our right, half a dozen helicopters were waiting to take off. They would film the competitors and pick up the injured. To the left of us were a few bare trees. And ahead was nothing but orange sand.

This stage was started in reverse order, a procedure that was new to the 2006 rally. It gave those of us near the back of the field an extra forty-five minutes to an hour of daylight – enough to get maybe eighty kilometres further down the track before sunset – but it meant we'd have to navigate the track ourselves until the top racers came pounding through.

After the start there were about a hundred metres of flat sand before a small ridge and a turn to the left led into some dunes that looked large but were mere foothills to the proper dunes lying twenty-nine kilometres ahead.

Like every rider, I roared off the start. With a couple of hundred spectators lining the first quarter mile some of the riders were showing off, leaping over the first ridge and gunning their bikes for all they were worth. I took it easy, then fell on the ridge at the first corner. A very bad start.

After that, it took me ages to calm down. Every rider around me seemed to be fired up by the day ahead and the reverse-order start didn't help. We soon bunched up and it felt like a motocross race as the faster riders caught up with the slower guys and the slower guys tried to ride faster than they normally would. Bikes collided and slipped all over the place. Only twenty or so kilometres into a six-hundred-kilometre special and it was already a mess.

MATT Although scared witless about the stage to Kiffa, I felt fine about the decision for Simon to press ahead if I slowed down. Any realist would have recognised it was the right thing to do and the only hard part for me was knowing that Si felt bad about it.

Starting thirty seconds behind Si, I couldn't help chuckling to myself as he went arse over bollock at the first ridge. After all, I was meant to be the one who struggled in soft sand. Then I thought: Oh fuck, I've got to follow Si through the same soft sand and he's just fallen off. I made it past Simon all right, he caught up and soon we were riding with Nick Plumb, trying to avoid trouble as the field bunched up.

There were bikes everywhere, people falling off and colliding all around us. Plummy, Si and I were riding close together, wading through other riders and cornering on some very soft dunes, when a bike swerved straight into my path. In such deep, soft sand there was nothing I could do. I had to maintain momentum. Unable to slow down or steer out of the way, I had to keep the throttle wide open and go where my bike was taking me – straight into a collision.

I heard the other rider shout out as my handlebar smashed into his navigational gear. Colliding full on at sixty kilometres an hour, there was little I could do except hold on tight and hope I'd be OK. Moving fast, and aware that Plummy was right behind me, I realised I couldn't turn around or look for an escape route because I'd either hit someone else or end up on my arse. It felt like the Charge of the Light Brigade. If you stopped you'd be run over in the stampede. I was just lucky to be on the bigger bike and moving in a straight line when he swerved into me. If the BMW hadn't been such a big old bus I might have been the one left lying on the floor.

'You wiped that geezer out big time!' Plummy yelled as we rode on together through the dunes.

It was all over quickly. I felt slightly guilty, but it was all part of the Dakar lottery.

Shortly before the end of the first major dune set, about ninety kilometres into the special, I lost contact with Simon and Plummy. The moment we'd both dreaded, when Simon would have to tell me he was leaving me behind, never happened. Instead, I went around one side of a dune, Simon went around the other, and, very soon, we were separated as the lie of the dunes forced us further apart.

Approaching the end of that first dune section I was feeling good, but the bike was losing power and struggling to get up the last few dunes, so I stopped to clean out my air filter. It was then, I think, that the gap opened up. By the time I reached the first checkpoint, which marked the end of the dunes, Simon was nowhere to be seen.

I was chuffed with how well I'd done. They were tough dunes and I'd done much better than I'd expected, probably because they came early on in the stage and I was still fresh and energetic. Fifty kilometres further I reached some fast stuff, a gravelly plain that needed to be taken flat out with the throttle on the stop to get as many kilometres in the bag as quickly as possible.

SIMON I didn't see a body, just a destroyed bike. But I knew from where it had happened and from the speed that I was riding – flat out on an open plain – that it had been a very big accident. I noticed it was a Repsol bike, so one of the top riders from one of the top teams. He would have been moving much faster than Nick or me and I immediately thought: He's probably dead. It sent a shiver through me, but the thought of a dead rider lying by the side of the track left my mind just as quickly as it had appeared. Two hundred kilometres into the stage, there's not much else to do but press on. That's the problem. You can't stop. You can't even decide to slow down. No matter what you see out there, you've got to keep going. Otherwise you'll be a statistic too.

But as I rode on I couldn't help wondering if the reverse starting order played a part in the crash. Judging by where it occurred, I suspected he might have been passing through another rider's dust, something which those of us at the back of the field dealt with on every day of the rally. But the stars at the front are not used to it. Always on fresh piste, chasing the dust of a handful of top riders racing at the same pace and rarely affected by the cars, they're not used to riding defensively. I'd become used to riding substantially slower than my capability so that I could keep out of trouble, but the top riders were in a different mindset, one that was only about riding as quick as possible all day.

Matt and I had done well through the dunes. Riding so much better than he had done three days previously, Matt was cracking on. I waited a couple of times when he got stuck or when he fell, and I might have picked him up once or twice, but I was also getting stuck and falling off, using valuable energy just to get myself sorted.

These were ergs, the worst type of dunes; shifting sand that moved with the wind. Often they weren't that large, but they were so soft the sand felt like flour. And because they were always shifting, like slow-moving waves, the softest part was often at the top, just where any rider would want to come off the gas and have a look around to choose the best line. If you did that you'd immediately sink.

Towards the end of the ergs we took separate routes through a large set. It was an area in which I couldn't stop. I needed to fight my way through until I got back on to firmer ground. At the end of it I waited a long time for Matt. When he didn't appear, and unwilling to ride back to find him, I realised the time had come for us to do our own thing, just as we'd agreed.

MATT When I hit the gravelly piste after the dunes I realised there was only one response: go for it. For an hour and a half I rode flat

Hanging out with some local dignitaries in Guinea.

This picture gives a small sense of the scale of the Dakar Rally. It's an astonishing feat of organisation.

A typical scene at the bivouac with the bikes parked outside the support truck – organised chaos!

Ingrained with the dust of Africa, our handmade clutch covers – a nice bit of kit!

Gareth works hard through the night to get Simon's bike ready for the next day's stage. This picture is one for the ladies – or so I'm told . . .

Scores of spectators line the road to watch the rally pass.

Tragically, Andy Caldecott died on this year's Dakar, doing what he loved most. Our thoughts and sympathy go out to those he left behind.

© Race to Dakar 2006

© Photo: DPPI

At the bivouac in Guinea. Simon and Nick Plumb were barely hanging in as they got closer to the finish line.

© Race to Dakar 2006

One of the best things about the rally was meeting all the other amazing bikers. Patsy Quick is a brilliant rider – this was her fourth rally. She's pictured here with her other half, Clive.

Left: Offering as much support as I could to our last rider in the rally, Simon.
Below: The secret hardship of the Dakar . . . nipple rash!

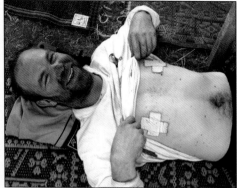

Spot the difference . . . The rally pushed us to the limits of our physical and mental endurance – every day.

Part of what kept Simon going was the thought of being reunited with his wife Linley in Dakar.

The first person I saw when I reached Dakar was Ewan. He'd flown in specially to congratulate the team – he'd been one of our greatest supporters right through our adventures.

Reunited with my beautiful girls, Doone and Kinvara.

I'd put my family through a lot – not only doing the Dakar but also training for it –
I owe them more than a big hug.

Celebrating with Simon on the podium in Dakar. One bike made it home but, despite broken hands and teammates lost in the desert, we all reached Dakar – what an achievement!

After a year's planning and two weeks in the desert, Russ and I had done what we'd set out to do – get to Dakar . . . though perhaps not the way I'd hoped to!

out, the throttle on the stop all the way. It was then that I passed a Repsol bike and realised one of the top riders had crashed. Parts of the bike were strewn across a large area and the body was nowhere near any of them. A medical helicopter had landed nearby; the body was on a stretcher, a blanket covering its face, and I thought: Fuck. It flashed through my mind – shit, someone's badly hurt, maybe dead, and it's a top guy – but I kept pushing. I took it in, but I couldn't let myself think about it too much. It was no time for emotions.

SIMON Thirty kilometres from the first refuel, my bike was dying. I should have been riding flat out, 130kph in top gear, but the fastest it would do was eighty. I needed a new filter but I'd swapped mine for a spare camera unit. It was time for a decision. Did I ride at eighty for the thirty kilometres to CP2, the next checkpoint, and clean the air filter at the same time as refuelling? Or did I change it now? Replacing the filter involved removing the petrol tank, taking out the filter, cleaning it, then reassembling the holder and replacing the tank. I decided to wait until the refuel.

Plummy was at CP2. He'd arrived just five minutes ahead of me, which was a relief because I thought I'd lost more time than that waiting for Matt. I removed my filter and scraped and banged it to clean out as much dust and sand as I could. I spent more time on it than it needed but I wanted to be meticulous and it paid off. Straight out of the refuel I was back to top speed, overtaking a gaggle of riders that had passed me on the stretch leading into CP2. About twenty kilometres down the piste, I passed a Euromaster team rider. He waved me down and, against my better judgement, I pulled over. He had a broken mousse so there was little I could do, but I did give him a tyre lever. While I was unpacking my tool kit, the riders I'd recently

213

overtaken all roared by. Just what I needed: another ten dust clouds to ride through. The Euromaster rider removed his tyre and I left him preparing to ride on the rim with the tyre around his waist.

By early afternoon, I'd reached the second major dune set, a 166-kilometre stretch of ergs. Riding on my own, I struggled through, frequently falling or sinking into the sand and pushing my bike as much as riding. My lungs felt ready to burst and the bike was overheating so I pulled up at the top of a small dune to take stock and decide which line to take. As I stopped, another bike pulled up on the same crest.

'Wotcha, mate!' It was Plummy.

I was too breathless to reply.

'Did you see Caldecott? I've heard he's dead.'

I hadn't realised it was a fellow Aussie. Plummy told me that when he went past he saw that a blanket covered Caldecott's body and the medics were walking away. The message was clear: there was nothing that could be done.

'I saw him,' I said, 'but I didn't know who it was.'

I thought back to the petrol station in Lisbon, where we'd bumped into Andy before the race. I didn't know Andy well, but I'd met him on previous Dakars and he was a nice guy with a reputation as a bit of a prankster. I remembered how he'd told me his wife was expecting their second child and it was a freak thing that he was in Lisbon. He hadn't been expecting to ride the Dakar and he hadn't trained for most of the year but one of the Repsol riders picked up an injury two weeks before the start of the rally, so the team offered him a ride.

It seemed incredible that another factory rider had been killed after Fabrizio Meoni died on the same stage the previous year. Usually it was privateers that died after getting lost in the desert. I'd always thought that was a more likely path to death than an accident while riding. Plenty of privateers had been left in the desert for several days with no water, freezing their nuts off at night and suffering heatstroke in the day. They were on their own with few resources, in motorcycle kit and boots which aren't particularly appropriate for traipsing across the desert.

A couple of days before the rest day, I'd seen the team riders go past for the first time. Although I was amazed at the speed at which they were riding I could see that just one mistake and they were in serious trouble. Andy would have been walking that tightrope without a safety net.

Endless dunes stretched out in every direction from where Nick and I were standing, all of them soft and featureless. We could see vehicles moving in most directions, plumes of sand spraying into the air as they churned across the ergs. The road-book was blank except for a compass heading and an instruction to follow the line between the white and the orange dunes, as if it was possible to tell them apart. Not knowing which way to go, we realised our only option was to take pot-luck. From our GPS we could see that we were within three kilometres of a waypoint, but in soft sand it was still a hell of a long way.

'We're here together.' I shrugged. 'Let's go together.'

The agreement was no more than security for the inevitability of either one of us getting totally bogged down. Most of the time we rode our own courses, digging out our bikes with our hands and getting them moving on our own, but keeping an eye on each other. It was the only way to do it – if we had helped each other every time one of us fell over we would never have moved on – and we helped each other only a couple of times in that set of dunes.

On one occasion, I'd sunk so deep into the crest of a dune that I just couldn't drag the bike over the top. Again and again I laid the bike down on its side, dug the wheels out, put it on a fresh patch of sand and then pushed like fuck while gunning the engine. And time and time again it sank up to the mudguards. I managed to turn the bike around and ride it back down into a bowl, which I intended to ride around until I'd built up enough speed to get over the crest of the dune, but the sand at the bottom was even softer than at the crest. Again I was stuck.

Nick appeared at the top of the bowl. The obvious line for him was to ride down into the bowl and over the next dune, but when he saw me stuck at the bottom he stopped.

While Nick and I worked out what to do, Patsy and Clive sped past on their lighter KTM bikes, skimming over the sand with apparent ease while our bikes lay buried.

CHARLEY Coming off the plane at Kiffa, I could tell something was up. An unusual atmosphere shrouded the airfield. As I approached the media and medical tents at the side of the airfield I bumped into Chris Evans.

'Charley . . . have you heard?' Chris looked shaken. 'Andy Caldecott's died.'

He told me what had happened and I immediately thought of Caldecott's pregnant wife Tracey, his daughter and the child Tracey was carrying. It would never know its father.

I imagined what Tracey was going through right then – the phone call we all dread coming in the middle of the night. She would have known something was up the moment she heard the caller's voice. In that moment, her life would have changed completely. One phone call and a family wrecked.

I thought of my family at home and burst into tears. It was difficult to make sense of my feelings. I thought of Meoni, who had won the Dakar twice but last year died of a heart attack after a crash, the second rider to die in that year's rally.

Shortly before the rally Meoni said in a magazine interview that he couldn't think of a better way for a racer to die than on the Dakar. I could understand what he meant. In a sense he and Caldecott would have died happy, caught in the moment of what they loved doing most, but that failed to take account of the utter devastation of their families.

It made me feel a selfish prick for risking my health and my life, even though the way I had been riding paled in comparison with the risks Caldecott or Meoni took. Nevertheless, in some ways it felt worse. Their job was to ride rallies and their wives knew the risks when they married them. I didn't have that excuse.

When I thought of the hundreds of wives, girlfriends and families at home, waiting and staring at their computer screens, watching the Iritraq symbols just to see if their husband, boyfriend or father was still alive, I couldn't understand why anyone wanted to do the Dakar. At a time like this, it felt a very dumb race.

A grim-faced Repsol team manager held an impromptu press conference on the airfield. Caldecott, he said, had crashed at about 11.30 a.m., about a third of the way into the special. The helicopter landed at five to twelve and he was confirmed dead two minutes later. Caldecott was the twenty-third competitor to die in twenty-eight Dakar rallies.

Everyone was very subdued, but there was also a spirit of the show having to go on. We didn't have time to think too deeply about the tragedy. We needed to check the whereabouts of Simon and Matt; we needed to set up the pits; and we needed to prepare for the rest of the day ahead.

MATT I reached the second dune set and it was hard. Really deep soft sand. I got stuck and fell off so many times I lost count – thirty or forty times at least. Mid-afternoon, stuck in a bowl and absolutely stuffed, I climbed to the top of a dune and lay down on the sand. Bikes were stranded everywhere around me. *Bollocks*, I thought, I've had enough of this.

Smaller, lighter bikes that I'd passed on the gravel plain, when I was riding flat out and putting my life on the line, were now zipping over the dunes. Lying on the top of the dune for about half an hour, I watched as a helicopter circled overhead filming the carnage.

I dug the bike out with my hands and got it going, building up speed until I reached a small dune. Taking it at speed, I jumped off the top and landed on the front wheel on the down slope. The front of the bike sank deep into the sand, stopped abruptly and sent me flying over the handlebars.

I wasn't hurt, but I knew I'd had enough. It was too bloody much. I clambered to the top of a high dune, where I sat staring into the distance. All I could hear was shouting, screaming and the whine of bikes getting stuck. I spotted Patsy and Clive in the distance, their bikes dancing over the sand, then called Jane, my girlfriend, using my satellite phone.

'Caldecott's dead,' Jane said as soon as she heard my voice. I realised then who I'd seen lying at the side of the piste.

We chatted for a short while and I told Jane I was exhausted but all right. After the phone call I started thinking about the reality of my situation. It was about half past four and I had maybe another two hours of sunlight. If I made it through this dune set before dusk I would have another hundred kilometres of fast riding on gravel in the dark ahead of me, then the final forty kilometres of dunes. I climbed on to a higher dune and looked ahead. I could see a truck moving across relatively flat terrain. If I can get there, I thought, then I might be OK.

But then I thought of Caldecott and realised what I was risking. I was already exhausted. If I kept going I'd have nothing left. And if I got stuck out in the dunes, injured or too weak to think about basic survival, I could get into serious trouble. I'm not going to do it any more, I thought. This is stupid.

I rang Jane again. 'That's it,' I said. 'I've stopped. It's over.'

'Thank God for that.'

I started to cry, I don't know why. It was probably relief more than anything. I was gutted after all the hard work and effort everybody had put in, but I'd given it my best.

I'd enjoyed it in a perverse way, but it had also been hell, taking everything I had out of me, emotionally, physically and mentally. Unable to imagine what kind of sadistic bastards had devised such a race I vowed never to come back.

I called the organisers. They told me the sweeper truck would pick me up, but I could see from the carnage that it was going to take a long time to reach me. I'd have to end my Dakar sleeping in the dunes.

SIMON At times the only way to get through the dunes was to turn the bike into a two-wheel drive, inching it forward at half a mile an hour with one of us at the front pulling the fork leg and turning the front wheel, the other at the back, pushing and revving the motor. Even then the back would suddenly slip down into sand and we'd have to dig out the bike. And when we did get the bike moving we would have to try to go from pushing to jumping on the thing but, more often than not, as soon as we got on the bike it started to sink again, so we'd either rev the nuts out of it or, if we could, pull it up a gear, increase the speed and rise on top of the sand. It would have been easy on a light bike but our Beamers weren't nimble enough to get up, so we stayed down in the gears, revving it. Although they'd performed flawlessly and been strong as oxen, they were just too much bike for the dunes.

219

On two of the many times I buried my bike in the crest of a soft dune a Dutch girl got stuck in the same place. We helped each other both times, then inevitably started to talk about what the hell we were doing in the desert. She was twenty-two years old and had always wanted to do the Dakar. She'd ridden only motocross until recently and had never ridden an enduro event. She had always thought she wouldn't have a go at the Dakar until she was in her thirties, but she'd finished studying and was living at home without a job or commitments so she thought she'd give it a go. With only three months' training, this slip of a girl was more than halfway through the hardest day of the rally. I thought she was amazing.

Towards the end of the second long dune set it all started to fall into place. Maybe it was a slightly better line or just one mile an hour more momentum, but I passed through the dunes beautifully and made it to the top of a section of high ground then stopped to look back for Plummy. I could see him struggling to cross a rise and watched him turn his bike around, sweep around the rise and blast back along the course, building up speed for another attempt.

Again Plummy got stuck, so he tried again, riding against the traffic and almost crashing head-on into a car coming blind around a dune. On the fourth attempt he made it over the rise and eventually we were approaching the end of the second major dune set.

My bike was making a horrible noise, like the chain was jumping off the sprockets, and I was exhausted, so I stopped on one of the last dunes. A stony plain was now in sight, stretching out into the distance. I walked back across some dunes, looking for Plummy. I spotted him struggling but still moving, and wanted to help. I'd taken my jacket off and replaced my helmet with my cap. My shirt was soaked and in the fierce heat I was dehydrating quickly. With less than a litre of drinking water left I was concerned we'd soon be suffering heat exhaustion. I helped Plummy get going. Then, as I started back towards my bike, I saw a helicopter coming in to land beside a truck that had broken down. I ran back to my bike, jumped on it and, with Plummy, altered our course out of the dunes to get across to where the chopper had landed. The pilot let us top up our water holders. With three litres of water on board things were looking up.

As soon as we got moving, my bike made a noise that was even worse than earlier, so I stopped. I tightened the chain – which seemed to solve the problem – then looked around. No sign of Plummy. I spotted some bikes about three hundred metres away, following a different line through the dunes. Maybe, I thought, Plummy had followed that route and didn't notice that I'd stopped to fix my bike. I walked over to the other track, then back to my bike. Still no sign of him. And all the time this was going on, a nagging voice in my head was reminding me that I needed to get moving.

We'd made a pact to stick together. Now I was worried that Plummy might think I'd deserted him. Not knowing whether he was in front or behind – and suspecting he was just as confused about my whereabouts – I didn't know whether to press on or to wait. Either option, if wrong, would increase our separation.

While I was wondering what to do, Mike, an American competitor riding with a broken wrist wrapped in plaster, passed nearby. I waved him down and asked him if he'd seen Nick.

'There's no one back there,' he said. 'I've not seen a soul.'

In a way, it was exactly what I wanted to hear. I really didn't want to ride back through the dunes in search of Plummy. Mike's answer gave me an excuse to press on.

Settled in a rhythm, I continued through the dunes, thinking I was doing well until I reached a deep bowl in which a television crew was filming some cars that were stuck. The only way out for

221

me was to ride against the traffic, like Plummy had done earlier, building up enough momentum to take me through the bowl by circling around it, then riding to the top, turning quickly at its lip hoping that no other vehicle was about to come over the crest, then riding as fast I could down the slope of the bowl, across a strip of grass at its bottom and up the far slope, over the lip and on to the next dune.

Trucks and cars were passing through the bowl all the time. Not knowing whether the next one was five minutes or ten seconds away I persuaded one of the television crew to stand lookout at the top of the dune while I begged one of his colleagues, a cameraman, to give me a shove to get out.

'We've got to go . . . we've got to go,' the cameraman yelled. A helicopter was whirring into action nearby, its rotors whipping up a sandstorm.

'Just give me thirty seconds of your time,' I shouted.

With his help I got on to the plain I'd seen in the distance earlier. Without the cameraman's help, my Dakar hopes might have ended in that bowl.

Ahead lay a long succession of gravelly plains, each stretching for about five kilometres and punctuated by short dune sections lasting maybe one or two kilometres. The plains gave me a chance to get my breath back and refresh my energy so that I could keep my head and pick good lines through the dune sections. I cracked on and got the miles done, but there was still no sign of Plummy.

The sun was starting to come down, my shadow stretching further in front of me as I rode on. I saw the occasional car but didn't see another bike for hours. As dusk approached, I was totally on my own, no other vehicle anywhere in sight. I was getting worried that no one would find me if I made a mistake or crashed, but I had to press on.

*

CHARLEY Russ was the first to hear that Matt had dropped out of the rally, but it wasn't from the most reliable source. An official told Russ that a friend of his who was working on one of the checkpoints thought one of our team had dropped out. When the official questioned it, his mate said 'not the one with the bandaged hands and not Simon Pavey, because I know him, but the other one.'

MATT Darkness was approaching and I was fading fast. Feeling wrecked, I was dehydrated and not quite sure what was going on around me. I thought I heard a helicopter land nearby. Then a woman, a medic I think, appeared and asked me if I was all right. Before I had a chance to answer properly I heard a shout from another rider some distance to the left of me and the woman ran off in his direction. A few minutes later the helicopter airlifted the other rider to safety and I was alone again.

Straining to shake some lucid thoughts into my head, I tried to face the facts. It would soon be dark. I needed to get my lifesaving kit and emergency beacons off my bike and set up somewhere I could safely spend the night. However, the kit was on the bike which was wedged in sand up to its mudguards and I couldn't dig it out.

'*Cent soixante-treize*! *Cent soixante-treize*!' I heard a male voice in the distance. Then I realised he was calling out my number. Maybe the medical team on the helicopter had alerted an ambulance on the ground.

Through my semi-delirium I spotted a young man approaching. He said something about dehydration then urged me to follow him to an ambulance. Hurrying me through the dunes, he explained the four-wheel-drive ambulance couldn't get to me because the sand was too soft.

'*Vite!*' he said. 'Quick! Before it's dark.'

Still dressed in my heavy protective clothing, wearing my

motocross boots and carrying all the electronic kit from my bike –
the GPS, Iritraq and communications equipment – I struggled to
keep up with him, sinking up to my knees in the soft sand as he
strode ahead. Every ten or fifteen steps the French medic would
stop, look back at me and gruffly order me to get a move on.
Warning of the dangers of getting caught in the dunes in the dark,
he never offered to give me hand with my heavy kit and clothing.
I felt like I was being punished for stopping.

A long slog through the sand later, I was safely ensconced in
the back seat of the ambulance, sipping water and feeling relieved
that I was on my way home.

SIMON Shortly before darkness fell I reached the second refuel,
111 kilometres from the end of the special section. With only a
handful of riders refuelling, and having lost so much time in the
dunes and not seeing Patsy and Clive since they shot ahead, I felt
I was lagging a long way behind the rest of the field. My fears
were confirmed when the Euromaster rider I'd met earlier arrived
while I was topping up my tank. Since I'd left him riding on his
rim he'd found an abandoned KTM bike, removed its rear wheel,
managed to bodge it on to his Yamaha, tied the brake calliper to
the outside of his bike's swing arm and somehow made it work.
Nothing, it seemed, was going to stop him finishing.

Before setting off for the final stretch to the liaison I asked the
refuelling officials if they'd seen Plummy. They hadn't. I felt bad.
I'd left him behind and part of me felt I should turn around and
find him. But I also knew that Plummy was resourceful and
determined, and that there was very little I could do.

By the time the sun was setting at 6.28 p.m. I'd made up some
ground but still had about eighty kilometres of alternating plains
and dunes to ride to the liaison. At least I was still on the rally, I
was still cracking on and there was still hope. The only problem

was I had now entered a section of dunes that were firmer than the ergs but almost as high as mountains. Beneath the drifting sand covering the dunes was hard stone that occasionally uncovered to create short stony paths at the top of a dune. Although the light was fading I could still see well enough to pick lines along the hard ridges instead of joining the many cars and bikes getting stuck on the long, soft climbs straight up the faces of the dunes.

By the time it was totally dark I'd reached a section of softer dunes and very soft sandy piste. At times the piste was so soft it was easier to ride to the side of it through camel grass, between stones and across harsh bumps. In an attempt to minimise the punishment any single part of my body was taking I swapped between soft piste and bumpy off-piste every few minutes. The bumps on the piste were less jarring but the softer sand was less forgiving and demanded greater commitment – I had to ride it faster and harder to avoid losing control of the front wheel. The off-piste bumps gave my legs a battering but I could be more reserved in my riding, chugging along in a lower gear, giving the engine a chance to cool down after the constant high-revolution labour necessary to keep the bike surging through soft sand. Chopping and changing tracks also kept my brain engaged through the many tens of kilometres.

Then the bike stopped. With no warning she suddenly cut out. Jacket off, helmet off, head torch out. Hoping there would be a simple answer, I went back to basics and checked all the main parts. Then I looked in the main tank. It was bone dry. I thought back to the refuel. I was convinced I'd filled it up to the brim, and with less than 120 kilometres from the refuel to the finish of the special there was no reason to run out.

I checked my front tanks. They were full, so there was obviously a problem with the fuel feed. I removed one of the front tanks, poured some gas in the main tank and the engine fired up straight away. Relief! Thank God it was something simple. I connected a long breather hose from the front tanks to the main tank and sat beside my bike for half an hour waiting for all the fuel to siphon between tanks.

'All right, boy?' It was Plummy. He'd turned up while I was sorting out my gas flow problems and he had a plan. Nick had rigged a full-power xenon headlight to his helmet. It was madness. He had zip-tied a huge high-intensity discharge transformer – labelled: 'Beware. 5,000 volts. Dangerous to Life' – to the jaw-piece of his helmet. The transformer was needed to punch a high voltage into the bulb to ionise the gas. But there was beauty in Nick's madness. Once it fired, the xenon lamp produced the equivalent of 150 watts of lighting power but drew only 35 watts from the batteries.

Other riders had tried similar systems but had failed to find a way of firing up the bulb with the transformer mounted on the bike. With a longer cable the voltage drop was too great. Nick, who had spent months developing his helmet light, had worked out the only solution: strap the transformer to your helmet.

We spent the best part of an hour stripping back wires to get Nick's light set up correctly. A medical team in a four-wheel drive gave us a terminal block to connect two sets of wires. Then, fortified with some food and water from the medical team, we set off into the dark.

Nick's light saved our skins. A few kilometres further on we came to dunes just as bad as the ergs in which we'd become separated that afternoon, but with Nick's light we could see for several kilometres from a high vantage point and choose the best lines. It was awesome.

MATT Inside the ambulance, a bottle of water and a ration pack in my hands, I felt immense relief that I was at last on my way out of the desert. Suddenly things looked a lot better. How bad is this? A taxi home? This Dakar's not so bad after all.

Despite its four-wheel drive, the ambulance got stuck in the dunes four or five times as we slowly moved ahead, passing race trucks, Unimog trucks, cars and bikes stranded in the sand or wedged in gullies. It looked like a war zone.

Every few hundred metres there was a sight that made my eyes pop out. Race lorries, supposedly capable of grinding through anything, were stuck. This was some race, the craziest thing I'd ever seen. People were lying on the ground, injured or tired out of their brains. It was more like a battle than a rally.

The doctor was a fantastic driver. When he couldn't find a firm route through the carnage he got out of the ambulance, climbed a couple of dunes and worked out a way ahead. Slowly but surely, he was getting through, even with a ton of gear in the back, while race vehicles were sinking deeper into the sand all around him.

About an hour after we set off we'd ground our way through a few kilometres when we came across a rider unconscious on the ground, his helmet cracked and his face a mess. There was blood everywhere. He appeared to have gone over his handlebars and was in a bad way.

Helping the medics by holding a drip while they stuck an intravenous needle into the rider, I could see the doctor who had picked me up was very concerned. Although I couldn't understand everything he was saying I spoke enough French to work out that he was trying to call in a medevac helicopter, which couldn't land because it was dark.

'We're going to have to take him in the ambulance,' the medic said.

It meant there would be no space for me. They somehow managed to squeeze the rider into the back of the ambulance Jeep, then assured me a sweeper truck would pick me up within the hour.

I climbed to the top of a nearby dune as the ambulance moved slowly away. All around me the night was lit up by batteries of spotlights on the top of stranded trucks. From every direction I could hear the sound of motors battling to drive vehicles through the sand.

After a few hours it became apparent that the promised rescue would not be arriving soon, if at all. The reason was simple: there were enough stranded competitors to fill a squadron of sweeper trucks. With the temperature dropping fast I realised I was going to be stuck in the desert for the night with nothing but the clothes on my back. Thinking I'd be picked up soon after the ambulance left with the unconscious rider, I'd left my water, rations and silver emergency blanket in the Jeep. And the medics hadn't returned all of my safety equipment. Without my GPS, Iritraq or balise emergency beacon, I couldn't determine my position, contact ASO headquarters or call for help. I didn't even have a watch. No one – including me – knew where I was and there was no obvious way for me to call for assistance.

A short while later I spotted a television crew in a four-wheel drive and begged them to take me out of the desert. 'I'm in the shit here. I've got nothing,' I pleaded with the cameraman. 'Please help me get out of here.'

The cameraman appeared sympathetic, but he refused. 'No . . . no, wait here. There'll be a *balai* along soon.' He was referring to the *camion balai* – the sweeper truck. 'Don't worry about it.'

A few other race vehicles passed by in the night. I waved them all down and asked those that stopped to give me a lift. All of them refused.

CHARLEY Lucy phoned shortly after dark to confirm that Matt had dropped out of the rally. All she'd been able to find out from ASO headquarters was that he'd been picked up by an ambulance but had been dropped off a few kilometres further down the track beside the bike belonging to rider 122 because the other guy was in a much worse condition. Things were very sketchy, but I was confident the ambulance people wouldn't have dropped him off without informing ASO of his whereabouts. And if that failed I felt sure the sweeper truck would pick him up, even if it took a long time.

I could only speculate about why he'd stopped. Maybe he was exhausted. Or maybe it was a mental thing, a lack of the experience that Simon had and which might have helped him to dig deeper, knowing the end would eventually come. But after seeing him at breakfast that morning, frightened about what lay ahead and appearing to think he'd be lucky to get through it, I wasn't surprised he was no longer in the race, not least because, by nightfall, it was apparent that most of the field was still stuck in the desert.

Inevitably thoughts of Caldecott's death returned as I waited for Simon – and maybe Matt – to return. Walking from the far end of the airfield, where I could monitor their positions on the Iritraq displays, to the far end of the bivouac where we'd set up our pits with the Bowler trucks, I couldn't get Andy's crash out of my head. None of it made any sense; it was just another unresolved emotion to add to the mess of thoughts surrounding the stresses, challenges and seeming futility of the rally.

At about 10 p.m. I approached the ASO tent, hoping to find out a bit more about Matt's whereabouts. The official had a much more detailed interactive map than that on the Iritiraq system and was able to pinpoint the position of bike 122, where I thought Matt was now stranded. I emphasised that although rider 122 had been picked up from his bike Matt now needed rescuing from the same position. If I told enough people, I thought, then maybe he'd be all right.

I phoned Lucy and told her to reassure Matt, the next time he phoned, that a lot of people were out there looking for him, but that it was likely to take a long time. Lucy said he'd sounded dehydrated and quite spaced out the last time she'd spoken to him. I reassured her that Matt would be in a much better state now. Surely, I told Lucy, the ambulance crew would not have left Matt without food, water, a blanket and communications equipment.

About half an hour later my satellite phone rang. It was Matt's father. He'd been trying to call Matt but had dialled my number by mistake. He sounded very worried. As with Lucy, I tried to reassure him that Matt was safe.

'Matt's fine,' I said, not knowing for sure if that was the case. 'He's not injured. And he might have been dehydrated earlier but they've left him with plenty of water and they know exactly where he is. He'll be picked up very soon and on his way to safety.'

Almost immediately after I finished speaking to Matt's father the phone rang again. It was Jane, his girlfriend. I could hear the panic in her voice, even though she was trying to put up a positive front.

'I promise you he'll be fine,' I said. 'He's OK. He's in good health. He's got water. Everyone knows where he is. He's all right.'

I could tell she was in bits. I only hoped that she couldn't tell that I didn't quite believe the reassurances I'd just given her.

As the long night wore on I became increasingly concerned about Matt and whether the organisation really knew that he was with bike 122. I spoke to Jim, who was as pragmatic as usual.

'How long's he been in the desert?'

'One day.'

'Nothing to worry about. It's when it gets to two days you got to worry.'

*

SIMON The last set of dunes were just as soft as the ergs we'd crossed at midday and again bikes, cars and trucks were strewn across every slope and stuck in every bowl. People and vehicles were everywhere, all of them privateers. Any factory rider still out there would have called for the helicopter and gone home. They'd be too far behind the race leaders to catch up with the rest of the top racers and they wouldn't want to risk injury in the dark.

With no obvious direction through the dunes Nick and I stuck to the main body of tracks, but at least we had Nick's xenon helmet light to find a route across them and over the ruts, rather than having to force our bikes through sand that had already been ground to a fine dust.

After seventeen hours on the stage we had a new problem. Our bikes were now overheating constantly because we were revving the nuts out of the engines to get the bikes through the soft stuff. And I felt the same as my engine – although the temperature in the desert had plummeted after sunset, I was baking hot and sweating inside my kit because of the extreme exertion needed to force my bike through the dune.

We'd heard from a Spanish guy on a BMW that two guys in his team had been forced out of the race when they kept going after the red light came on. They blew their engines, so we were determined not to ignore the warning to stop. We'd ride for ten minutes, praying all the while that our engines wouldn't blow up, then we'd stop for just as long to let our engines cool, but it seemed to do little good. Within a few minutes of moving off the red warning light would come on again. And we'd already seen several KTMs that night which didn't have warning lights and had been forced to stop after their cooling systems boiled over. That was the worst that could happen. It would mean using valuable drinking water to cool the bike down.

While this was going on, we came across a rider standing in the middle of a stretch of piste between the dunes, waving us down.

'Please help me,' he yelled. 'My bike's in a hole.'

I looked at Plummy. He shrugged. 'OK . . . right, yeah, let's just do it,' he said.

'Where is it?' I said.

I was expecting to be led into a bowl between the dunes, but the rider took us along the piste and pointed at the ground. Just as he said, his bike was in a hole. A perfect bike-sized hole.

As we looked at it, I couldn't think what the hell to do. Then I realised there was nothing for it but brute force. Plummy, the rider and I heaved and dragged until we got the KTM out of the hole.

'There you are,' I said. Plummy just nodded. I could tell he wanted to get going.

'Oh please wait while I get it started,' the rider said. 'I can't start it unless you hold the bike up.' His electric starter had broken, but he couldn't kick-start it without standing on the foot pegs.

'Just get off it!' This hapless rider was starting to exasperate me. 'I'll start it.'

'Si, don't wear yourself out,' Nick insisted.

'I just want to start it because I want to go . . .'

Having ridden KTMs for years I thought it would be easy, but he had left the fuel on while his bike was upside down in the hole so the engine was flooded. Nothing for it but to push in the decompressor, crank the throttle fully open and keep kicking it until all the fuel had cleared out. It took at least forty kick-starts to empty the stale fuel out of the cylinder, then another ten or fifteen kicks in a normal starting procedure to get the engine going.

By the time I'd started his bike the rider had run out of ways to thank me. He rode with us for a stretch of the dunes, until we reached a high point where he signalled for Nick and me to pull over.

'I've got the unblocking code for the GPS,' he said. 'Come with me. Follow me. It's only twenty-five or thirty ks to the liaison. We'll just go on the GPS.'

Plummy and I answered as one: 'Naaaa . . .'

Having looked at the road-book, which indicated a track in the opposite direction to the bearing given by the GPS, we were determined to stick to the official track.

'No . . . no, come with me,' the rider insisted. 'It's only thirty kilometres straight line, but forty-five on the road-book.'

We turned him down again and he rode off. It was his first Dakar and he thought he was doing the right thing, but I was totally convinced our method of sticking to the road-book was best. There would be a reason why the road-book didn't match the GPS and was showing forty-five kilometres. It would take us round the worst of the dunes.

Having lost at least half an hour helping him we were determined to press on, but two kilometres further into the next set of dunes two more guys on bikes waved us down in a bowl. This time we couldn't stop. At some point we had to make that horrible decision not even to look at stricken riders and to drive straight past. This was that time. We had our momentum and we had to keep going for as long as we could before the overheating engines forced us to stop.

'You know that was Tom back there?' Nick said the next time we stopped. Tom was a South African rider we'd met on previous Dakars.

'I didn't see who it was,' I said. He'd been just some guy with a pair of jump leads in his hands, stuck at the bottom of a sand bowl. 'Sorry, but there was no way I was stopping on this bike. I'd never get out myself.'

Nevertheless, I hated riding past stranded riders. It was heartbreaking to ignore their pleas for help but, having spent so much time digging out that rider's bike and getting it started, we now needed to think of ourselves.

We continued through the dunes, caning the arse off the Beamers to get them across each dune then stopping for short rests to give our engines a chance to cool. At one stop, a Swiss rider came over.

'I've broken my clutch,' he said. 'I've got a spare one but I don't know how to fix it.'

After so many maydays, I'd had enough. 'Right? So what are you saying here? You want me to fix your clutch?' I said. 'It's not that hard. You just take the side cover off. It's obvious what to do.'

'OK, I'll wait until first light,' he said.

The further we went, the more I felt sorry for those riders who'd been forced to stop. It wasn't just the frustration of having made it further towards the end of the special; it was also because the further you were down the piste, the longer it would take for the *camion balai* to pick you up. And when it did arrive, there was a greater chance of it being full. Towards the end of the special there was only one option if you wanted to get out of the race quickly: jump on your own arm. With a broken arm you could call a helicopter for evacuation. That was why many riders joked that broken ribs were the best injury because you could fake them. With an arm or a leg, you actually had to break it.

We continued, riding for hours by the light of the helmet light until – and I'd thought I'd seen it all on the Dakar – we came across a group of Italian tourists standing beside ten four-wheel-drive cars. In the middle of the night, thirty to forty Italians stood cheering on the rally in the middle of the desert. It was such a surprise that we rode over to them and Plummy collapsed on the ground in front of them. They loved it and were fantastic, cheering us and patting us on the back.

'It's only eight kilometres to the finish,' one of the Italians said. 'You've just come over the last dune.'

I could just see a flashing orange light in the distance. It indicated the end of the special.

'You've done it, bro!' another of the Italians said.

They gave us food and water, but the best thing they passed on to us was their spirit of boundless optimism. It did us good.

'Keep going!' they shouted. 'Nearly home!'

'Thanks, guys, thanks,' I said. It meant a lot to us. They picked Plummy off the ground, we took a few photographs and then we cruised to the finish, the sound of their cheers fading in the distance.

Chapter 13

10 AND 11 JANUARY
Kiffa to Bamako

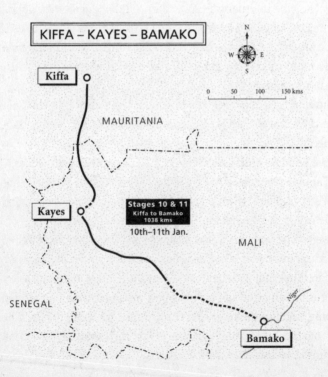

KIFFA – KAYES – BAMAKO

N
W E
S

Kiffa

0   50   100   150 kms

MAURITANIA

Kayes

Stages 10 & 11
Kiffa to Bamako
1038 kms
10th–11th Jan.

MALI

SENEGAL

Niger

Bamako

CHARLEY Quarter past three in the morning and I was hating every moment of the waiting game. With no news from Matt since early evening and no idea of Simon's whereabouts since the Iritraq screens at the airfield were switched off at 10 p.m., I was in bits. All the crew – Russ, Gareth, Wolfgang and Jim – were up and waiting for news of our boys. I struggled to find anyone from the organisers' team and, when I did, they didn't speak good enough English for me to be convinced they were the right person to help me.

I felt I'd had more than enough. It was the pits. The uncertainty was more than I could handle and I was so anxious I couldn't eat. Even if Simon arrived fairly soon he'd be able to have only four or five hours' sleep before setting off on the next stage. Then the infernal waiting game would begin all over again. The organisers had cancelled the stage from Kiffa to Kayes as a mark of respect for Andy Caldecott, but Simon would still have to ride more than three hundred off-road kilometres. They just wouldn't be timed.

I thought I'd got over the panic and anxiety after I crashed out of the rally, but the waiting was even worse for my nerves than competing. A horrible feeling.

Clive Dredge, husband of Patsy Quick as well as her mechanic and team manager, tried to console me. This was his fourth Dakar with Patsy and he'd spent many more long nights than me waiting for his riders to come home.

'Every time you hear a bike you pray it's yours,' he said. 'When they're out there you just don't know where they are and I'm sure you can think of a thousand scenarios for Si. But you have to try and brush them aside and say: No, he's just on the side of the road sleeping because the road's so straight now he'll fall asleep if he stays on the bike. You've got to stick with that. If you think anything else you'll go mad.'

They were wise words indeed and just what I needed to hear in the small hours.

SIMON Reaching the end of the special was really no more than a false dawn. Although we could stock up on food rations, fuel and water at the checkpoint we still had more than 240 kilometres to ride to the bivouac. In some ways the fact that it was a fairly good tarmac road made it worse. Dog-tired, the thought of having to ride for another three or four hours on a monotonous path was a scary one. And if you fall asleep on a bike you're going to make a mess of yourself.

Nick and I had something to eat, then I set the alarm on my watch and we kipped for an hour by the side of the road. When we woke up, and just as we were pulling on our kit, the rider that we'd pulled out of a hole and who had decided to follow the straight line indicated by his GPS turned up. Judging by the time he'd taken to catch up with us we'd been right to stick to the road-book.

'Please help me!' he begged. 'I need help.'

He was starting to sound like a scratched record, but it transpired he just wanted someone to ride with. However, we needed to get going so we left him getting ready to sleep by the road.

After about eighty kilometres, I had to stop again. 'Plummy, I'm sorry, mate. If you want to go on, then go. I've got to stop. I just need ten minutes to get my helmet off and wake myself up a bit.'

I lay down at the side of the road, still with all my kit and helmet on. I fell asleep immediately. Completely gone. An hour later I woke up. Plummy was asleep beside me. I woke him and we climbed back on our bikes for what we hoped would be the last leg. This time Plummy struggled to keep awake but eventually we arrived at the bivouac. No fanfare. No fireworks. Just the satisfaction that we'd done it. Gareth, Wolfgang, Charley and Russ were ecstatic as we rolled into our little encampment. They all jumped up and dived in to sort us out. Charley got some food; Wolfgang and Gareth started servicing the bikes straight away. A tent was ready for us to crash out in for a couple of hours before the ride to Kayes. Providing we departed by 10 a.m., we'd still be in the rally.

CHARLEY Awake all night waiting for Simon and Nick, thinking every minute they might arrive, I'd convinced myself that one of them wasn't going to make it. When they both rode into the pits I felt like crying.

I made them chuck some breakfast down their throats before sleeping then brought them some more food when they woke up. In the meantime, Simon's bike had been given the minimum service but, thanks to Gareth and Wolfgang's quick work, it was ready to tackle the next stage.

As I watched Simon and Nick ride out of the bivouac I felt enormous pride and confidence in Simon and his ability. I knew he wouldn't do anything stupid and that he would know when to stop. Even at 6 a.m. he'd come in with a smile cracking his face. He was an incredibly tough fucker. My only worry was that the bike was going to let him down, or that the tyre mousses would give way; something that would be a cruel blow for all of us. I was desperate for him to finish, not just because it would be good for the team but because I'd come to see how much it meant to him.

MATT I must have fallen asleep at some point. When I woke up, it was light, maybe 5 or 6 a.m. Everything and everyone was gone. All of the lorries and cars that had been stuck had now disappeared.

Paranoia set in. I started to analyse my situation, going through what had happened. I reasoned that if the medics hadn't recorded the GPS point at which they dropped me off nobody would know where I was.

I went through my options. I got through to Lucy on the satellite phone and relayed a message that I was still out in the desert. After the farce of chopping and changing vehicle, it was a relief to know someone was making efforts to alert the authorities to my position.

Nearby were two broken bikes. One of them belonged to a Spanish rider on the Gauloises team who'd taken a big crash. His bike was smashed to pieces, yet another warning sign that this was a sport for crazy men. Looking at his bike and my predicament, I didn't think I'd ever be back. It was too hard, too fast and too dangerous.

The other bike looked like it might work. If the worst came to the worst, I decided, I could at least try to ride it out of the desert. But in which direction? I didn't have any navigation equipment. And, without a watch, when would I know that the worst had come to the worst?

I got up and looked at the damaged bike. Shivering in the post-dawn cold, I noticed it still had its road-book in it, so I could navigate to some extent without recourse to a GPS. As I was standing there, wondering how long it would take for the sun to rise high enough to take the chill off the desert, it started to rain. I couldn't believe it. I was stranded in the Sahara desert, famous for being one of the most arid places on the planet, and it was raining. Not just a light drizzle, but proper English rain. It was pissing down. Now I was wet as well as cold, with no shelter in sight.

Scanning the horizon for somewhere to get out of the rain, I spotted some kids' heads popping over the tops of dunes. These young nomads showed little sign of being interested in me – they must have seen dozens of stranded riders and vehicles already – and gave no indication of wanting to help. I then spotted another bike, about five hundred metres across the dunes. Brilliant, I thought. I could get to that bike and team up with its rider. Even if the authorities had lost track of me surely they would know his whereabouts. If we sat together they could pick up both of us. Everything would be sorted.

Approaching the bike, I could see bits of road-book and debris scattered across the desert. It turned out to be the bike of a KTM rider who'd had a huge crash the day before. He'd been carted off and I was still on my own. At least I now had two bikes to cannibalise if I needed to ride out of the desert. The factory KTM, I thought, had to be the best option. My only problem was I had no safety gear and might get myself deeper into trouble. I didn't know what to do.

Thirsty, but not particularly hungry, and with no better option than waiting to see if I was picked up, I sat down and waited. And waited. And waited some more. After a while I established a deadline. If they didn't rescue me by midday, which I hoped to judge by the position of the sun in the sky, I'd have to take things into my own hands.

CHARLEY As soon as Simon and Plummy left on the next stage I got on the phone to Lucy. The bivouac was packing up, the vehicles were pulling out of town, the aircraft were about to take off for Keyes and I was only now realising the extent of Matt's problems. He had no GPS, no water and it didn't look like he was going to be picked up soon. Worried that Matt's plight could quite easily tip into dangerous territory I went steaming up to the ASO tent at the airfield.

'I'm really worried now,' I told one of the officials. 'Matt has been moved from one bike to another. You guys have taken his GPS, Iritraq and balise so he's got no way to contact Paris. You've left him out there after the doctors said he's dehydrated and he hasn't any water. The guy's going to fucking die if you don't sort it out.'

Already in a panic because half the field was lost on the stage into Kiffa, the organisers were very nice after I'd vented my anxiety.

'We absolutely know he's there,' said one of the officials. 'We know exactly where he is and we know the *camion* is heading towards him, but it's going to take a few hours.'

Russ, who was about to leave in the X5, was calmer but definitely concerned. He wanted to get Matt to the bivouac at Keyes but he couldn't do it himself. He had to get on the road. I also needed to get moving. The circus was moving on.

MATT Shortly before my midday deadline, I heard a voice calling over the dunes in French. I stood up to find a woman walking towards me, shouting my number. Rushing towards her, I was overjoyed that help seemed to be arriving at last, but as I got closer I could see she wasn't pleased. In fact, she looked like she had a right hump with me.

'You are *cent soixante-treize*?'

'Yeah, that's me.' I wanted to hug her and tell it was fucking excellent that she'd turned up.

'Oh gee, they told me you were half dead. But look at you, there's nothing wrong with you.'

I was speechless. Totally deflated. Now the last thing I wanted to do was hug her as she spun around and walked off.

'What happens now?'

'I'm stuck back there . . . half a kilometre away,' she said. 'You sit and you wait here.'

'What? Wait here with this bike?'

'Unless you want to come and dig.'

After her offhand treatment of me I was determined not to help her dig out her vehicle. 'I'll sit here.'

About an hour later I was still sitting on the sand. Worried that she had left without me, I trudged off in pursuit, following the woman's tracks until I found her beside a four-wheel-drive ambulance hopelessly wedged in a bowl. A man, who I later discovered was her husband, was standing nearby.

'We'll have to wait for the lorry,' the woman said. She explained that she'd been radioed the previous evening to collect me but they'd got stuck every twenty metres on the way. I could see that she and her husband weren't in the best of moods, having spent the night in the dunes, but at last I had reason to feel safe. The woman's husband was in a worse state than me. I didn't know if it was dehydration or exhaustion, or maybe both, but, sitting in the back of the ambulance, I could see he was struggling to stay conscious while his wife took his blood pressure every half-hour.

A couple of hours later I heard the sound of a truck approaching. With witches's brooms strapped to the front two corners of its cab it was obvious what this truck was all about. It was the *camion balai* – the sweeper truck. My ticket out of the desert. Behind the driver's cab was a steel box like a small prefab building and a flat loading platform. The platform was chock-a-block with broken bikes picked out of the desert by a hydraulic grabbing arm. Climbing up on to the truck and opening the door to the steel box, I was introduced to a world of suffering I hadn't anticipated when I saw the *camion* approaching. It was full of riders who had been lifted out of the desert like their bikes and were now also strapped to the truck. It also contained three car drivers with their co-drivers. All of them were totally exhausted and dejected, but bound by a spirit of camaraderie in adversity.

With all the bucket seats occupied, I found a place on the floor and was immediately welcomed into the fraternity. A Portuguese driver and his navigator, both fruitcakes, and a mad rider from the Canary Islands were really getting off on the craziness of the experience, something that I struggled to comprehend after my night alone on the sand.

'What are you so happy about?' I said.

'Well, it's not so bad in here,' said the Portuguese driver.

'I slept in the dunes.'

'My God.' The Portuguese driver laughed. 'I've left a hundred thousand pounds' worth of racing Toyota in the dunes. I rolled it three times and I'm happy to leave it there. So what are you worried about?'

I realised he had a point.

While we were talking another sweeper truck turned up. Half of us transferred to the other *camion* while the semi-conscious ambulance driver was strapped into the front of one of the trucks. The Portuguese driver and his co-driver climbed into the ambulance Jeep with the French medic and drove off with a manic grin.

Inside the steel cabin eight competitors sat in two rows of bucket seats, facing each other and sharing a space no larger than ten foot by six. Each seat had a four-point harness, many of which were faulty and didn't fit. We strapped ourselves in as best we could and piled what gear we had (in my case none) on the floor in the middle. Bolted to the truck chassis, directly above the gearbox and with only a single tiny window for ventilation, the box was a sticky, sweltering hellhole. With all the dust and sand blowing outside, we couldn't open the window. It stank.

One of the other evacuees was a Spaniard, who told me that *balai* sounded like the Spanish word for washing machine. That summed it up well as the truck bumped and ground across the desert.

With only one pack of water bottles and ration packs of peanuts and sugary snacks such as nougat, we drove all day, not knowing where we were being taken. Eventually, at a toilet break, we were told we'd be taken to Kayes to catch up with the rally. I quickly phoned Lucy so that she could pass on the news to Charley and Russ. Things were looking up.

CHARLEY Looking out of the aeroplane window at Kayes, I spotted a familiar face above a bare chest and a pair of shorts. Skipping under the plane, right under my window, it was Tony Woodhams, Simon's friend from Wales, nicknamed Rubber Band. He was helping a bunch of people push the plane backwards.

'All right, Charley!' said Tony as I jumped off the plane. It was delightful to see him. A few months earlier he'd taken me aside and given me a pep talk about the Dakar. 'I think it's amazing what you have decided to do,' he'd said. Coming from Tony, who never said anything he didn't want to say, I was touched.

Now, a few months later, Tony looked like he'd had quite a rough ride since I'd last seen him. He'd left home in Croydon to ride through Africa, but he'd found north Africa a lonely place. Having spent a lot of time on his own since he set off in November, he'd decided that he was better suited to more densely populated places, like Thailand.

'I'm missing people. I need hugs,' he said.

I put my arms round Tony and looked at him with amazement. I had thought we might bump into him on the rally but I'd underestimated his resourcefulness. Around his neck was a pass that allowed him access to everywhere on the bivouac and airfield.

He'd arrived a day earlier and befriended the course openers. After sharing dinner they'd given Tony a rider's pass and shown him where everything was kept. He knew about the showers, the food and refreshment supplies. Out of everyone at the bivouac, Tony was probably the best person to help me sort out the team's problems.

The team was splitting up, I said. I was in Kayes. Simon was somewhere on the stage from Kiffa. Gareth was hopefully on his way to Kayes aboard a Bowler truck. Russ, Jim and Wolfgang were with the X5. And, worst of all, Matt was somewhere in the desert east of Nouakchott.

With some luck, we might get Matt to Kiffa before the X5 departed but, with a marathon stage approaching, when mechanics and assistance would be banned from the bivouac, it looked like we'd soon be even more scattered across a thousand kilometres of west Africa and I couldn't see a way of pulling the team together. Like an advancing army, the ASO circus kept moving on. Nothing would impede its progress to Dakar. Anyone who didn't keep up simply got left behind in the swirling dust.

Tony had an idea. First, Russ, Jim and Wolfgang should head directly for Tambacounda when they'd fitted the new turbocharger. It made little sense to drive a car that was becoming less reliable every day over some of the rougher off-road tracks of Mauritania, Mali and Guinea when there was an asphalt road from Kiffa to Tambacounda, a distance of about 350 kilometres.

And as for Matt, Tony offered to track him down then carry him to Dakar on his bike. He wanted to head for a beach south of Dakar and had a suggestion for what he could do with Matt if they arrived in Dakar before the rally. 'We'll go and have a day surfing. Never mind surfing the sand, we'll go and find some nice blue water, Atlantic Ocean-style.'

With that, Tony ran off – he rarely walked anywhere, it seemed – to fix or fetch something, just as my phone rang. It was Lucy with news that Matt was in the sweeper truck bound for Kayes. At last, something good. The only snag was that he didn't have any credit cards or money and would be stranded if he arrived in Kayes after the Dakar army had advanced. Maybe Tony's offer was the best solution.

I called Russ, who was still in Kiffa. 'Try to get him here,' he suggested. 'Then he can join us for the drive to Dakar.'

I searched out one of the ASO officials who'd helped us when the X5 broke down near Zouérat. An expert in logistics, he was the one person I thought I could rely on to find a way to get Matt to Kiffa instead of Kayes. I explained the situation.

'Absolutely impossible,' he said. 'There is no way he is going to be able to catch up with them in Kiffa today, or even tomorrow. That guy is going to spend a lot of time going completely in the wrong direction.'

'Isn't there anything you could do?'

'We're not going to do anything,' he said. 'And before you ask, I'm not going to send the plane back to pick him up.'

That was that, it seemed. Back to the drawing board.

By mid-afternoon, Simon and Nick had arrived, exhausted, filthy and very smelly, but much more relaxed than on previous days. I found them lying on rush mats in the most comfortable bivouac so far, bickering about who should get the cups of tea before falling asleep.

When they woke up, Tony was lying beside them. 'I thought when I was coming into Kayes that you might be here,' said Simon. 'It's the kind of place that Tony would appear.'

'Listen,' said Tony. 'I can get you anything. *Anything*.'

'How about a towel and some soap?'

While Tony went in search of the request, Patsy Quick and

247

Clive Towne arrived. Patsy was filthy and her hair was matted. Her face black with dust, except for a bright white area around her eyes where her goggles had been, she looked like an inverted version of a panda.

SIMON The fact that the special had been abandoned didn't make the slightest difference. We still had to ride the same route and we wouldn't have ridden it any faster or slower if the special had not been cancelled. Although short, it was more technical than the longer sections, which had one benefit: it slowed the cars, which hadn't caught up by the time we stopped at the refuel at the halfway mark.

Whenever we stopped, we heard tales of riders who had not reached Kiffa by the start of the next stage but who were nevertheless allowed to proceed to Kayes. It was a sign that ASO was rattled by the number of riders who had dropped out on the long stage after the rest day and was concerned that fewer than the target 30 per cent of motorcyclists would arrive on the beach in Dakar.

About ten guys that we knew had spent the night sleeping in the last dune set. At sunrise, they'd ridden out of the dunes, finished the stage, were checked by the doctors at the bivouac in Kiffa then started the stage to Kayes late in the afternoon with the intention of riding through the night to reach Kayes by the start of the following stage.

We heard about a Spanish rider whose bike got stuck in sand. Unable to dig it out, he was sitting beside his bike wondering what to do when a tiny African girl popped up over the top of the dune and offered to dig it out for five euros. Looking at her, he thought there was no way she could do it. He was a grown man and he'd failed, but he agreed to her suggestion. The girl disappeared and returned fifteen minutes later with at least a dozen children. Working together, they got the bike out of the sand then scarpered when he started the engine because they were scared of it.

We also heard an amazing tale about Tom, the South African rider Nick and I had passed without stopping. His bike broke down in the dunes after a piece of his carburettor fell off. Eventually, he stopped a truck. The driver said that he'd seen another bike some way back in the dunes. Tom took off his boots and started looking for the other bike, walking until he was too exhausted to take another step. He then lay down and went to sleep. When he woke up, he walked some more, covering about twenty kilometres until he found the abandoned bike. He climbed on the bike. It started straight away. Wearing neither boots and socks nor helmet, he rode the abandoned bike back through the dunes in the dark to his bike, fitted its carburettor to his bike and rode out of the dunes. By the time he'd caught up with the rally he'd been going for forty hours non-stop.

It was a classic Dakar tale. After that kind of effort and determination to keep going, he deserved every break he could get. A big part of the rally was about never giving up, and the organisers would often find an excuse to cancel a stage the day after a particularly tough special. This year was no exception. With around eighty competitors stuck in the dunes overnight, I suspected the rally organisers would have cancelled the stage to Kayes. Caldecott's death gave them the excuse they needed.

Cancelled stages still had to be ridden in full but it allowed competitors who had failed to finish the previous stage by the deadline more time to start the next day. We were probably the last riders to make it out of the dunes and arrive in Kiffa within the official time.

Now, riding up a twisty section of track, we were being caught by the first cars so we decided to stop for twenty minutes to let the fastest pass us.

Seated under a tree, Plummy and I ate our rations, had a little siesta and then cruised down to the finish. Nick and I had tried to ride and finish side by side on several previous rallies but had never both made it to Dakar on the same rally. Now we were four days from Dakar and somehow we'd ended up together, mainly because we'd decided to help each other on the big dune day out of Nouakchott. It meant we started the following day consecutively and, because we rode at roughly the same pace, it seemed inevitable that we'd remain shoulder to shoulder all the way to the end.

MATT At 6 p.m., just as it was getting dark, the two *camion balai* stopped and the drivers told us to get out. Since setting off around midday we'd picked up several other stranded competitors and all seats were now full. As we milled around beside the trucks one of the drivers made an announcement in French. All the French competitors immediately climbed into the cabin of one of the trucks. Then he repeated the announcement in English. One *camion* would now take a fast route to reach Kayes within twelve hours; the other would continue on the special, taking twenty-four hours to reach the same destination. That explained why all the French competitors had jumped on the fast truck.

'We've got space for ten on the fast truck,' the driver said. 'Decide amongst yourselves who's going on it.'

Fortunately I understood English rather better than the Japanese competitors and managed to grab one of the last spaces on the fast truck. I strapped myself to a seat and made it clear I was going to move for no one.

It was pitch black in the cabin and absolutely unbearable. The truck lurched from side to side, tossing us around like rag dolls. The driver was taking no prisoners. Every few hours, he'd stop the truck, chuck some ration packs at us, slam the door shut and drive on.

Some time in the middle of the night we stopped and the doors swung open. Outside it was blowing a gale. Dust and sand whistled into the cabin as dozens of emaciated faces appeared at the door – a side of Africa we'd not seen when we'd still been within the safe embrace of the rally and bivouac. We threw out whatever remained of our ration packs, then watched, somewhat shocked as the Mauritanians scrabbled in the dirt

I felt like we were space travellers, dressed in high-tech clothing and strapped into a metal capsule, transported through space and time to somewhere totally alien, where we were surrounded by people who regarded us with both fear and amazement. I could see wonder in their eyes as they tried to make sense of the *camion balai* and its occupants. Then I noticed they were all carrying plastic bottles bound in rags. They were pointing at the bottles. They wanted water, it seemed, but none of us had any to spare. I then noticed that they weren't fighting over the food; they were sharing it out amongst themselves. Before I had time to work out what exactly was going on and what they must have thought about us, the door was slammed shut and we were moving again.

Trying to sleep as we rumbled through the night and the wind whistled around the cabin, I lost track of time. The mad rider from the Canary Islands had also managed to hitch a lift on the fast truck and would try to amuse us by switching the light on and off, but it served only to irritate everyone else in the cabin.

At about 6 a.m., I woke up. Feeling dazed and confused, I spotted a sign through the small window – hotel, it said – as the truck came to a sudden stop. What the hell is a hotel doing out here, I wondered. Don't stop, please keep going, I silently urged the driver. I want to get to the bivouac at Kayes. But then the door swung open and the driver beckoned for us to get out of the cabin.

A filthy tent had been erected in the car park of the hotel. We were hustled inside it. Mosquitoes buzzed everywhere. Thin, grubby foam mattresses were scattered across the floor.

'You can sleep here until ten o'clock when taxis will come and take you away,' said the driver.

'What do you mean, taxis?' I said. 'Where are the taxis going to take us?'

'The taxis will take you where we tell them to take you.'

'I want to know where I'm going. You told me we were going to Kayes.'

'You're not going there.'

'So what happens now?'

I never got an answer. The driver walked off. As far as he was concerned, by getting us to this tent he'd done his job. It was now up to us to find our way home. So much for the fast *camion*. It turned out to be the going-nowhere-fast *camion*.

CHARLEY Still trying to work out where Matt was headed, I could see no end to the anxiety. If anything, it was becoming worse with each passing day as the team approached Dakar and I had to explain to more of our supporters that I had crashed out of the race on day five. I'd now spoken to Herbert at Touratech. He was very supportive, but I could hear the disappointment in his voice. He reassured me that it didn't matter, he was pleased to have supported us, but all the time he was talking I was thinking: I've failed you; I've failed everybody.

I'd signed up for a bike ride, not for the mind games involved in being a team manager, but I also knew that it was important for everyone that the team, Matt and I included, reached Dakar. I'd heard soldiers say the worst thing after an injury was to be left behind by their advancing unit. They needed to go through the process of finishing the mission, then winding down and returning home with their fellow soldiers. Although our experiences were hardly comparable to soldiers in battle, I felt we shared that need to end the experience together. Russ had already said that, whatever happened, we had to get Matt to Dakar. Even if we had to drive into the desert to fetch him. I fully agreed with Russ, but ensuring Matt would get to Dakar was proving to be difficult.

Then I realised there was very little I could do. I had to let events take their course. Matt could only contact Lucy and so I needed to let Lucy sort out his passage to Dakar. If Lucy could get a wishbone to the X5 stuck in the Sahara desert, she could certainly get Matt to the finish.

SIMON At last the rally was becoming enjoyable. The first stage fully in Mali took us along narrow tracks through a sumptuous sequence of forests and savannahs, with a mercifully short 231-kilometre special, book-ended by 471 kilometres of liaison, most of which was on tarmac or hard piste.

Nick and I had a good day, our Beamers ideally suited to the long stony mountain pass at the beginning of the special where we overtook lots of other riders. It was very technical and a lot of fun. Riding over slippery stones, our engines had so much more grunt than other bikes. In first or second gear it thumped us steadily up the slope, stable as a carthorse.

After the rocky climb there was lots of twisting through the trees on a hard piste. Again it was great fun, sliding round the corners and taking jumps. It was a beautiful stage, almost perfect until, five kilometres from the end of the special section, a rider in front of us hit a deep ditch, went down like a sack of cement and skidded across the track on his back.

Plummy and I stopped and went to his assistance.

'Jesus – only five kilometres to the end . . .' the injured rider said. 'I was just looking at my road-book . . .'

He was one of the competitors who had ridden straight through from Nouakchott; he'd been on his bike for forty hours and was exhausted. Unable to refill his water bladder, he'd ridden the last 150 kilometres back through the stinking heat without any water. If he hadn't been so tired and dehydrated he probably would have seen the ditch coming and avoided it. Now he had a broken ankle.

Nick contacted the organisers by pressing the emergency button on the injured rider's GPS unit. After a while, a voice came out of it. Nick explained that the rider of the bike on which he was calling had injured his leg.

'Could you please send a helicopter as soon as possible,' said Nick.

'You'll need to speak to a doctor first,' said a Frenchwoman. 'Could you please hold.'

Nick and I stared at each other with disbelief as piped on-hold music played out of the injured rider's bike while we stood on a dirt track in Africa waiting for medical attention. Eventually a doctor came on the line. He spoke no English and we spoke no French.

'I think he's broken his foot,' said Nick, referring to the injured rider. 'Please send a helicopter. It's an emergency.'

The doctor cut off and the line went dead. A few minutes later, the Frenchwoman we'd spoken to earlier rang back. 'Sorry, we couldn't contact an English-speaking doctor. Could you please hold again . . .'

'Just send the helicopter. It's an emergency,' Nick insisted.

'You'll need to speak to the doctor first.'

The music started again. Eventually we got to speak to an English-speaking doctor who agreed a helicopter was needed to evacuate the poor lad. While we waited for the chopper to arrive another two guys nearly wiped out in the same ditch. It reminded me that, like Charley, you could still get badly bitten on what appeared to be a relatively easy day.

The helicopter arrived and spotted a clearing in the bush only slightly wider than the span of the chopper blades. The pilot made several attempts to land. Then, realising he couldn't squeeze it into such a small gap, he hovered a few feet above the piste while two doctors jumped out. The medics ran over to the injured rider while the helicopter flew off, nearly blowing my bike over in the process. Within five minutes the medics had strapped up the lad's ankle, the helicopter had found somewhere else to land and we were back in the rally, albeit almost at the back of the field after the delay.

According to the rally rules, anyone who stopped to aid an injured competitor should have their lost time deducted from their total time, but that rule appeared only to apply to the frontrunners. It seemed too much work for the organisers to credit those of us at the back of the field with our lost time unless we made a massive fuss about it. In some ways it didn't matter. I didn't care about my position. All I wanted to do was reach Dakar. But, as a result of helping the injured rider, Nick and I would have to start the next day near the back of the field. That meant riding through lots of slower riders' dust and getting caught by the cars earlier in the day.

By the time we were approaching Bamako in the late evening I'd entered a paranoid state that I knew from previous rallies. Having dealt with the worst terrain that the Dakar could throw at me and knowing that my BMW was ideally suited to the long stony passes that remained our only major obstacle, my worry now was that the bike would break. All it would take was a silly little crash or a minor mistake. Dog-tired after almost a fortnight in the saddle, I was making more mistakes than I would have done if I was fresh and rested. Every day I'd have several little moments that I wouldn't have had on day three or four. It was so easy to lose concentration and roll too far sideways or whack my head on a tree.

Having come so far, I couldn't bear the thought of something stupid taking me out of the rally. The previous year Gary, a good Irish friend, was wiped out by a car and broke his femur two days from Dakar. He'd done everything to deserve to be at the finish, but one small incident and it was all over.

MATT Losing my wallet at some point the previous day had left me with two problems. First, I had only twenty euros to my name and I was stuck somewhere near either Kiffa or Atar – no one could tell me which one. Second, my malaria tablets were in my wallet and I was now being circled by a swarm of mosquitoes.

With my jacket over my head as protection from mosquito bites, I grabbed a couple of hours' sleep on a mattress. At about 9 a.m. I woke up and wandered outside. In daylight it looked even worse. A small hotel and a parking lot stood beside a dusty highway. There were some ramshackle concrete buildings nearby and that was it.

Most of the dumped competitors were sitting on a low wall running along the side of the parking lot, staring into the distance or chatting quietly. I couldn't understand why I was the only one trying to demand anything and they were being so submissive. I wanted to shake some sense into them and shout: What are you doing letting yourself be treated in this way? But it was probably just fatigue. We were all dehydrated and hungry. No one had eaten a proper meal since breakfast two days earlier.

I entered the hotel, hoping to find somebody who might be able to help me. As I walked into reception a Spanish BMW rider was walking out. I'd met him with Simon two days earlier. When we'd all been stuck in the dunes somewhere between Nouakchott and Kiffa I'd helped him push his bike out of the sand.

'Hey, *hombre*, how you doing?' One glance at me must have told him I was not too happy. 'What's the matter?'

'I've just been on this *camion balai*. I'm exhausted. I've lost my wallet. No credit cards. No money. Nothing . . .'

'Oh? You need money, it's not a problem.'

'Thanks, but I can't take your money.' I'd met this Spanish rider only briefly and I didn't want to impose on him, particularly as I didn't need to borrow just fifty euros; I needed a big lump of money to get me out of trouble.

'Have you had a shower?' he asked.

'No. Nothing.'

'Here's the key to my room. You go in there. You have a shower. Then you have breakfast with me and my friends.'

After several days of being treated like an animal such generosity was overwhelming. He felt like a knight in shining armour. Half an hour later I was sitting with him at a table, clean, relaxed and happy, filling my belly with bread, jam and coffee.

Competitor number 178 his name was Manuel Garcia and, like me, he was a privateer on a customised BMW F650 Dakar bike. Unlike me, he had an escape plan.

He had rented a car with some other Spanish-speaking riders and was going to drive to Dakar, taking in some of the sights on the way and getting there in time for the rally's arrival on 14 January.

'You are more than welcome to come with me and my friends,' Manuel said.

I didn't doubt his sincerity but I could tell that his mates, although friendly, were slightly reluctant to have another body crammed into the back of the tiny pick-up they had hired. The rally organisers had also promised to provide taxis for the seven-hundred-kilometre ride to Nouakchott, so I turned down Manuel's kind offer.

'I'm going to Nouakchott anyway,' he said. 'Any problems when you get there, we can meet up again. You're probably better off going in the taxi with the ASO.'

'Great,' I said. 'I'll see you in Dakar.'

'You need some money. How much?'

I couldn't tell him I needed at least five hundred euros. It was too much to ask of a stranger.

'Look, here's one thousand euros,' Manuel said. 'And here's my telephone number. Ring me when you get to Dakar.'

I couldn't believe it. 'Are you sure?'

'You'd do the same for me, wouldn't you?'

'Yes,' I said. 'I would.' But I really didn't know. I'd never given a stranger more than a few quid and I didn't know if I would have done the same for Manuel. One thing was certain, however, the Dakar had a habit of bringing out the best in people.

ASO arranged taxis through the hotel owner and shortly after midday we were headed for Nouakchott on tarmac and dirt roads. The taxis were two old Toyota 4x4s, essentially solid but their engines were clapped out, with a top speed of no more than sixty kilometres an hour. The Portuguese competitor was in the other taxi with two other Dakar drop-outs. I shared with a Frenchman and a Belgian called Rene, who was in his fifties and totally disillusioned with the Dakar. He'd done it a few times but was convinced it was no longer an adventure for normal people. It had become, he said, a hardcore race for professional race teams.

The Mauritanian taxi drivers were great. Although they'd received only a fraction of the seventy-five euros we'd each paid to the hotel owner they insisted on stopping after a few hours and buying us lunch. When we passed through villages they bought us bottles of water and loaves of bread as none of us had local currency. Shortly before midnight they dropped us at the Mercure hotel in Nouakchott, where the Portuguese competitor had booked rooms for all of us.

'It's four star,' the Portuguese guy said. 'It's going to be fantastic.'

Civilisation at last, I thought. I couldn't have been more wrong. The hotel was a major disappointment. Although it provided a bed and a much-needed shower, there was nothing to eat. However, by now my five fellow Dakar escapees and I had become travelling buddies and so I stuck it out with them until I could work out a way of getting to Dakar.

Chapter 14

12 AND 15 JANUARY
Bamako to Dakar

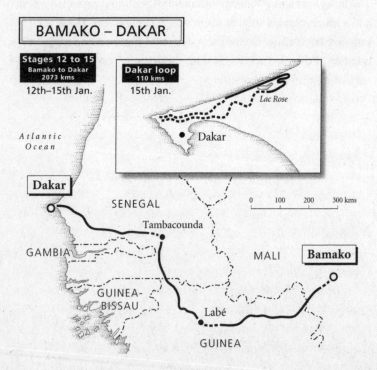

BAMAKO – DAKAR

Stages 12 to 15
Bamako to Dakar
2073 kms
12th–15th Jan.

Dakar loop
110 kms
15th Jan.

Lac Rose

Dakar

Atlantic
Ocean

Dakar

SENEGAL

Tambacounda

GAMBIA

0   100   200   300 kms

GUINEA-
BISSAU

MALI

Bamako

Labé

GUINEA

CHARLEY The next couple of days were going to be a test for us. Assistance crews were banned from the next bivouac. While competitors travelled from Bamako in Mali to Tambacounda in Senegal via Labé in Guinea, all assistance vehicles were directed straight from Bamako to Tambacounda. Riders and drivers would have to service and repair their own vehicles in Labé, relying only on a small crate of spares and tools that would be airlifted to the next bivouac. The organisers called this the marathon stage.

The previous night I'd checked with Gareth that all the most important spares had been loaded on to the aeroplane for Labé, including tyres and wheels, the most essential of all spare parts.

Then I'd fussed around Simon, who was anxious about the marathon stage and the growing pressure on him as he rode closer to Dakar. Every night, as Simon arrived, I worked hard to make his time in the bivouac as easy as possible for him. Having worried about him all day I'd be so overjoyed that he was back that I would do anything. I made his bed, cleaned his goggles and helped him correct his road-book. Whatever needed doing, I did it. Then, feeling like his nursemaid, I'd tell him it was time for bed.

'Charley, can you just come over and talk to me for a minute,' Simon had said as he was heading for his sleeping bag the previous night.

I sat down beside Simon lying on the floor and listened more than talked. He told me that on the way to the special the previous day, he'd been overcome with emotion and had burst into tears. The little bubble in which he'd kept himself cut off from the pressures of the team had burst and he'd started to feel overwhelmed by the whole experience. Once he'd got a couple of hundred of kilometres into the special, he'd got over it and was whooping, shouting and laughing.

'Thanks, Charley, for being here,' he said. 'I just needed to have a little moan and to hear some encouraging words before I went to sleep. Just so I could wind down and get to sleep.'

It was a lovely moment. After everything we'd been through together over the last year, at last I could help him. It was nothing compared with what he'd done for me, but it was great to be able to identify with what he was going through. Anybody could see Simon's determination and ambition, and he could also be quite moody – when Simon was in a bad mood, you knew to steer well clear – but this was the first time on the rally that I'd seen his gentle side.

After Simon had departed the next morning I flew on to Guinea. Approaching Labé, I glanced down at the ground. With much more vegetation than Mali or Mauritania, I thought it looked like Surrey with a hose-pipe ban. There were rows of houses with gardens of parched grass and plants behind them, a stark contrast to Mauritania where there'd been nothing to see but sand, tents and maybe a shack or two. As we descended, it became apparent that some of the houses were little more than concrete shacks with corrugated iron roofs, but still there was a sense that Guinea was much more affluent than Mauritania or Mali with everyone having their own home – however modest – and plot of land.

The airport was colourful and bustling. Smiling and relaxed, the locals appeared much friendlier than those we'd met so far on the rally and the president was there to greet us, surrounded by local women. It felt like a carnival compared to the austerity of the desert in Mali and Mauritania. The vibrant colours of the locals' costumes, the sounds made by hundreds of people talking and wandering around recharged my senses and reminded me why, at heart, I was a city boy. I needed the stimulation and excitement of activity and the scene at the airport provided it by the bucket load.

The locals and organisers had made a special effort with the bivouac. Usually it was no more than a canvas tent with carpets on the floor, but in Labé they'd built it from bamboo with grass matting on the roof. And, because the mechanics and trucks were absent, there was a completely different vibe For once all the competitors were on the same level. Even the top guys had to service their vehicles and prepare for the next day, a welcome novelty for all of us.

After securing a spot at the bivouac for our pit and kit, I walked into Labé with Claudio. The police had cordoned off a large circle around the airport and were keeping a road clear so that the bikes, cars and trucks could reach it without impediment. Just outside the cordon was a marketplace selling the usual tourist tat, such as T-shirts, bags and plastic items.

Claudio and I were standing at the side of a road watching the world pass by when we noticed that the police were being very heavy-handed with the locals. Thousands of spectators had gathered along the route to the cordoned-off bivouac and airfield. Any who stepped on to the road were immediately set upon by police wielding long truncheons. Even people innocently wandering back from the market with bags of shopping, who didn't care about the rally, were getting clubbed by the police when they tried to cross the road.

Claudio ran off into the crowd to film the police brutality while I watched from a distance. Suddenly it kicked off. Rocks and sticks flew through the air as the crowd vented their anger at the heavy-handedness of the police. With inflation running at more than 40 per cent, the president accused of corruption and the rally returning to Guinea for the first time since a little kid was killed by a rally vehicle ten years ago, maybe it wasn't such a surprise that tensions were running high.

I spotted local people in trees to the side of the rally route, throwing rocks and taunting the police who were wading through the crowd, indiscriminately clubbing whoever was in their path. Several dull thuds heralded the arrival of rubber bullets and the crowd immediately scattered, panicked people running in all directions.

It wasn't a pretty sight, but it was over quite quickly. The remaining people calmed down, Claudio returned from his positioning roaming amidst the rioters and we could walk down the road as if nothing had happened.

It was all very sad, but I didn't know who to blame. The police had clearly been heavy-handed, but there had been an atmosphere of a crowd wanting to start a fight. Maybe it was yet another ugly consequence of the uncomfortable juxtaposition of the extreme affluence of the rally and the extreme poverty of the countries through which it passed. All the Guineans I met were very pleased to see the rally return to their country. It brought in much-needed foreign funds and attention, but there was a downside, which we'd seen on the streets of Labé. There was no easy answer.

SIMON Guinea was beautiful. A revelation. Having not been there before, I thought it would be similar to Senegal, twisty savannah tracks that were fun to ride, but it was completely different. With its mountains, bush tracks through banana plantations and monkeys running across the track, it was just gorgeous and reminded me of home in Queensland.

Our brakes hadn't been tested as much on the rest of the rally as they were in Guinea. We crossed big mountains, riding uphill for fifteen or twenty kilometres, then the same distance downhill. I tried to film as much as I could of the stunning scenery, particularly the final three-hundred-kilometre liaison on tarmac into Labé. It was beautiful. And the villages were just as good, the streets packed solid with people, the route just a handlebar-width through the crowd, which shouted and egged us on, encouraging us to pull wheelies as we passed through them.

The crowds weren't just in the villages. They appeared by the piste in all sorts of places – on the sides of mountains, in the bush, along rivers and on the open savannah. It was awesome.

Coming down a mountain, on a fast dirt road about halfway through the special, I spotted an old broken-down car parked on a corner with a Union Jack on its bonnet. I wanted to stop and say hello, but I couldn't. Instead I gave them a big wave, mindful that the 872 kilometres from Bamako to Labé was one of the longest stages of the rally and I still had a long way to ride.

Later on we had to wheelie over a water pipe in the middle of a village in which every house and hut had washing hanging out. Everything was filthy and covered in dust. I hated to think what the state the washing would be in by the time the cars and trucks passed through.

The only fly in the ointment came early in the day on a rocky downhill track. I couldn't steer the bike and I was struggling to keep it on the track. The front wheel was pushing in the corners, as if the tyres were trying to roll off the rim of their wheels, but I was fatigued after twelve days on the rally so I didn't know if my front mousse had gone or I was just having a bad day on the bike.

Nearing the bottom of the hill, I lost control and ended up on the left-hand edge of the track, among trees, stumps, stones and termite mounds. Suddenly my left leg was torn backwards. I'd hit something hard, but it had been so fast I hadn't seen what it was. My whole leg hurt. I wobbled a short distance down the track and pulled over. I got off my bike and gingerly bent my knee to assess the extent of the damage. It hurt like hell but it was all still working.

As I rode on the swelling and pain got worse. A couple of times I rode past medical assistance vehicles and thought I should stop to get it examined, but then I thought I had better stay on the bike and keep moving. I was worried that, once off the bike, I wouldn't be able to get back on it. And by the time I'd taken my trousers off, the medics had looked at it, sucked their thumbs for a while and given me some painkillers, I would have lost fifteen valuable minutes. Not losing time was the one mantra that every Dakar rider needed to keep firmly at the front of their mind.

MATT Stuck in Nouakchott while the rally was running full steam ahead to Dakar, I called Lucy in the hope she'd be able to arrange a flight. The only available seats involved flying via Paris, a ridiculous option when only around six hundred kilometres separated the Mauritanian and Senegalese capitals. Without a driving licence I couldn't hire a car. The only alternative was a taxi. I hunted around for the cheapest price, but most drivers harped on about the border and were reluctant to take me to Senegal. Eventually I found a driver who would do it for 550 euros – a fortune when I considered I'd come 700 kilometres for 150 euros the previous day.

The driver, Khan, had a nice car, a 4x4 with a good sound system and he said it was the fastest car around. It was certainly the best car I'd seen in Mauritania apart from the brand-new Porsche Cayenne S that belonged to the owner of that hotel in the middle of nowhere at which the *camion balai* had dumped us the previous day.

'It does one hundred and ten kilometres an hour,' Khan boasted as we got in the car.

'All right, let's go for it then,' I said.

Trundling down the coast road, I was enjoying myself. At last,

I thought, I'm doing it. I'm on my way to Dakar now. I felt I'd overcome all the hardships, come through the darkness and seen daylight. It was great to be away from everybody and in control of my own destiny for the first time in a very long time.

What I saw of Mauritania on that stretch of the journey was not pretty. It was littered with rubbish. However, the sea of plastic bags was dotted with fascinating people, their self-built houses and some amazing Mercedes buses.

After a few hours we arrived at a town that felt wrong from the moment we entered its first streets. Prostitutes stood on every street corner. Destitute children were lying in the gutters. The local population looked disease-ridden and dangerous. The buildings were all run down.

'What's this place?' I asked Khan.

'This is it,' he said. 'This is the frontier.'

Now I knew why so many taxi drivers were reluctant to make the crossing into Senegal.

We came to a large iron gate with several thousand people crowded in front of it. Khan honked the horn, a small kid opened the gate and we drove into a dirty car park lined by military police and border guards. Ahead of us was a ferry and a river, the border between Mauritania and Senegal.

Immediately the police surrounded the car. '*Cadeau*? *Cadeau*?' they all said.

I'd heard the *cadeau* refrain dozens of times before from street urchins and beggars, but it had never come from anyone in an official position. Here, in this godforsaken place with its atmosphere of evil and decay, even the police were asking for a 'present'.

'No,' I said. 'I'm with the rally.' I held up my left wrist to show the orange wristband given to rally competitors. The police immediately stepped back and stopped hassling me.

Then they started on Khan. They demanded to see all his

267

papers and insisted that he got my passport and gave it to them. They fired dozens of questions at him, too fast for me to understand. After a few minutes a couple of policemen grabbed Khan and dragged him off into one of the nearby shacks. I hadn't a clue what was going on.

Spotting a bunch of motorcyclists on BMWs, I went in search of help. The riders were Czech tourists following the rally but they said they couldn't help me. They had even less of a clue than I did about what was going on. I walked up to one of the policemen and managed to persuade him to return my passport. Then I walked back to the Czech rally fanatics.

'Has he given your passport back?' one of them asked.

'Yeah, but only after I hassled him for a long time.'

'They've had ours for three hours and they're refusing to give them back.'

Keeping an eye on the door to the police shack, I chatted with the Czechs while watching the police turn Khan over. I saw him hand over a wad of cash then get hassled for more.

'Hey! *Hombre*!' shouted a familiar voice. I turned round. It was Manuel, the Spanish BMW rider who had lent me a thousand euros. 'Have you got your passport back?'

'Yeah, I've got my passport. It's great to see you.'

'Did you give them money?'

'No.'

'Good. Come with me.'

'But they've got my driver.'

'Don't worry about that. Come with us. Sit down and have some tea.'

Hoping the police would release Khan before the last ferry to Senegal left at 3 p.m., I sat with Manuel at the side of the parking lot. At ten to three Khan was still being hassled when a Mauritanian came up to me.

'I support Arsenal,' he said in a perfect English accent. We chatted for a while about football, then he asked what was keeping Khan.

'I don't know,' I said. 'Do you what it's all about?'

'They are saying the car is not registered in his name. They won't let him take it across the border.'

'So what do we do?'

'Nothing. Don't worry. It will be fixed.'

A short while later, the police came over to where Manuel and I were sitting in the dirt.

'*Cadeau*,' said one of them, holding out his hand.

I asked the Mauritanian to speak to them and translate.

'They are saying you can go, but the car doesn't go,' the Mauritanian Arsenal supporter explained. 'They said they know you've paid this man to take you, but he's not going so you've wasted your money.'

'What's it going to cost?' I asked.

Before the translator or the policeman answered I pulled out twenty euros and – hey presto – suddenly everything was bright and shiny. Khan was released from the police building and we were whisked on to the ferry like a couple of VIPs.

CHARLEY After returning to the bivouac from the riot I walked up to the medical tent where a doctor changed my dressing. Resting the tip of his thumb on the back of my hand to tighten the bandage and giving it a good yank, he managed to re-break one of the bones in my right hand.

I was in agony. His remedy was to give me some painkillers and ply me with vodka, a very effective treatment I remembered being advocated by Vasiliy Nisichenko, our Russian doctor on Long Way Round.

Fortified by drugs and booze, I went in search of the spare parts for Simon's bike. I found the crate inside a transport aeroplane, opened it and discovered the spare wheels were missing. I'd seen Gareth tie our wheels together, put tape around them and write Simon's race number on the bundle before they were loaded on to the plane. Now they just weren't there. On my hands and knees I searched through the plane. Then I examined every single wheel and tyre I could find to check it wasn't one of ours. The one thing that Simon was paranoid about was the mousses in his tyres disintegrating, particularly if he was going to be riding a lot on tarmac. Not changing his wheels would increase the chance of that happening.

After making some enquiries I worked out that our wheels and tyres were on another plane that had leapfrogged the Labé bivouac and flown on to Tambacounda. There was nothing that could be done about it.

I phoned Lucy to check everything else was OK. She said Plummy's rear shock had exploded and that he thought there was a spare shock on the Bowler T4 support truck, an assistance vehicle that was registered as a race truck and therefore allowed to come to the bivouac. That support truck would also have spare wheels for bikes on it, I reasoned. Even if it didn't arrive until 4 or 5 a.m., we'd still be able to swap the tyres.

SIMON By the time I reached the refuel my knee was causing me serious trouble. The pain was excruciating but I had no other option but to hobble around, topping up the bike and looking for water which, for some inexcusable reason, the organisers had failed to provide. Annoyed by the lack of water and distracted by my knee injury, I rode off without putting my fuel cap back on properly. A few kilometres down the track I realised my mistake and stopped to stuff a wad of toilet paper into the open top of the fuel tank. Not a big deal but another irritation in what was becoming a tiresome day.

I rode on. Seventy kilometres from the end of the special, Plummy stopped. His rear shock had broken. With no suspension, his bike was riding like a Harley Davidson Hardtail chopper and he needed me to lead him along the track. With me in front he'd get more warning of potholes. If he hit a deep hole he'd go for six.

Just after the end of the special I was so hot, sweaty and claustrophobic inside my helmet and goggles that I had to stop. The sun and humidity had become oppressive, so I waved Plummy on. He had around three hundred kilometres to ride to the bivouac, but at least it was all tarmac now that we were on the liaison. I pulled over in a small village, took off my helmet and sipped some water. Less than a minute later I was surrounded by people staring at me, none of them venturing any closer than ten feet away. The crowd parted as a tall man came walking through and approached me. He spoke a little English.

'I am Ibrahim,' he sad. 'This is our village Foum Doum.'

Ibrahim told me he was studying tourism and was going to be the local tourist officer, although I couldn't for the life of me think where his customers were going to come from. He introduced me to all his family and said he had friends all over the world.

'Where are you from?' he asked.

'Australia. Near Sydney.'

'I know someone from Australia. His name is White Man.' We spoke for a little longer, then I realised Ibrahim's friend was called Mr White. Needless to say, I didn't know him, but it was great in the midst of the madness of the rally to spend a short time with these calm, friendly Guinean people who lived in what was, by Western standards, abject poverty, but absolute beauty. Ibrahim lived in a small round house that I guessed was made of mud with a pointy grass roof. Situated in the middle of the mountains, the

271

view of the valleys stretching from Foum Doum to the horizon was spectacular.

After leaving Ibrahim I rode the rest of the liaison slowly. Even though night was approaching I cruised slowly along the beautiful, winding tarmac road, just wanting to take in as much of the scenery as possible and frequently stopped to film the route. I wanted to be able to show viewers of the documentary that the Dakar rally was about more than what they got to see on Eurosport or other sports channels. The 300-kilometre liaison into Labé would never feature on Eurosport, but it was one of the most spectacular parts of the rally. For a privateer, it was very much part of the journey.

When darkness fell I was still about 150 kilometres from home. Everything changed as the scenery disappeared into the night and the gentle liaison turned into something that looked more like a stock-car video game.

When a car passed me at around 130kph I glued myself to its tail lights and bombed into Labé. Sitting far enough behind the car to allow my headlights to fill the gap in front of my bike and using the car's headlights to pick out animals straying on to the road far further ahead of the car than any bike's lights could shine, I made good time. He was driving so fast I had to push my bike to its limit. It was a windy road, but the car driver was cutting all the corners and going ballistic in the straights, while I was working up and down the gearbox, revving the bike to the red line. It was completely mental. Eventually he caught up with a slower car and I switched allegiances, riding on the tail of the slower car all the way back to the bivouac.

MATT Half an hour after boarding the ferry we docked on the Senegalese side of the river. We were immediately hassled by vendors trying to sell us stuff, something that hadn't happened in

Mauritania, where it seemed they were so poor they didn't have anything to hawk.

'Change money? Change money?' one of the black-marketeers pestered me. 'You wanna woman? I get you woman.'

Khan ran up to a large bloke in uniform and threw his arms around him, then grinned at me. The border guard was Khan's mate and he immediately whisked us into a hut in which officials were sitting in a row of booths with piles of passports. Everyone on the ferry had to pass through this office and queue at a tiny window to get their papers stamped.

Khan and I sat at the back of the office watching arms and heads poke through the windows of the booths, most of them pointing at us as if to say it wasn't right that we were given preferential treatment. Khan's mate flicked through all the passports until he found mine, then stamped it and waved us on our way. Oh, to have friends in high places.

The road was terrible, much worse than in Mauritania, but Khan didn't drop the speed below his promised 110kph as we left the hordes at the border – including Manuel and his mates – far behind us. After about an hour and a half of racing through villages and the scrubby countryside I started to relax and enjoy the journey again.

The border had been bizarre. There was such a massive change in cultures between the Islamic Republic of Mauritania and Senegal; it was almost like stepping from the Soviet bloc to Jamaica. Mauritania had been very stark, but its people had been very proud and decent. With thick vegetation, colonial buildings and lots of people milling around, Senegal felt immediately wealthier and more vibrant, but it also came across as more cynical and seedy.

Rolling on through villages of decaying buildings and littered countryside, I spotted a huge bird flying across the road about a mile ahead. Another big bird followed in its wake. At least three foot tall, they were the largest birds I'd ever seen. I assumed they were vultures. About twenty of them were feasting on a dead cow in the road, ignoring completely any passing traffic. Just as we were about to pass, one of them took off, beating its wings lazily as it caught the breeze and crashed into Khan's side window.

There was a squeal of hot tyres on tarmac as glass shattered. Khan tried to regain control of his car, which was careening down the road. We'd travelled half a kilometre by the time we'd stopped skidding and swerving.

Relieved that we were stationary, I looked at Khan. He had cuts down his arm and across his hands. I could feel glass in my hair and was worried that Khan might start bleeding from his head. Above all, I felt guilty. I'd made Khan drive all day for a measly amount of money and several hours' hassle at the border. Now I'd ruined his pride and joy, a car that had been immaculate. The wing mirror and window were trashed and the inside was a mess.

Khan looked upset about the damage the bird had done, but he didn't let it get in the way of our progress to Dakar. We brushed all the glass off the seats and ourselves, then got moving again. Twenty minutes down the road, Khan started laughing hysterically, cackling about the bird colliding with his car.

'It's bad for us,' I said when he'd stopped laughing. 'But it's worse for that vulture. It's dead.'

'No,' said Khan. 'It's not. I saw it fly off.'

Soon after the crash it got dark and Khan started driving like a man possessed. With only fifty kilometres remaining, I didn't want a crash to end the journey. I hadn't gone through everything I'd experienced over the previous few days only to be rammed into the back of a bus in the Dakar suburbs, but I didn't feel I could say anything.

'Where are you staying?' said Khan as we approached the centre of Dakar.

'The Novotel.' I expected Khan to give me a blank look in response.

'OK.'

Khan weaved through a maze of back streets, took a sudden right turn and drew up in the Novotel's car park. He dropped me off, then drove off, presumably all the way back to Nouakchott. After the emptiness of the desert, the nightmare of the *camion balai*, the commotion of the border crossing and the madcap race with Khan down the coast to Dakar, I couldn't quite get to grips with standing outside a quiet, orderly four-star hotel. It felt unreal.

Forty minutes later I was in the bar, a beer in front of me. I was the first Dakar competitor to arrive and everyone wanted to hear my story. In spite of crashing out of the rally on the ninth day, I felt totally content with my achievements and very lucky to have seen and witnessed some amazing things over the last few days.

The stage from Nouakchott to Kiffa had pushed me to my limit in a way I'd never been challenged before. Although I was physically capable of riding further, I'd reached the end of my emotional capabilities. Seeing Caldecott's body had been a big turning point. I was part of the same race and all of a sudden I became disillusioned with it. I couldn't work out what the hell we were doing risking our lives in the desert. The races in which I competed every weekend also had the potential to cause serious injury, but it would be a freak accident. In the Dakar every competitor was dicing with death. And for what?

Anyone who wants to compete in the Dakar has to face the fact that they will be riding at their limit for quite a lot of the rally. In the nine days I was in the race, I'd had many moments each day when I was just a whisker away from a very serious accident. Every couple of minutes I put myself in a situation where I could

275

have died or wound up in a wheelchair. Sitting safe in that bar in Dakar it all seemed stark raving mad. And, having spent three days travelling more slowly across parts of Africa that the rally tore through like a marauding army, I was having doubts about the ethics of the whole enterprise.

Mauritania, in particular, had seemed a very innocent country. And I felt we had abused it, our huge lorries, powerful cars and dangerous bikes thrusting through its countryside. All the locals with whom I'd spoken welcomed the rally. It was excitement and money for them, but in their situation I would have been surprised if they didn't welcome anything that brought a brief respite to the harshness of their lives.

On the plus side, I'd met some amazing people, the best of whom was Manuel. I didn't know if I'd see Manuel ever again, but the next morning I went down to the hotel reception and asked the manager to reserve a room for him. The hotel was fully booked, but I was determined to pay back Manuel's good deed in the desert. After several hours of negotiation in the manager's office I'd secured the room. Walking out of the office, I bumped straight into a familiar face.

'Hey! *Hombre!*' It was Manuel.

CHARLEY Looking really freaked, Plummy arrived at the bivouac panicking that he had no spare shock in his box. I ripped open Simon's crate of spare parts and immediately spotted a spare shock absorber, only seconds before Nick spotted it and started hovering over the box, trying to wangle it from us. Fortunately Simon arrived a few minutes later. He'd whacked his knee on a tree and was really sore but there didn't seem to be any problems with his bike, so I handed the shock over to a very relieved Nick, then set off to get him some food.

Returning with two heavily laden plates, I insisted that Nick sat down to eat and recoup his energy before starting to repair his bike. Then I went in search of Simon. I found him in the medical tent, where the doctors had given him a clean bill of health. Simon had bruised his kneecap but not damaged any ligaments. They'd strapped up his knee, given him some him painkillers and anti-inflammatory pills then declared him fit to ride the next stage.

We returned to the pits and, while Simon changed the air filter on his bike, I got him his dinner. With nothing wrong with his bike, he quite happily accepted the fact there were no mousses. While he finished eating and repairing his bike, I went on guard duty. The previous night, some local kids had stolen some of my things and I was determined to make sure we didn't lose anything else. Simon fell asleep beside his bike after servicing it and once I'd checked all our belongings were safely stored away, I found a patch of soft ground to sleep on. As soon as I dropped off a huge generator thundered into action beside me. Too tired to move, I turned over, jammed my iPod headphones into my ears and went straight back to sleep.

SIMON I felt I could smell the finish when I woke the next morning. But first I had to ride 567 kilometres to Tambacounda, then 634 kilometres to Dakar. It didn't let up.

With fewer riders still in the race, the manic activity that had characterised the early morning starts earlier in the rally had gone. Now we could take our time getting to the start. We'd roll up, hand in our time-cards and almost wander into the stage. Charley was up before me, fussing around the camp and helping us to get going. Charley, Plummy and I discussed the race over breakfast; in particular how well all the female riders were progressing. Two days remaining to Dakar and only one woman had dropped out, an astounding finishing rate. It proved the rally was not about strength or power. It was a mental thing.

After eating I got dressed in my racing kit, then went over to my bike. During the night someone had moved it by about ten yards. I hit the start switch. Nothing. The engine wouldn't start. My heart was in my mouth and I couldn't breathe for a few seconds. Eventually I got it to start, but it would only keep running with the throttle fully open. Plummy came over.

'Stop it,' he shouted over the roar of the engine. 'When it's off slowly pull the throttle fully open, then slowly back, then slowly open again.'

It worked. Somehow the computer controlling the fuel flow had become reprogrammed during the night. Going through Nick's procedure helped reset it but I was worried, particularly as, because it was a marathon stage, we didn't have Gareth or Wolfgang with us to sort out any technical problems.

Like the previous day, the stage was a beautiful ride with long technical climbs up mountains almost a thousand metres high. About thirty kilometres into the special, I spotted the Euromaster Yamaha belonging to Ludivine Puy, a female factory rider, lying by the side of the track. A little further on, Ludivine was lying on the ground with her leg poking skew-whiff. It looked like she'd had a really nasty crash, just after we'd been remarking how the female riders were faring much better than most male competitors.

The accident had happened on a stretch on which I'd been tiptoeing along, feeling pretty nervous. This fast dirt road with rain ruts at crazy slants was very dangerous for bikes. If we hit a rut at the wrong angle it would pull the front wheel sideways. I heard later that Ludivine had crashed trying to avoid a child that ran across the track. She'd broken her hip. My knee injury had already forced me to ride slowly. I could still stand on my pegs but I was finding it harder than usual to turn the bike and larger bumps were forcing me to slow down and roll with them rather than wheeling into them. Seeing Ludivine injured made me slow down even more. She was a cool operator and it was so close to the end. At this stage of the rally, when the only objective was to protect that Dakar finish line, I was quite happy to take it easy if it meant I wouldn't make some silly, nervous mistake.

CHARLEY I was struggling to roll up and stuff Simon's sleeping bag into its compression bag with my broken hands when I heard a helicopter come juddering over the bivouac. It landed nearby and an ambulance pulled up beside it. As they lifted a body out of the back of the helicopter I could see from the racing suit that it was a Euromaster factory rider. Then I spotted the blonde ponytail. It was Ludivine.

The ambulance departed for the medical tent. A few minutes later another helicopter hovered overhead. Dangling Ludivine's Yamaha from a rope, the chopper flew to an open area of the bivouac, descended until it was about thirty metres above the ground, then released the bike. Ludivine's bike hit the ground with an almighty thump.. A couple of officials ran over to the bike, cut the fuel pipes and watched as the petrol spurted all over the ground. Within the hour it would be packed into one of the cargo aircraft and on its way home. Meanwhile, the helicopter tilted then thundered away to pick up more of the injured and their steeds

A few minutes later, a rider on a KTM came tearing through the bivouac. Spattered with oil from head to foot, he was shouting that he had a leak. He rode over to the Locktite truck and persuaded them to help him. They sealed his leaky nut then patted him on his back as he raced off to the start.

SIMON One hundred kilometres into the special, I came to the first long, rocky climb. By the time I reached the top of the mountain my fairing was shaking badly. Two brackets on the left side had broken. I stopped and zip-tied it together, but my handiwork held for only five minutes. The zip-ties were going brittle in the sun. I strapped it up again then rode on to a village on a small plateau, where I secured it with a thicker BMW tie-down strap. While I was working on my bike the head honcho of the village wandered over, pitching in, helping me and shouting in French.

He wasn't much help, but he was so friendly that I didn't have the heart to ask him to stop.

'*Moto*.' He pointed at himself and revved an imaginary bike throttle.

I smiled and raised my eyebrows. I didn't have a clue what he was trying to say. My only worry was that he wanted a ride on my bike.

He ran off towards some huts, returning on a moped and holding a piece of thick rubber band. The *moto* part solved – clearly he meant his moped – I now wondered what he was going to do with the rubber. A few moments later I got the answer as he tied it around the front of my bike and knotted it. It didn't make any difference, but I thanked him effusively. He smiled, then patted me as I got on my bike and, with a wave of his arm, wished me on my way. For the life of me I couldn't imagine how he had managed to get a moped up those rocky slopes to the village, but obviously that is what he had done.

Towards the end of the special, I stopped at a village to take some photographs and have a rest. Sipping my water, I heard another bike approaching. A Yamaha XT500, a relic from the 1970s, pulled up. A Dutch competitor called Henno Van Bergeik swung off it and started talking. He was an off-road fanatic with a garage full of XT500s, the original classic desert dirt bike. Every year he'd go off on a bike tour on his own. He'd crossed

Mongolia and he'd traversed Algeria twice – once without a guide, just sneaking across the border and finding his own way through the desert.

Wearing old leather gardening gloves that had cost him maybe three euros, he was now doing the Dakar on a bike that first saw action in the race about thirty years earlier.

'This is the most organised holiday I've ever been on.'

That's the quote of the rally, mate, I thought as soon as he said it. We were busting our guts to get to Dakar in one piece, but Henno thought it was a leisurely jaunt.

'They give you the route every morning. They provide all the food and a place to sleep. There's water and fuel provided every few hundred kilometres. If anything happens to you, there are doctors and helicopters to rescue you. It's never been like this for me before.'

While most of the other people on the rally were thinking it was the most dangerous thing they'd ever done, this Dutch rider on the most inappropriate bike, wearing the most inappropriate clothing, was cruising through it, thinking it was the safest fortnight's holiday he'd ever had. He told me he'd shot several hundred photos along the route and we'd worked out he'd spent at least seven hours just taking snaps.

Nine kilometres from the end of the special, a French rider stopped me and asked if I'd tow him to the finish. His engine had stopped. I nearly said yes, but I decided it was too much of a risk. It would take me hours and I was nursing an injured knee. I decided against it. He would never have stopped for me and I shouldn't even have hesitated in refusing, but I found it hard to say no to a Frenchman I'd never met before.

As I approached Tambacounda, a huge scrub fire lined both sides of the route, jumping across the road. We had to ride through it, but after everything we'd been through it seemed like small fry.

Of more concern within the bivouac were the local children who tried to steal just about anything that wasn't bolted to a vehicle. Sneaking under the fence, they were grabbing whatever they could find. Every few minutes there would be a shout and we'd see thirty people chasing a little kid, shouting at him to stop. The kid would be clutching a bag or a piece of kit, probably with no idea about what it contained or its purpose. After the easy-going vibe at the last two bivouacs in Guinea and Mali, it was a shame to be put on the back foot as soon as we arrived in Senegal. It turned the rally into an 'us and them' situation.

The mood was lifted by Russ, who had found the first hot shower in days – a little bit of much-needed bliss for a mere five euros – and by Clive Towne calling out as he arrived at the bivouac: 'Can I hear the fat lady singing yet?'

Everyone reacted immediately. 'No! No! You can't.' We were all too superstitious to think about the end of the rally too much. 'Don't relax. Keep your concentration boy!'

CHARLEY While Simon was out on the stage news reached the bivouac that a Guinean child had been hit by a rally car six kilometres outside one of the villages. He'd died while being airlifted to a nearby hospital. The details were sketchy – no one knew if he'd ran across the piste – but it was a tragedy, and made all the worse because this was the first time the rally had passed through Guinea in a decade.

The atmosphere in the camp was considerably different from the mood four days earlier, when Andy Caldecott had died. We could all rationalise a racer losing his or her life, but an innocent child was different.

I felt terrible for the little kid and his family, but I also felt for the driver who had hit him. I thought of the kid watching the cars and motorbikes racing past, probably excited by the spectacle.

Driving through villages, I'd seen how easy it was for accidents to happen. Kids ran everywhere and it was surprising there weren't half a dozen accidents every day. It was an unavoidable fact that it was impossible for the rally organisers to make the route absolutely safe to the local population.

With only one stage remaining until we arrived at Dakar, I'd also become aware of the damage the rally was doing to the local environment. Every day it moved on, leaving behind a barren wasteland and several tons of litter. The organisers made sure it was all bagged up and put into piles, and we were repeatedly reminded to use the bins they provided. But, even before the caravan departed, I'd see the locals rooting through the bins and emptying the rubbish bags, scattering our detritus everywhere in the hope of finding something of value or some food, while we slowly packed up our last belongings for the leap to the next bivouac.

The organisers sourced as as possible much locally. I'd heard that 70 per cent of the food and beverages were bought in the countries through which we passed. They also tried to employ as many locals at each place the bivouac stopped, but because they were running a perfectly oiled machine and because they needed to maintain a high standard of food preparation most of the skilled staff and helpers were European, while the low-paid jobs, such as security guards or litter collection, went to the indigenous population.

Tambacounda was the first bivouac for several days at which the whole team came together. I met Gareth, Wolfgang and Russ in a pit surrounded by all the Bowler trucks, some of which we hadn't seen since Kiffa. With only a relatively short hop remaining to Dakar and the Iritraq indicating that Simon was making good progress at last there was a sense of a fortnight's pressure lifting off my shoulders. I sat down with Russ and Clive Dredge, Patsy's husband, drank a large bottle of beer, smoked too many cigarettes and chewed the cud for a while over a lazy lunch, our shirts off in the sun.

With the end in sight, barriers between the teams and privateers were coming down, the bivouac was becoming a more friendly place and I started to notice things that I'd previously been too stressed or preoccupied to register. For two weeks I'd watched riders climb out of their sleeping bags every morning, strap on body armour, pull on dust-encrusted trousers and shabby jackets and get ready for the next stage with little thought about where they came from. Now, as I watched the riders cruising into the bivouac at the end of the day's stage, I realised there was something very remarkable about an event that brought together people from forty-one countries, all united by the goal of reaching Dakar before they ran out of time, energy or luck.

Assured that their riders and drivers were now likely to reach the finish, team managers and mechanics on other teams were letting down their guards and I was getting to know some of the other faces around the bivouac. There was a feeling that we were all united in our excitement about the finish and about the amazing trip we had all shared. I realised then the rally was not just about my team but about all the teams and privateers. We had all been through hell and now we could all taste achievement and could dare to think about the end.

However, by late evening Simon was a long way behind Patsy Quick, Clive Towne and Plummy on the Iritraq and immediately the panic returned. Worried that it was all about to go wrong on the penultimate day, I was in an edgy mood throughout supper with Russ and could hardly eat my food.

'Let's just go and ring Lucy,' I said to Russ. 'I just want to make sure Simon hasn't called in with a problem.'

I disappeared for a few minutes to sort out some errands. When I got back, Russ had phoned Lucy.

'Simon's sixty-five kilometres away according to the Iritraq,' he said.

'Really? That far? What the fuck's happened to him?'

Fretting about Simon, I walked into the pits and there he was, standing by his bike, his jacket off as he chatted to Gareth and Wolfgang. I couldn't believe my eyes. I ran up to him and threw my arms around him like a wife who hadn't seen her husband for ten years.

'Thank God you're here,' I said.

'No worries, mate,' said Simon. 'No worries. It's a pleasure to be here.'

'Fucking hell! All my chickens are home.'

SIMON Having ridden 8933 kilometres so far, the riders' reaction to the penultimate stage, a 634- kilometre ride from Tambacounda to Dakar, was unanimous: a doddle. Maybe it was the relief of being able to see the end in sight, but somehow it didn't seem quite as far as stages of similar length had felt earlier in the rally.

It was a lovely stage with some tricky navigation, but the 254-kilometre special seemed to pass in the blink of an eye. It was a long way in the grand scheme of off-road riding, but by Dakar standards it was a walk in the park, particularly as the last thirty-five kilometres was a big wide dirt road on which we could quite easily cruise at 130kph.

The main danger on the stage was the number of local people who had turned out to watch. Racing along a sandy winding track at eighty kilometres an hour while passing through crowds of people separated by a space not much wider than the bike's handlebars was madness. But the team riders could not afford to slow down because their race position would be jeopardised. And the privateers couldn't ride any slower for fear that in the soft sand we'd lose momentum and control of the front wheel.

In all the years I had been riding the Dakar I'd not managed to work out my feelings on the risks of the race to the local population. The sheer size of the crowds was an obvious sign that tens of thousands of locals wanted to see the race and be part of it. They had hiked miles into the bush just to see the vehicles race past. And it was beautiful for the riders too; after a fortnight's hard work through the desert it felt great to be cheered on by thousands of people. But there were risks.

At the end of the special, I let Plummy shoot off on his own – wherever possible, he felt compelled to ride roads flat out at 130kph – and waited for Patsy and Clive. Patsy had reminded me several times on each day of the rally that her dogged determination to finish the Dakar, a quest that had dragged her to Africa for four years now, was all my fault. She said that if I hadn't enthused about the rally at her kitchen table all those years ago she would never have entered.

The night before, at the Tambacounda bivouac, Clive had come up to me and said it to me again.

'You bastard. This whole thing for four years has been all your fault.' Then he gave me a big hug. 'Thanks very much!'

Patsy deserved to have reached Dakar in each of the years she entered, but she'd had the worst luck. Ridiculous things always seemed to happen to Patsy, and even this year she'd faced one technical mishap after another. To be able to ride into the finish with Patsy and Clive was something very special for me.

After 175 kilometres of tarmac liaison, the road-book took us on a 30-kilometre detour on sandy piste. Towards the end of it we came to a heart-shaped track that had been built in remembrance of Fabrizio Meon.

A trust had been set up in memory of Meoni, which had built the Fabrizio Meoni school for agriculture, arts and crafts in Senegal. The heart-shaped track had been set up beside the school. Climbing off our bikes to sign our names on a memorial board, we pulled off our helmets and Patsy was instantly mobbed. Realising she was a woman, everyone wanted their photo taken with her. Patsy spent ages signing shirts and pieces of paper for locals and Italian rally enthusiasts, then we took it in turns to ride the memorial track. The heart-shaped circuit was a few kilometres of sandy, twisting piste that Dakar riders could ride if they wanted. I was thrilled to ride it but, like everyone else I spoke to who followed its short course, I spent a lot of the circuit thinking what a cruel irony it would be to crash on this optional section of track and not reach Dakar.

Riding around the track, my mind was full of memories of many riders I'd known who had died, particularly John Deacon, with whom I'd set up our BMW off-road riding school and who had died shortly afterwards on the Master Rally in Syria. As one of the best enduro riders in Britain, John had a factory contract but we'd entered the Master Rally as privateers. With a couple of bikes in the back of John's van, we set off to do it just for the fun of riding together. We didn't have a mechanic and, with no sponsorship, John had to borrow his bike from BMW.

On the day we left home, John promised my wife that he would look after me. A few days into the rally John was found lying dead on the ground beside his bike. The bike was not damaged and it was on a stretch of the piste where it was impossible to ride fast. He would have been riding at walking pace, in first gear. The post mortem found no sign of a heart attack, and the coroner couldn't decide what had killed John. To this day, no one has been able to work it out, but it left his wife Tracey devastated and his friends in shock.

CHARLEY Simon left quite early and by 6.45 a.m. I was inside the X5 for the final leg to Dakar. I'd wanted to travel in the X5 on the last day to experience what it had been like to follow the rally in the car. I soon discovered it was awful. Sitting in a cramped bucket seat was really painful – I added a back injury to my broken hands – and very boring. Bikes were zipping past while I trundled along, getting stuck in traffic and wishing I was on two wheels. The X5 squeaked and croaked over every bump. I was terrified it wouldn't reach the finish. We drove slowly into Kaolack, just over halfway between Tambacounda and Dakar. We pulled into a little hotel, drank some coffee and then I went in search of a toilet. For the first time in a fortnight there was a proper loo with a seat and a flush. Now used to holes in the ground, I'd almost forgotten what to do.

Leaving the hotel, our last stop before a return to civilisation in Dakar, I caught sight of the four of us – Russ, Wolfgang, Jim and me – in a mirror. We were all filthy. When one of the hotel staff held the door open as we exited the hotel, I noticed he was holding his breath. Clearly we stank.

Riding on to Dakar, I was consumed with just one thought: shall I ring them yet? I knew Olly and my children had arrived in Dakar the previous night and couldn't wait to speak to them, let alone hold them in my arms. It had been only two weeks, but it felt like years. The stage finished at the Meridien hotel in Dakar. I had butterflies in my stomach; I was so desperate to get there and to see my family again.

By early afternoon we were rolling into Dakar and stuck in a heavy traffic jam, which prolonged the agony, but at least it allowed me plenty of time to phone Olly and the kids to give them notice to get across town to the Meridien with Matt and Linley, Simon's wife. I'd also be reunited Ewan and David Alexanian, the fourth member of the Long Way Round circle, who had flown in from London and Los Angeles to be at the finish. It would be the first time in a long while that the four of us had got together.

Eventually I could see the Meridien hotel coming into view. Cracking up at the sight of a squadron of Repsol cars being washed on a petrol station forecourt (they rarely failed to arrive spotlessly clean, even transporting water out to the desert on donkeys to clean cars that would be covered in dust the next day), we were all in high spirits. Only minutes remained until I'd see my family again.

Arriving at the gates of the Meridien, I jumped out of the car and ran into the car park in front of the hotel where drummers, dancers and stilt-walkers had created a carnival atmosphere. I ran through the crowd, searching for Olly and the kids. I ran up to the hotel and looked through the bars and restaurants, but still couldn't find them. Desperate for my family, I ran out of the gate of the hotel and along the queue of traffic in the road for about a quarter mile. Still no sign. The street was packed with people and I was peering into every passing taxi, expecting any moment to hear shrieks and shouts of 'Daddy! Daddy!' from Doone and Kinvara, but still nothing.

Disappointed that I'd beaten Olly, the kids and the rest of the party to the Meridien, I walked back to the hotel car park.

'CHARLEY!' I spun round and there was Ewan.

'Ewan! Great to see you!' I felt like crying as I hugged him.

'Great to see you too, mate. Well done. Congratulations!'

'I can't believe we did it. I thought we'd never get here. And now look!' Over Ewan's shoulder I saw Olly approaching with the girls. I ran over to her.

'I was so worried about you,' I said as I hugged and kissed my wife.

'You've got your beard again!' said Kinvara as I bent down to hug her and Doone. 'And you *smell*.'

I showed my wife and daughters my broken hands. The girls were fascinated, wanting to know exactly which bones were broken.

Matt was there too, looking a lot more relaxed than when I'd last seen him leaving the bivouac at Nouakchott.

'It looked so hard,' said Ewan, who had been watching the rally on television. 'You had such bad luck. If you hadn't fallen . . .'

'My riding was good. I was capable. I took the lead on the first sand dunes. Simon was following me. I found it quite difficult, but I was managing, then I waved Simon forward and we just cruised together. If only I hadn't fallen . . .'

'It's insanity, isn't it?' said Ewan. 'It's pushing you beyond the bounds, really, isn't it?'

I was so pleased Ewan had come to the finish. And although I could see he was concerned about my injuries I could also see he was insanely jealous that he hadn't been part of it. Although Ewan had always said the Dakar was not his thing – he preferred doing things at his own pace rather than having to keep up with hundreds of riders in a rally – he knew it had been great fun. It might have been hard, but it was an adventure.

'It's crazy,' I said. 'You're doing London to Edinburgh off-road every day. Some days it's even further.'

'Do you think you'd want to do another one?'

'I don't know,' I said. 'I only did five days, so . . .' But already I was starting to think about it. It was the craziest, toughest, most dangerous thing I'd ever done and I was deeply relieved to have survived without serious injury, but there was something about it that had me hooked. Although I knew it would be extremely foolhardy to make another attempt I couldn't look anyone in the eyes and promise I wouldn't return.

In the background I could hear Matt relating his experiences in the desert to Russ.

'. . . there were eleven of us in the back of the *camion*,' Matt said.

'No! Eleven?' said Russ. 'But there's only seats for ten . . .'

'Anyway . . . Have you got any money?'

'Yeah.'

'Have you got a thousand euros? I had to borrow a thousand euros off a Spanish guy in the middle of the Mauritanian desert.'

'A *thousand*?' Some things never changed.

We walked up to the gates at the entrance to the Meridien to wait for Simon, Nick Plumb, Patsy Quick and Clive Towne. I wanted to greet them all.

Plummy arrived first, of course, with news that Simon, Patsy and Clive were not far behind him.

'Simon and I have tried three times to do it all the way to Dakar together,' he said. 'This year we managed it so it's time to close the book, hang up my kit and get on with my life. Time to spend time with the family and go on holiday when the Dakar starts next January.'

'Typical Simon,' said Matt as we waited. 'Always late. *Always*. It'll be bloody good to see him. The last thing I saw was his arse disappearing into the distance . . .'

'My little chickens are returning,' I said.

'We're all coming home to roost,' said Matt.

Patsy and Clive arrived about twenty minutes later. Just behind them, lurking in the background so he wouldn't steal Patsy's moment, was Simon. Tears in her eyes, Linley ran over to him and hugged and kissed him. Then, when we'd all congratulated Simon, Linley jumped on to his pillion and rode off with him to the pits, clearly a very happy and proud woman.

SIMON The first time on the Dakar that I'd ever had a proper welcoming committee and it was brilliant. Having Linley there crowned what had been the best Dakar for me ever, no question about it. And Charley had been such a diamond for the last two weeks. Every race has always been about the finish for me but this

291

year, knowing Linley was going to be there, I was desperate to reach Dakar.

Riding in with Patsy and Clive, and with Plummy a few kilometres ahead, was beautiful and felt very special. Getting back to the hotel, having a hot shower and a proper bed were all fantastic, but having Linley waiting for me crowned it all.

CHARLEY Although we'd all reached Dakar, the rally wasn't over. The next day Simon, Nick, Patsy and Clive had to ride the final stage, 110 kilometres out of Dakar and back for a quick circuit of the *Lac Rose*, a lake in which, at certain times of the year, the water turned pink when an unusual algae bloomed.

This last stage was in many ways a tiresome formality. Only thirty-one kilometres of it was a special, all of that on the beach along the lake, and the timing of the special had been abandoned after it emerged that a second child had been killed as the rally passed through Guinea. The twelve-year-old boy had been hit by an assistance truck near the town of Kaffrine. Quite how an untimed stage would honour the two African children who'd been killed, I couldn't quite work out. If the rally had really wanted to hold a tribute to the children they should have scrapped a stage that was, after all, no more than a formality for the sponsors and big teams.

'It's not going to bring them back, it's not going to change their deaths,' said Matt, who was angry about the hollowness of the organisers' gesture. 'It won't mean the rally won't be here next year. It won't mean the rally participants will be more careful. It doesn't mean anything. It's just about the organisers trying to come out of a tragedy looking a bit better.'

It was particularly ridiculous as the final forty-one kilometres of the stage took place after every finisher had ridden up on to the podium to collect their finisher's medal. To most of the recipients, that medal meant more than anything else in the rally. Many, including Simon, didn't know their finishing position. A lot of them had only a passing interest in the news that Marc Coma, a Spaniard with central-casting good looks on a Repsol KTM, had won the motorcycle section, or that Luc Alphand and Gilles Picard had won the car section in a Mitsubishi. Coma, who had taken fifty-five hours, twenty-seven minutes and seventeen seconds to complete all the specials from Lisbon to Dakar, was an hour and thirteen minutes ahead of the second-place rider and forty-three hours, twenty-two minutes and thirty-six seconds ahead of Simon, but that didn't matter. All that really mattered was getting there.

It had certainly been the hardest thing I'd ever done, much harder than Long Way Round because it was so intense and every problem was potentially so massive that if it wasn't solved the rally might be over for the whole team.

As we waited for Simon to take his turn on the podium Russ asked me what advice I would give to anybody wanting to do the Dakar. All I could think to say was that however hard you might think it would be, and however well you prepared for it, it would never be enough. It was an emotional, physical and mental rollercoaster that demanded total devotion. If you needed to ask about it, you probably shouldn't do it.

I asked Matt if he'd ever do a Dakar again. His answer was immediate: 'No.'

Then he paused. 'Not unless you did one, Charley. Then I'd do it with you.'

Great friendships had come out of the race. Not just with Matt and Simon, but with people such as Lee Walters and Paul Green back in Wales. It had enriched my life more than I could have imagined before I embarked on my crazy quest to ride with the world's best across the desert to a former colonial town on the Atlantic coast of west Africa. What we'd been through in two weeks had been amazing. Absolutely nuts. Mechanical faults, a car breaking down in the desert, my injured hands and Matt's saga after leaving Nouakchott. And I still didn't know why I had done it. All I knew was that Simon had made it to Dakar and it had been a worthwhile ride.

As Simon rode up on to the podium everyone present who had been involved with the team in some way – Chris Evans, Doone, Ewan, Gareth, Jim, Kinvara, Linley, Matt, Olly, Russ, Wolfgang and I – followed him. Simon answered a few questions from the host of the awards ceremony and accepted his medal. As I glimpsed his medal covetously and listened to him talk into the host's microphone in the glare of dozens of camera flashes and television cameras, thoughts of the last year flashed through my mind.

It had been an extraordinary twelve months and I was just as proud of the lows as the highs. The injuries and exhaustion at the end of long, cold days training in the Welsh mountains; the disappointment in myself when I couldn't finishing enduro races; the frustration and pain after breaking my collarbone; the anxiety that haunted my first few days in the rally; and finally the despair and agony when two broken hands ended my race dreams five days into the race – all of them were worthwhile setbacks on the road to Dakar. Because without them I wouldn't have had the highs that made it the ride of a lifetime.

I'd learned that when we push ourselves to the limit, there's always somewhere deep inside us where we can find more strength to keep going. And much to my surprise I'd discovered that when it was over, there was something – I didn't quite know what – that made us want to do it all again.

I knew I would never forget the people I'd met, the places I'd seen and the experiences I'd had since persuading Russ that he should help me enter the 2006 Dakar rally. There was something very special about an event that brought everyone together. As well as all the people on the podium around Simon and me, and our invaluable event managers Lucy and Asia in London, there were dozens of supporters and friends who had helped us reach the start line in Lisbon. And although by the end all our hopes had rested on Simon's shoulders, because of everyone who had participated and helped us, our race to Dakar was very much a team effort and a team triumph. And, as a team, we'd made it.

APPENDIX 1 – ROUTE AND DISTANCES

Date	Stage name	From	To	Liaison	Special	Liaison	Total	Assistance
31 Dec	The tracks of Alentejo	Lisbon	Portimão	186	83	101	370	356
1 Jan	The ridges of Algarve	Portimão	Málaga	65	115	387	567	0*
2 Jan	Something new to the east	Nador	Er Rachidia	237	314	121	672	687
3 Jan	Gateway to the desert	Er Rachidia	Ouarzazate	56	386	197	639	302
4 Jan	The wadi road	Ouarzazate	Tan Tan	187	350	282	819	682
5 Jan	Southbound	Tan Tan	Zouérat	336	444	12	792	742
6 Jan	A tricky pass	Zouérat	Atar	10	499	12	521	309
7 Jan	Hole shot	Atar	Nouakchott	34	508	26	568	434
8 Jan	Rest day							
9 Jan	The well track	Nouakchott	Kiffa	30	599	245	874	612
10 Jan	The great savannah	Kiffa	Kayes	1	283	49	333	291
11 Jan	Wednesday in Bamako	Kayes	Bamako	50	231	424	705	626
12 Jan	The river track	Bamako	Labé	197	368	307	872	919
13 Jan	Sarakole country	Labé	Tambacounda	7	348	212	567	0**
14 Jan	Westward bound	Tambacounda	Dakar	107	254	273	634	476
15 Jan	Delivery	Dakar	Dakar	38	31	41	110	0***

* = assistance travels Lisbon to Málaga; ** = no assistance (marathon stage); *** = assistance stationary

APPENDIX 2 – GLOSSARY

Bivouac – Nightly camp for riders to rest in, which moves from stage to stage

Camel grass – Tough tuft of grass, found in the desert

CP – Checkpoint

Enduro races – Motorcycle race that tests endurance

Factory team – Professional sponsored team

Fairing – Windshield at front of bike

Fesh fesh – Fine sand, equivalent to cement dust. A grey/white colour

Front fascia – Exterior accessory added to the front bumper

Gas Gas – Spanish bike manufacturer

Hare scrambles – Type of race format. The winner is the person to do the laps in a certain amount of time

Iritaq – GPS tracking system attached to each vehicle

Liaison stage – Section of the stage before and after the special stage

Monocoque construction – Construction technique that uses the external skin of an object to support some or most of the load on the structure

Parc ferme – Designated area where race vehicles are out of bounds to the competitors the night before the rally begins

Privateers – Non-professional racers

Scrutineering – Process undergone before the rally of examination and verification of all race vehicles and competitors' documentation

Sentinel – Alarm that warns that vehicles are approaching from behind

Special stage – Timed race stage

Tyre mousse – Foam inserted in the tyre instead of air, which prevents punctures

Wadi – An old river-bed

Ending With a Sense of Hope

My many adventures on motorbikes have provided me with memories and stories that I will enjoy and dine out on for years to come. Some are hilarious; some are terrifying – either way they seem to make me smile.

The most vivid are the memories of the people I met along the way: those who gave such a warm welcome despite living in the middle of nowhere; those children who waved and chased me along the side of the road, shouting and laughing as only children can do. It made me realise that children are children wherever you are in the world and they deserve to have opportunities for a decent and happy future.

During Long Way Round in 2004, I saw how UNICEF was doing life-changing work around the world to put smiles back on the faces of those children who had lost all sense of their childhoods because of poverty, exploitation and disease. UNICEF gives children a better chance in life, giving them the things we take for granted – education, clean water, protection and care.

I have pledged my support to UNICEF and I hope you will do the same.

Charley Boorman

unicef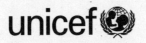

UNICEF is the world's leading organisation working specifically for children, protecting and promoting their rights. It works in 157 countries of the world to help every child realise their full potential through long-term and emergency work on child health and nutrition, quality basic education for all boys and girls, and the protection of children from violence, exploitation and AIDS.

By working in partnership with others, from governments and teachers, to youth groups and mothers, UNICEF is a driving force for people throughout the world working to ensure a world fit for children.

UNICEF receives no money from the UN, and we rely entirely on donations to fund our work for children worldwide. We need people like you to help us protect children. You can make a difference. You can donate, or purchase UNICEF cards and gifts, or become a volunteer or campaigner.

If you are in the UK and would like to find out about giving, purchasing cards and gifts, volunteering or campaigning, please visit

www.unicef.org.uk

You can also donate by calling the 24-hour credit card hotline on **08457 312 312**, or by sending a cheque payable to 'UNICEF' to

UNICEF
Freepost CL885
Billericay CM12 0BR
United Kingdom

If you are outside the UK and want to find out how you can get involved in your country or make a donation, please visit

www.supportunicef.org

Acknowledgements

Special thanks to:

Race Manager
Russ Malkin

The Race Team
Simon Pavey, Matt Hall

The Race Support Team
Wolfgang Banholzer, Gareth Edmunds, Jim Foster and Claudio von Planta

Race Team HQ
Lucy Trujillo, Asia Mackay, Liz Mercer, Robin Shek, Lisa Benton, Louise Houghton and Ollie Blackwell

BMW UK
Pieter de Waal, Tony Jakeman, Mark Harrison, Adrian Roderick, Gavin Ward, John Beckley, Kylie Maebus and Martin Harrison

Race Partners
Arai – Wendy Hearn
Cotswolds Outdoor – Mike Gurney
Dome – Neil Miller
Michelin – Paul Cordle
Snap On – Sean Derrig and Terry Barcham

Sonic Communications – David Bryan, Liam Thornton and Darren Roper

Touratech – Herbert Schwarz and Jochen Schanz

Invaluable Support

Anthony Henry, Chris Evans, Craig Gunn, Dave Newman, Dave McBride, Emily Malkin, Jane Prior, John Shirt, Lee Walters, Linley Sullivan-Pavey, Llewellyn Pavey, Paul Green, Richard Gunn and Sean Linton

ASO

Etienne Lavigne, Armal Canet, Frédéric Lequien, Gael Colloc'h, Christophe Marchadier, Virginie Soulaire, Matthieu, Vladimir Gasic and everyone at ASO, especially the medical team for patching me up and looking after me!

BMW, Lisbon, Portugal

Carlos Ludovino and everyone at Baviera – Comercio de Automovers

BMW, Mauritania

Sid Ahmed and Mr Yuseffa

Bowler Spirit

Keith Banyard, Ben Gott, and all the Bowler Boys

Thanks also to: Jenny Fry, Zoë Gullen, Antonia Hodgson, Caroline Hogg, Marie Hrynczak, David Kent, Alison Lindsay and Duncan Spilling at Little, Brown Book Group, and Robert Kirby at PFD.

Alpine Stars, AST, Gas Gas, Giali, Goskirk and McGinty, Jebel Ali Hotels, RG Engineering, Royal Brunei, Scorpion Racing, Scott Racing and Visa Express.

Other bestselling titles available by mail:

☐ Long Way Round Ewan McGregor and Charley Boorman £6.99

The prices shown above are correct at time of going to press. However, the publishers reserve the right to increase prices on covers from those previously advertised without further notice.

———————————————— sphere ————————————————

SPHERE
PO Box 121, Kettering, Northants NN14 4ZQ
Tel: 01832 737525, Fax: 01832 733076
Email: aspenhouse@FSBDial.co.uk

POST AND PACKING:
Payments can be made as follows: cheque, postal order (payable to Sphere), credit card or Switch Card. Do not send cash or currency.

All UK Orders **FREE OF CHARGE**
EC & Overseas 25% of order value

Name (BLOCK LETTERS) . . . .

Address . . . .

. . . .

Post/zip code: . . . .

☐ Please keep me in touch with future Sphere publications

☐ I enclose my remittance £ . . . .

☐ I wish to pay by Visa/Delta/Maestro

Card Expiry Date | | | | | Maestro Issue No. | | |